Living with Strangers

Pananiapapi (Struck by the Ree) and Shunkanonpa (Two Dogs),
from a sketch by Valentine Francis Rowe, 1874.
(Saskatchewan Archives Board, R-A22972.)

Living *with* Strangers

The Nineteenth-Century Sioux *and the* Canadian-American Borderlands

David G. McCrady

UNIVERSITY OF NEBRASKA PRESS • LINCOLN AND LONDON

Set in Minion and
Copperplate by
Bob Reitz.
Designed by Ray Boeche.
Library of Congress
Cataloging-in-Publication
Data
McCrady, David G.
Living with strangers: the
nineteenth-century Sioux
and the Canadian-American
borderlands /
David G. McCrady.
p.   cm.
Includes bibliographical
references and index.
ISBN-13: 978-0-8032-3250-1
(cloth: alk. paper)
ISBN-10: 0-8032-3250-0
(cloth: alk. paper)
1. Dakota Indians—
Migrations.   2. Dakota
Indians—Wars.   3. Dakota
Indians—History—19th
century.
4. Canada—Ethnic relations.
5. Canada—History—19th
century.   I. Title.
E99.D1M46   2006
978.004'975243—dc22
2005009278

My heart is not bad, my heart is glad to see the English,
the English are good, but the Big Knife is bad,
they kill our children.

Two Dogs to Valentine Francis Rowe, 1874

CONTENTS

ILLUSTRATIONS

Following page 72

MAPS

The story of Sitting Bull's sojourn in Canada unfolded before me as I sat on the floor of the McPherson Library at the University of Victoria reading the annual reports of the Canadian Department of the Interior, the ministry charged in the 1870s with the administration of Indian affairs. I was surprised. I was reasonably well versed in Western Canadian history, yet I had no knowledge of these events. How could I be unaware that Sitting Bull, one of the most famous American Indians to have ever lived, spent four years in what would later become southern Saskatchewan? I began to understand that, as an *American* Indian, Sitting Bull had no place in *Canadian* history. By researching the life of Sitting Bull and comparing what I had learned with how historians had related these events, I started to realize that the boundary separating Canada and the United States had had a profound impact on the way historians—still generally of European origin—had thought and written about aboriginal history. Stories like that of Sitting Bull and the Sioux had not been told very well.

When this project began, several years later, as my doctoral dissertation at the University of Manitoba, I set myself the task of trying to write the history of those Sioux who ventured into the area on both sides of the Forty-ninth Parallel during the nineteenth century. I would write about the Dakotas, or Eastern Sioux, who left Minnesota after the warfare of 1862 and went to Rupert's Land, and the Lakotas, or Western Sioux, who entered the North-West Territories (as Rupert's Land came to be known after it came under Canadian control) in the 1870s, having defeated Custer at the Little Bighorn. To understand this history, I would also have to take account of the Yanktons and Yanktonais. But foremost I wanted to learn how the Sioux—not just in wartime, but in peacetime as well—had come to understand the boundary and to use it for their own purposes.

I discovered while I researched and wrote that the boundary, and how it had partitioned academics, had created several problems that I now faced. Would readers steeped in the history of one country know as much about the other?

People interested in Western American history would know about Lewis and Clark, the Bozeman Trail, and the Black Hills gold rush. But would they know about Gabriel Dumont, the Honorable James McKay, or the North-West Rebellion? Those interested in Western Canadian history could explain the significance of the Canadian Pacific Railway. But could they do the same for the American frontier? How would such a divided audience receive this work? My research touched on some well-known episodes in the history of the American and Canadian Wests—the Dakota Conflict of 1862, the March West of the North-West Mounted Police in 1874, the Battle of the Little Bighorn, and the Great Sioux War of 1876–77—and certainly some well-known personages are here—Father Pierre-Jean De Smet, Louis Riel, Sitting Bull, and George Armstrong Custer. Yet the background literature had so little to say about the topics that I was covering. There seemed to be so much that I needed to know to complete my work, yet where was it? Much has been written, for example, about the Métis and the Red River Resistance, but very little about the Métis who lived on the plains away from Red River, and almost nothing on Métis communities in the United States. It was difficult, also, to find good maps in the published literature, that is, maps that gave equal weight to places on both sides of the boundary. In the end, by putting together material from a number of sources on both sides of the border, I hope that I have said something new and significant about Sioux history.

Betraying the fact that I am Canadian and that the Canada–United States boundary has shaped my intellectual toolshed, I use Canadian spellings for the names of aboriginal groups. Unless quoting documents that use American forms, I refer to the Blackfoot and Ojibwas, not the Blackfeet and Chippewas. In keeping with Axtell's dictum, plural forms of aboriginal group names conform to the rules of Standard English—except in the case of *Blackfoot*, which is the usual singular and plural form in Canada.[1]

I have not made corrections to any of the documents that I quote. The spelling, grammar, punctuation, and errors appearing in quotations are in the original, so I do not use *sic*. Any errors in spelling, grammar, punctuation, interpretation, or fact in the rest of the text are my own, not those of anyone who has read the manuscript or offered comments and advice.

The University of Manitoba, the Social Sciences and Humanities Research Council of Canada, and the Canada–United States Fulbright Program provided financial support for this research. I would like to thank them all.

A number of people offered insight, inspiration, and support. First of all,

I must thank Jennifer Brown, who supervised my graduate studies and my dissertation. She has been a mentor and a dear friend. Let me also extend my gratitude to Ken Coates, Francis Carroll, David Reed Miller, Maureen Matthews, and Michael Gourlie. I reserve a special thank-you for Ray DeMallie, who gave me a home for a year at the American Indian Studies Research Institute at Indiana University, granted me access to his huge collection of archival photocopies and microfilm, and made me feel completely welcome. Without his help, advice, and support, this book could not have been written. Garth Clarke, Gerhard Ens, Molly Clark, Brian Hubner, and Thelma Poirier all pointed me to important sources. The staffs at the Provincial Archives of Manitoba, the National Archives of Canada, the Montana State Historical Society Archives, and especially the Glenbow Archives have been encouraging and helpful. I wish to thank my family, Eileen and Carolyn McCrady, for their ongoing support. This project has taken a great deal of time, and, for preparing its index and giving me her insight and clarity through it all, I must thank, above all, my partner, Susan Gray. She made everything possible.

A NOTE ON
SIOUX GROUPS AND LEADERS

This study refers to a constellation of individuals and groups. To bring some order to the panoply that follows, a thumbnail sketch of the borderland Sioux and their leaders may be useful.

By the early to mid-nineteenth century, the Sioux inhabited the territory stretching from the forests and prairies of modern-day Minnesota and Iowa to the grasslands as far west as Montana and Wyoming. Although the nineteenth-century Sioux considered themselves a single people, they did not live as a single political entity. People lived in bands, which in turn were parts of larger entities, of which there were at least thirteen in the nineteenth century.[1]

The Mdewakantons, Wahpekutes, Sissetons, and Wahpetons (using English forms) called themselves the Dakotas and are also collectively known as the Santees or the Eastern Sioux. The Mdewakantons and Wahpekutes, who generally lived along the Mississippi and lower Minnesota Rivers, are often referred to as Lower Santees, while the Sissetons and Wahpetons, who lived along the Minnesota River to its headwaters and on the prairies to the west, are the Upper Santees. Those Upper Santees who lived closest to the Minnesota headwaters had considerable contact with and close cultural ties to the Yanktonais farther west.

Burnt Earth (Sisseton) and Waneta (Sisseton born but the leader of a Cut-head Yanktonai band) were among those Dakota leaders who attempted to open a trade with the British along the Red River of the North after British traders evacuated Sioux territory following the War of 1812.

Standing Buffalo (Burnt Earth's nephew), White Cap (Wahpeton), and Little Crow (Mdewakanton) were among those who led their followers onto the plains and then north into what is now Manitoba during and after the Dakota Conflict of 1862. Little Crow's grandfather, also named Little Crow, had allied his people with the British during the War of 1812. Standing Buffalo, White Cap, and others continued west into what is now Montana and Saskatchewan. Standing Buffalo was killed in a fight with the Crows in 1871. Most of his band then followed his son, the younger Standing Buffalo. Standing Buffalo's and White Cap's people eventually settled principally on reserves in Saskatchewan. Others resided on the Fort Peck Reservation in Montana.

The Yanktons and Yanktonais are collectively the Yankton or Middle Sioux, although they, too, call themselves Dakotas. At midcentury they inhabited a swath of territory between the Santees and the Missouri River. The Yanktons lived in the southern part of this territory, while the Yanktonais lived to the north. Struck by the Ree (Yankton), Two Dogs (Yanktonai), Medicine Bear (Yanktonai), and others brought their people up the Missouri River into what are now North Dakota, Montana, and Saskatchewan during the 1860s. Most eventually settled on the Fort Peck Reservation, while smaller numbers joined Standing Buffalo's and White Cap's people on their reserves.

The Oglalas, Brulés, Minneconjous, Two Kettles, Sans Arcs, Blackfeet, and Hunkpapas (again, using English forms) call themselves Lakotas and are collectively known as the Tetons or the Western Sioux. The Lakotas lived beyond the Missouri River and were moving west in the nineteenth century as buffalo along the river became increasingly scarce. Sitting Bull and his uncle, Four Horns, and cousin, Black Moon (all Hunkpapas), Spotted Eagle (Sans Arc), and Crazy Horse (Oglalla) were among the most prominent leaders of the nonreservation Lakotas in the 1860s and 1870s. Four Horns and Black Moon entered Saskatchewan in the months following the Custer fight on the Little Bighorn. Sitting Bull joined them the following May. Big Road and Little Hawk took the remainder of Crazy Horse's band north to Canada in early 1878, following the murder of Crazy Horse in 1877.[2]

Lakota refugees began returning to Montana soon after the food crisis became acute in 1879. By 1880, the trickle south was a stream. Sitting Bull surrendered at Fort Buford in July 1881, the last major leader to return. The Lakotas who surrendered to American authorities were transported down the Missouri River to reservations in North and South Dakota. Several hundred remained in Saskatchewan and were finally granted a reserve at Wood Mountain in 1910.

1. INTRODUCTION:
PARTITIONING SIOUX HISTORY

The Sioux are generally conceived of as "American" Indians. The feather-bon-neted, tipi-dwelling, horse-riding, buffalo-hunting Sioux warrior is, for many people around the world, *the* image of the American Indian. By the 1870s, most Sioux had entered into treaty relationships with the American government—northern Lakota bands under Sitting Bull and other leaders being major ex-ceptions. In so doing, the Sioux became American Indians in the eyes of the American government and in the eyes of subsequent scholars and the general public. This designation has determined, in many ways, how the history of Sioux peoples has been written.

In the United States, the history of the nineteenth-century Sioux has been largely the history of their opposition to American encroachment onto their lands. Sioux opposition to the reduction of their reservations in Minnesota pro-duced the Dakota Conflict of 1862. Their opposition to army posts constructed to protect American travelers on the Bozeman Trail to the Montana goldfields culminated in Red Cloud's War in the 1860s. Opposition to gold miners in the Black Hills and to railroads in the Yellowstone Valley led to the Great Sioux War of 1876–77. The Ghost Dancers were massacred at Wounded Knee in 1890, thus putting an end to any further Sioux resistance. By the end of the century, the Sioux had been exiled to reservations.

The Sioux appear more briefly in Canadian history as refugees from warfare in the United States in the 1860s and 1870s. Once across the border they generally disappear from the pages of American history, where, often, little more than a sentence or two acknowledges their activities in Canada. They are simply no longer subjects for American history. Canadian historians pick up the history of the Sioux once they appear in Canada—only after they have become subjects of Canadian history. The result is the creation of two separate histories—the first ending at the Forty-ninth Parallel, the second beginning there. That the boundary itself and the opportunities that its presence created might be an important issue in Sioux history is missed by both.

The overwhelming popular and academic interest in the Sioux, their place in the history of the American West and in Sioux-American conflict (the Custer battle in particular), makes any conception of them as anything other than American Indians seem absurd. Yet the writing of Sioux history does profit when we recognize the Sioux, not as American Indians, but as a people of the "borderlands."

Borderlands can be an ambiguous concept. Historians and other scholars use the word in different contexts and for their own purposes, and the term can be and is used to cover more than one concept. The evolving literature on the nature of borderlands is also complicated by references to *frontiers* and *boundaries*, also seemingly straightforward on the surface but elusive when probed.

Borderlands is used here in two different but related contexts. In the first instance, it is used to suggest a social, cultural, and economic interface between aboriginal peoples and others. In the eighteenth century and for much of the nineteenth, notwithstanding European treaties indicating so-called Spanish, French, British, and, later, American and Canadian territorial boundaries that cartographers dutifully superimposed on their maps, no physical trace of these boundaries existed on the ground. Instead, foci of European settlement were separated by vast hinterlands—really the heartlands of aboriginal nations— in which European and aboriginal traders, soldiers, families, and others came face-to-face and forged relationships spanning the continuum from hostility to trade, accommodation to intermarriage and community. There was a geographic dimension to every borderland, but it might range from the immense Ohio Valley to the more localized environs of a trading post on the shores of Hudson Bay. All cultural encounters have an element of borderlands within them.[1]

Great Britain and the United States agreed in 1818 that the Forty-ninth Parallel would serve as the boundary between their respective territories from the Lake of the Woods to the Rocky Mountains. This boundary was not demarcated on the ground until much later in the century, and the borderlands consisted of a shifting set of relationships between the people of the western interior and the American, British, and Canadian traders who ventured into the area.[2]

The Sioux, for their part, developed a stronger attachment toward the British, and, to cement this relationship and to prevent the encroachment of American traders into Sioux lands, their young men fought alongside the British during both the American Revolution and the War of 1812. At the conclusion of the latter, some Sioux groups traveled to Saint Louis to sign treaties of peace with the U.S. government, while others wished to remain trading partners of the British. They were regular, if usually unwelcome, visitors to the British colony on the Red River of the North. The movement of Sioux peoples to the northwest, and into the Canadian-American borderlands, became more pronounced as the century progressed.

The nature of the borderlands on the Northern Plains also changed over the course of the nineteenth century. While the social, cultural, and economic aspects of aboriginal-European encounter continued, they were given physical expression as the boundary between the United States and Canada became visible on the ground. By the 1860s, when Sioux groups were moving into the border country, the Métis and their ubiquitous Red River carts were creating a trail from Pembina and Saint Joseph (just south of the Forty-ninth Parallel) to Wood Mountain (just north of it) that corresponded, roughly, to the international boundary. The Wood Mountain trail was not the Oregon Trail, with its deep wagon ruts and piles of discarded goods, but it bore evidence of the passage of hundreds of Métis to and from these settlements. With each passing year Métis hunts headed west along this trail, and it grew steadily more distinct. Then, between 1872 and 1874, British and American surveyors followed the same trail as they physically marked the boundary with iron stakes and mounds of earth. Also in 1874 the newly formed North-West Mounted Police used the same trail on its march west. To any observer, this was a physical symbol of the social and cultural borderlands on the Northern Plains.

The term *borderlands* is, then, also used here to describe the boundary, the territory on both sides of it, and the set of relationships between aboriginal peoples and others that its presence made possible. The Sioux, like other borderlands populations, exploited the boundary tactically. The decision of some to move to British territory in the 1860s and 1870s following periods of warfare in the United States was based on the knowledge that Americans troops would not follow them across the boundary. Sioux leaders petitioned representatives of both the Canadian and the American governments for land, testing which government would grant them the better treatment. And the Sioux took advantage of trading opportunities that were made possible by their location in the borderlands: Métis traders from Canada supplied the Sioux with goods that were contraband in the United States, such as firearms and ammunition, because they were close enough to the border to evade American authorities if they were pursued.[3]

Indigenous peoples throughout the colonial world were acutely aware that they could take advantage of the existence of separate colonial economies and economic policies either by selling goods in whichever market offered the better prices or by trading in contraband goods. Métis-Sioux trade shared characteristics of this kind of borderlands trade.[4]

By the mid-nineteenth century the borderlands Sioux were readily identifiable groups. They were Dakotas under leaders such as Standing Buffalo and White Cap who fled to the borderlands after the Dakota Conflict of the 1860s and who visited settlements in what are now Manitoba, Saskatchewan, North Dakota, and Montana. They were Yanktonais under Medicine Bear and Yanktons and Yanktonais under Struck by the Ree who had entered the area from farther down the Missouri River and who were moving into the Milk River country of Montana and the adjacent parts of southern Saskatchewan. They were northern Lakotas, especially Hunkpapas, under leaders like Black Moon, Four Horns, and Sitting Bull who had recently taken possession from the Crows of the country to the south, between the Missouri and Yellowstone Rivers.[5] The borderlands Sioux inhabited the plains, badlands, and river valleys from the Qu'Appelle River in the north to the Yellowstone River in the south. Fort Peck, run by the American firm of Durfee and Peck, was a favored trading post, although even as early as the 1860s Lakotas and Yanktonais traveled north in hopes of trading at the Hudson's Bay Company's Fort Qu'Appelle. When Sitting Bull and other Lakota leaders took their followers north to Canada following the Great Sioux War, their pathway was already in place and well traveled.

By the end of the century, the once permeable Canada–United States boundary became impermeable to aboriginal movement. More than anything else, the collapse of the buffalo economy left aboriginal peoples, including the Sioux, dependent on foodstuffs doled out by Canadian and American government officials. Native peoples had lost the freedom to pursue their own objectives by using the boundary as a tool. The Canadian-American borderlands had become *bordered* lands.[6]

There is a voluminous literature, both popular and academic, on the Sioux. Some topics have, of course, received more attention than others. The stories of the Great Sioux War and of Lieutenant Colonel George Armstrong Custer's defeat at the Battle of the Little Bighorn, for example, have become entrenched in the mythology and historiography of the American West. The interpretation and analysis of each event, but most notably the Custer fight, have become cottage industries.[7]

The best recent ethnohistorical material attempts to give voice to Sioux perspectives. Raymond DeMallie, in particular, has been instrumental in publishing manuscripts written or dictated by Sioux people and in demonstrating their value for the ethnohistorical method.[8] The Plains volume of *The Handbook of North American Indians* contains concise and authoritative chapters on the Sioux people and a comprehensive bibliography.[9]

Despite this vast amount of work the literature on those groups that moved into the Canadian-American borderlands does not acknowledge the boundary as a factor in their history. At the same time the extensive literature on borderlands people rarely contemplates the aboriginal societies of North America. The most highly developed borderlands literature focuses on Africa, where every colonial and successor state boundary partitions ethnic groups.

The history of Sioux peoples in the Canadian-American borderlands has been largely overlooked owing to the national perspectives of historians. Much of the research on the Dakota Conflict focuses on the war itself, not on the activities of those Sioux who fled to the plains during its aftermath. The career of the elder Standing Buffalo gives ample evidence of this: Canadian historians have been interested only in Standing Buffalo's interviews with Canadian government officials, while Americans have looked only at his talks with American authorities, Mark Diedrich's biography being the notable exception.[10] Gary Clayton Anderson's biography of the Mdewakanton leader Little Crow concluded with a chapter on his people's flight to Rupert's Land in the 1860s—but went no further.[11] Anderson's account of Dakota-European relations in the upper Mississippi Valley also ends in 1862 and mentions the migration north of Dakota peoples even more briefly.[12] Although Peter Douglas Elias's study of the Dakotas in Canada begins with the archaeological record of Dakota peoples in what is now Canada, his discussion of modern Canadian Sioux communities begins with their departure from the United States following the warfare of 1862, where his American counterparts' works generally end.[13]

Robert M. Utley's excellent biography of Sitting Bull examined the years the Hunkpapa leader spent in Canada more fully than any other. Yet Sitting Bull was presented as an American Indian who took his people into the Grandmother's Land (i.e., the land of Queen Victoria) after 1876, not as the leader of a borderlands people who had had extensive contacts with communities on both sides of the boundary long before the events on the Little Bighorn.[14] The writing of

Dakota cultural history is also affected by the boundary. When Alice Kehoe conducted fieldwork in Wahpeton Dakota communities in northern Saskatchewan in the 1960s, she was surprised to discover them practicing a modified form of the Ghost Dance. American historians had assumed that the Ghost Dance came to an end at the Wounded Knee Massacre in 1890, when many participants were killed: they had paid no attention to Canada and so had overlooked the Canadian history of this religious movement.[15]

Historical problems, when defined by modern political boundaries in North America, limit the kinds of questions and approaches that we bring to the study of aboriginal history. Boundary populations and their history remain marginal to the concerns of Western American and Western Canadian historiography. Yet a borderlands paradigm offers new vistas. Borderlands people, unlike those living in areas deep within the territorial limits of a newcomer state, interacted with two different settler societies. They were confronted by—among many things—two different sets of government policies regarding Western lands and Western Indians, two distinct groups of missionaries sent from different Eastern cities, and two different experiences with European forms of law enforcement. Studying borderlands experiences offers fresh perspectives on the ways in which aboriginal peoples responded to settler societies.

In some ways, aboriginal peoples tended to ignore the boundary. They moved repeatedly back and forth across the border, continuing to hunt and trap and gather foods, just as they had always done. But they also began to use the boundary for their own purposes. Sometimes, entire bands presented themselves to government agents in both countries for rations and presents. Occasionally individuals signed treaties in both countries. The nineteenth-century Sioux used the boundary both as a shield against oppressive policies and as a gateway to new opportunities. Certainly the study of these transboundary populations offers fresh insights into the way aboriginal peoples responded to the imposition of European institutions and settlement.

This book is a preliminary attempt to explore the history of the Sioux peoples in the Canadian-American borderlands. It started as an idea, an intellectual puzzle regarding aboriginal peoples and the boundary. The idea led to research that surprised me by revealing documents that told a story that had not been written before and adding new material to events that we thought we already knew.

I believe that this book says things about Sioux history that were not known before but that should have been known. Why did we not know about trade ties between Sioux and Métis? Historians certainly know a great deal about trade between the Sioux and American traders. But they do not acknowledge Sioux trade with the Hudson's Bay Company. Louis Riel is famous in Canada as a founder of Manitoba, but his attempts to remove the Sioux from the borderlands remain completely unrecognized. This information was there all along, but we missed it. Theories of all academic walks of life and disciplines let us see some things and not others. They show us some things while hiding others. Boundaries, being a part of our intellectual framework, serve as equally effective filters.

The Sioux cannot be pulled away from Western American history. The histories of the Sioux and the American people are admittedly intertwined. But, once historians recognize that the boundary was an important element in Sioux history, the way in which they view that history changes forever. And, if Sioux history can be changed when scholars notice the border, imagine the impact that a borderlands awareness would have on those groups that academics already recognize as partitioned peoples. On the Northern Plains this includes the Blackfoot, Assiniboines, Ojibwas, and others. Many groups are partitioned by other stretches of the Canada–United States boundary. Historians have, as yet, failed to realize the potential of looking beyond the border.

2. FROM CONTESTED GROUND TO
BORDERLANDS, 1752–1862

In the roughly half century between the outbreak of the Seven Years' War in 1752 and the close of the War of 1812, Sioux lands were contested by empires, both old and new. At first France and Great Britain and then Great Britain and the emerging United States struggled for paramountcy in the *pays d'en haut*.

For the Sioux these years were times of change and opportunity. Sioux territory had become a borderland in which Sioux actively pursued their own goals and chose allies from among the newcomers on the basis of what best served Sioux interests. The Eastern Sioux usually traded and sometimes fought with the French before the Seven Years' War and sent their leaders to Québec and Montréal to meet and discuss trade and military issues with the governors of Canada.[1] At war's end, France relinquished Canada to the British and ceded Louisiana to the Spanish lest it, too, fall into Britain's hands. British traders soon approached the Sioux in hopes of establishing trade ties.

The British government knew very little of the western interior when it acquired Canada from the French at the close of the Seven Years' War in 1763. Jonathan Carver was part of an unofficial expedition organized in 1766 by Robert Rogers, the commander at Michilimackinac, to gain knowledge of these new lands and to promote trade with the Indians. The expedition members traveled separately to the *pays d'en haut* but intended to rendezvous during the winter. Carver missed the appointment and wintered instead with a band of Dakotas on the Minnesota River. In the spring of 1767 he invited Dakotas from both the river and the plains bands (probably Upper Santees or Yanktonais) to visit the British at Michilimackinac. The Dakotas were interested but preferred that the British come to them. At a council held on 1 May 1767 the Dakotas informed Carver that, as he reported, they "wish[e]d I would encourage the English to come among them and trade and settle near them and insisted upon my returning again to their country and bring fire arms & tobacco."[2] British traders complied in the years to come, and the Anglo-Sioux alliance proved durable.

By the end of the eighteenth century the Sioux had incorporated the Montréal-based North West Company into their trade network. European fur traders writing in the 1790s and early 1800s recorded that Dakotas visited Canadian traders on the Minnesota and Des Moines Rivers, exchanging peltries for guns, kettles, pipes, bows, and other items. These Eastern Sioux then attended the annual Sioux trade fair held between the Mississippi and Missouri Rivers, at which they exchanged iron goods for horses and leather goods with the Yanktonais and Lakotas. Finally, the Lakotas traded some iron goods to the Arikaras for horses, mules, corn, beans, and native tobacco.[3] The British presence in the region troubled the governor-general of Louisiana, who complained to the Spanish secretary of state that the Sioux, Ojibwas, and Assiniboines were partial to the English and hostile to Spanish traders on the upper Missouri River.[4]

British and Canadian traders were important parts of the Sioux economy, and to protect their economy the Sioux supported Great Britain during the American Revolution and the War of 1812.[5] The basis of Anglo-Dakota relations was not war but economics, a fact made clear by the Mdewakanton leader Wabasha in the spring of 1812, before war had been declared, when he noted that the Dakotas "live by our English Traders who have always assisted us, [and we] have always found our English Father the protector of our women and children."[6]

At the end of the War of 1812, Britain informed its Native allies that, owing to American objections, British traders would be withdrawn from so-called American territory. The Dakotas were horrified, and, during a council held on Drummond Island in June 1816, the Mdewakanton leader Little Crow told the British that this would seal the fate of his people.[7] The removal of British traders after so many Dakota men had abandoned their crops to fight the Americans would bring starvation. At a second council held at the end of June Wabasha revealed that the British had deserted their Native allies during the peace negotiations and predicted that the Americans would fill the void left by the British and build forts on Sioux lands.[8]

While the end of British trade in the Old Northwest prompted some Dakota groups to sign peace treaties with the United States, others traveled to the Red River Settlement, founded in 1812 at the forks of the Red and Assiniboine Rivers in what is now southern Manitoba, to open negotiations with British officials there. During the winter of 1816–17 two Ojibwa women arrived at Pembina from the Sioux country with an invitation from the Sioux to the Ojibwas to make peace. News of this peaceful overture soon reached Robert Dickson. Dickson had been a trader in the Old Northwest and had facilitated Sioux support for the British during the war. He now resided in the Red River Settlement, from which he sent a message to the Sioux, asking them to visit.[9] Twenty-two Sioux men arrived in the summer of 1817 and held discussions at Fort Douglas; the result was a short-lived peace between the Sioux and Ojibwas.[10]

Relations among the Sioux, the Ojibwas, and the Hudson's Bay Company (HBC) at Red River were volatile. The company made efforts to trade with the Sioux, arguing that trade promoted peace between the Sioux and the Ojibwas and, thus, helped protect the Red River Settlement from Native conflicts. The Ojibwas, however, were furious that the company traded goods and ammunition to their enemies. Parties of Sissetons and Yanktonais visited Fort Douglas in 1817, 1819, 1820, and 1821 to trade and to negotiate peace agreements with the Ojibwas, but hostilities continued. The Sioux killed three members of the Ojibwa delegation during an incident in 1817, and the Ojibwas stole the Sioux delegations' horses in 1819. In August 1821 a confrontation between a party of fifty Ojibwa warriors and the Sioux delegation nearly ended in a battle. A Métis shot a member of the Sioux delegation and wounded another while the Sioux were in the settlement, and, in retaliation, the Sioux killed a family of Ojibwas near Pembina while on their way home. In the aftermath of these disturbances the HBC abandoned the Sioux trade.[11]

The Sioux attempted to renew trade ties with the HBC after its merger with the North West Company in 1821, but the company was reluctant: the Ojibwas were adamantly opposed, and the HBC, acting in its own interest, sided with them. When a party of Sioux was seen near Pembina in September 1822, one colony official recorded the change in the company's attitude toward them. "We are kept in a constant state of alarm by reports concerning those Scoux [Sioux]," he wrote. "They were seen only two days ago near Pembina, & I greatly fear they will yet do some serious mischief to the Colony Settlement. . . . I know very well that mischief will follow, if we do not purchase their good will by presents; and this will displease Pegowis [Peguis, the noted Red River Ojibwa leader] & his people, who are already much discontented and greatly inclined to be saucy."[12]

Violent incidents often marked Sioux visits to the Red River Settlement after 1821. To prevent a group of Cuthead Yanktonais under Waneta from coming to the settlement in May 1822, a group of HBC traders and the missionary John West went and met them at the company's post at Pembina, just south of the newly declared boundary between the United States and Rupert's Land. Three Assiniboines had come also "to smoke the calumet" with the Sioux. That night, Waneta shot one of the Assiniboines in retaliation for the theft of one of his horses by an Assiniboine about a year before, and the Sioux hastily departed.[13]

A visit to Fort Garry from the Sisseton leader Burnt Earth and thirty-five of his men in 1834 nearly resulted in a battle with the Ojibwas. The visit proceeded cordially until the arrival of a large party of Ojibwas who had lost relatives in a Sioux attack a year or two before. On the departure of the Sioux, a small number of the Ojibwas set out on the Assiniboine River in hopes of intercepting them. Accounts of the incident disagree. According to Sir George Simpson, the governor of the HBC in North America, the Ojibwas were determined to attack the Sioux; the retired fur trader Alexander Ross, however, later argued that the Ojibwas had no hostile intent and that they had entered the river only to have a "parting peep" at the Sioux. The Ojibwas, he wrote, believed that it was the whites who intended to attack the Sioux.[14] While the documentary evidence leaves this matter unresolved, it is clear that incidents such as this made the Sioux more cautious. When Waneta returned to the settlement in 1836, he brought a much larger contingent, some 250 men. According to Thomas Simpson (George's cousin), his delegation had come to ask the HBC to establish a post in Sioux country.[15] Waneta had concluded that his people would no longer be able to trade at Red River.

Relations between the Sioux and the Red River Métis during the nineteenth century were equally volatile, alternating between war and peace. As the Red River official and former fur trader Alexander Ross commented: "Every year, in fact, treaties of peace are made between the half-breeds and the Indians, and every year they are as regularly broken."[16] While Sioux leaders such as Burnt Earth were eager to trade with the HBC and courted peace with the Métis, others strongly opposed Métis hunts on Sioux lands. John McLean, an HBC trader, noted in his memoirs: "The Indians of the plain [undoubtedly the Sioux] view the encroachment of the strange race [the Métis] on their hunting grounds, with feelings of jealousy and enmity. They are, accordingly, continually on the alert; they attack detached parties and stragglers; they also set fire to the prairies about the time the 'brulés' set out for the hunt, and by this means drive the game beyond their reach."[17]

Internecine conflict between Sioux and Métis groups over access to the hunt continued throughout the 1840s and 1850s. During the summer hunt of 1840 Métis hunters under Jean-Baptiste Wilkie Sr. traveled south to the Missouri

River, where a party of twelve Sioux killed Louison Vallé when he was separated from the camp. In response the Métis pursued the Sioux, killing eight. In July the Métis were near the American Fur Company's Fort Union on the Missouri River, and some forty went to the fort to trade. The camp moved west, where it encountered Burnt Earth's Sioux. Burnt Earth and his band visited the Métis camp and discussed the Vallé affair and the eight Sioux who had been killed. Burnt Earth accused the Métis of wanton cruelty—eight Sioux had been killed in retaliation for only one Métis death. The Métis made a small collection and gave it to Burnt Earth. To all outward appearances the Sioux and Métis parted amicably—although the Métis kept a strict watch day and night.

This armistice did not last long, however. The Métis were returning home and had reached the Sheyenne River by late July. Some forty or fifty Ojibwas, "attached as camp-followers to the expedition," and one Métis, Parisien, went off to attack a small Sioux camp. A fight ensued in which seven Sioux and three Ojibwas were killed and three Sioux and four Ojibwas wounded. The Ojibwas then retreated to the Métis camp. The following day, three hundred Sioux, "armed cap-a-pie," arrived at the Métis camp and challenged the Ojibwas to come and fight. The Ojibwas refused, and, with the Métis "acting as mediators between them, a sort of peace was patched up, and the Sioux returned [to their camp]—we may be sure, far from well pleased."[18]

Skirmishes were not uncommon for the rest of the decade. In August 1845, when a group of Sioux visited Fort Garry, an Ojibwa whose brother had been killed by the Sioux in 1844 fired a shot at one of the Sioux, killing him. The ball also passed through the body of an Ojibwa, who also died, and grazed a white man. The Ojibwa was tried for murder and hanged in September 1845.[19] The following year a party of Métis hunters who were traveling west beyond Turtle Mountain encountered a group of Sioux who had come to negotiate peace. While negotiations proceeded the body of a Métis was brought into camp. The death was attributed to the Sioux, and a fight occurred three days later in which eight Sioux were killed.[20]

Of all the engagements between the Sioux and the Métis, the most famous is the Battle of the Grand Coteau. The engagement took place in the summer of 1851 somewhere west of the headwaters of the Sheyenne River. Its exact location is no longer known. In June 1851, Métis hunters from Red River and the White Horse Plains (an area just west of Fort Garry) rendezvoused at Pembina and then headed west (although they continued to operate independently). After encountering small groups of Sioux, the White Horse Plains party stumbled on a large Sioux camp at the Grand Coteau in mid-July. The Sioux attacked the Métis on 13 and 14 July and then withdrew. The identity of these Sioux is open to debate. The historians W. L. Morton and George Woodcock have both written that they were Lakotas, but this identification appears to be guesswork.[21] It is possible that these Sioux were Yanktonais. In his description of the Sioux (written in 1855 and 1856 at Fort Union) the fur trader Edwin Denig referred to conflict between the Sioux and the mixed-blood hunters from Red River only when he discussed the Yanktonais.[22] The engagement was a victory for the Métis, who lost only one man. It is less clear how many Sioux were killed. Father Albert Lacombe, who accompanied the Red River party, recorded eighteen Sioux deaths; Rudolph Friedrich Kurz, an artist who sojourned at Fort Union between September 1851 and April 1852, was told by some Métis (and later reported the account in his diary) that the Sioux had lost eighty men.[23]

Reflecting on the warfare between the Métis and the Sioux, Denig noted: "It appears that the Half Breeds get the better of the Sioux. At least they are not afraid to continue their annual excursions into their country, and [they] are known to be as good if not better warriors than the Indians."[24] In the historiography of the Métis, the engagement at the Grand Coteau has come to symbolize the superiority of Métis arms over the Sioux: after this battle, the Métis were the "masters of the plains wherever they might choose to march."[25] But this is the stuff of myth. In reality Métis-Sioux conflicts continued. In 1854 Father Georges-Antoine Belcourt informed the American commissioner of Indian affairs that the Sioux had raided Saint Joseph each year between 1852 and 1854 while the Métis were away on the hunt. Individuals were killed in both 1851 and 1852, and some thirty horses were stolen in 1854.[26] Apparently the Sioux called for peace, and Belcourt, acting in concert with a number of Sioux mixed-bloods (Rainville, Lafrenière, Larocque, and others) whose sympathies lay with the "Métis sauteux [Ojibwas]," successfully mediated negotiations in 1854. This peace broke down in the summer of 1855, however, when Métis and Ojibwa hunters were attacked by an assembly of Sioux belonging to three "nations."[27] In the autumn of 1857 Cree guides on the Canadian Red River Exploring Expedition demanded that the company be increased before traveling along certain parts of the Assiniboine River. Yanktonais had been stealing horses from Métis hunters coming in from the plains and had been crossing the boundary and raiding the Crees and Ojibwas.[28]

Small HBC trading posts were not immune to the threat of Sioux attack. In July 1858 H. L. Hime, the photographer and assistant surveyor to the Assinniboine and Saskatchewan Exploring Expedition, passed by the HBC post near the Little Souris River. The post was operated in the winter but abandoned in the summer "on account of the Sioux who then come here." Hime remarked in his diary that two of the huts had recently been burned. [29] Métis hunts, especially those emanating from Pembina and Saint Joseph, inevitably infringed on Sioux lands; given the location of the herds the Métis had little choice about where to hunt, so, despite continued Sioux opposition and retaliation, the Métis attempted to make peace with the Sioux. In the summer of 1859, for example, one Father Mestre went on the annual hunting expedition from Pembina and Saint Joseph and, according to Alexandre-Antonin Taché, the Roman Catholic bishop of Saint Boniface, was instrumental in concluding a peace treaty. [30]

Scholars can say little about the actual negotiations for peace that transpired between Métis (and English mixed-bloods) and Sioux peoples during the nineteenth century as the documentary evidence is so limited. The most detailed record of Sioux-Métis peace negotiations dates from the winter of 1844–45. The Sioux had killed several Métis during an aborted peace conference in 1844, and subsequent Métis retaliation resulted in the deaths of at least eight Sioux (four Sissetons and four Yanktonais). In November 1844 Burnt Earth of the Sissetons and several other leaders sent a letter to the Métis of the White Horse Plains in which they regretted the state of affairs and asked for four cartloads of goods to serve as compensation for the four dead Sissetons. Cuthbert Grant, the leader of the White Horse Plains community, replied for the Métis in December, saying that the Métis wanted peace but that they refused to pay the compensation as the deaths were the fault of the Sioux and the demand was unjust. The Sioux held council over this message for three days before deciding that it was a peaceful overture. They replied in February 1845 that the Sioux who had lost relatives in the recent conflict wished to adopt the Métis who had done the killings. Creating these kin ties brought peace to the two groups and lessened the prospect of future warfare. Peace was restored, Burnt Earth's and Grant's followers hunted together in the summer of 1845, and a party from Burnt Earth's group paid a friendly visit to Fort Garry. [31]

The nineteenth century was marked by periods of war punctuated by local truces among various groups of Sioux and Métis. Peace was never universal but was sometimes achieved by paying compensation for the dead or by voluntarily extending kinship relations to members of the deceased individuals' families. None of these local truces lasted, and periods of conflict alternated with periods of peace right up to—and after—the Dakota Conflict of 1862. As late as

September 1861 a group of Métis under William Hallet had a rendezvous with the Yanktonais under Medicine Bear. According to the newspaper in Red River: "The holding of a peace Conference with Mettonaka (The Medicine Bear) a Sioux chief, was one of their first performances. . . . There was plenty of smoke and palaver, and many were the pledges of amity exchanged."[32]

The *pays d'en haut* during the seventeenth and eighteenth centuries was a world characterized by shifting political alliances and fluid social structures. The arrival of Europeans added new sets of players but did not immediately change the rules. Natives and newcomers were caught up in a process of evaluation, misinterpretation, and accommodation that led ultimately to the creation a new society, what Richard White called *the middle ground*—"the place in between: in between cultures, peoples, and in between empires and the non-state world of villages."[33] It was on the middle ground that the Sioux became expert in promoting their own goals by taking advantage of opportunities offered by different groups of newcomers—the French, British, and Americans. Their position in the middle ground also required that they fend off challenges from the Métis, who also profited in this milieu. The Sioux were drawn into the borderlands stretching from Minnesota to the plains by the chance to hunt and trade. After 1862 they were drawn there for refuge as well.

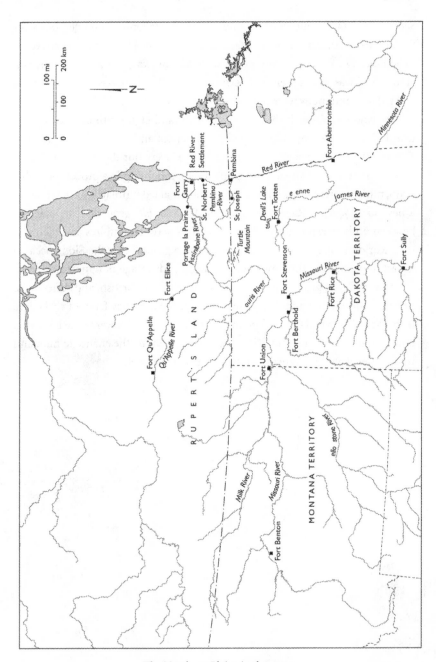

The Northern Plains in the 1860s

3. THE DAKOTA CONFLICT OF 1862 AND THE MIGRATION TO THE PLAINS BORDERLANDS

In the wake of the Dakota Conflict, Dakota people moved up the Minnesota River and onto the plains beyond. This exodus has often been presented as if the refugees fled either to the Dakota Territory or to Rupert's Land, as if the boundary presented a real barrier once crossed. In reality, Dakotas fled to the borderlands and then moved back and forth between American and British territory. Although the boundary had not yet been marked on the ground (this would not happen until 1873–74), Dakota peoples were very much aware of its existence, and they took advantage of the opportunities it offered during the 1860s. Dakota leaders from Minnesota sought sanctuary from Hudson's Bay Company (HBC) officials at Upper Fort Garry, while at the same time they discussed peace with American army officers. When American troops approached camps on American soil, the Dakota leaders fled across the border, using it as a shield, and throughout this period they traded with the Red River Métis for arms and ammunition. By the end of the 1860s the Dakotas had constructed a host of relationships with their borderlands neighbors. Many formed close ties to the Yanktonais and remained with them on Sioux lands. Others negotiated with the Ojibwas for access to Ojibwa lands. Most continued to trade with the Métis. These new relationships were pivotal to the success of the Dakotas in the borderlands.

The movement of Dakota people across the boundary into Rupert's Land in 1862 was prompted, undoubtedly, by the need for supplies. The Dakotas were at war, and they needed firearms and ammunition to fight the Americans as well as to hunt. The HBC was a potential source of such munitions, so several Dakota leaders and their followers traveled to the Red River Settlement in late 1862 and early 1863 to renew ties to the British crown, represented by HBC officials, which they hoped to do by focusing on past Anglo-Dakota relations—relations forged during the War of 1812. Less visible in the sources is the fact that the Dakotas also aimed to open negotiations with the Métis. From both the British and the Métis the Dakotas hoped to receive arms and allies.

On 10 December 1862 Father Alexis André wrote from his mission at Pembina that the Dakotas at Saint Joseph, a Métis settlement on the Pembina River, would soon be joined by some six hundred others from Devil's Lake and that the combined assembly intended visiting Fort Garry to get munitions. The sources do not identify the leaders of this delegation, but it is likely that the Sisseton leader Standing Buffalo was among them.[1] According to John Christian Schultz, a prominent member of the "Canadian Party" at Red River, the Dakotas had sent a peace pipe to Alexander Grant Dallas and then a message saying that they wanted to come to trade.[2] Dallas, the governor-in-chief of Rupert's Land, and Father Alexandre-Antonin Taché, the bishop of Saint Boniface, replied that they wanted nothing to do with them, but on 27 December over one hundred Dakotas arrived at Saint Norbert, a village just south of Fort Garry. There they were met by nearly eight hundred Métis and by Dallas, William Mactavish (the governor of Assiniboia—that part of Rupert's Land that contained the Red River Settlement), and Taché. The Dakotas announced that they had come to renew the friendship that existed between their forefathers and the HBC. The following day they attended a mass at which both Taché and Dallas asked them not to go to Fort Garry. They proceeded to Fort Garry anyway, arriving later that day.[3]

Eighty men and six women from the Dakota delegation arrived at Fort Garry on 28 December and met HBC officials in the courtroom. Governor Mactavish and Joseph Hargrave, Mactavish's secretary, noted that they had come to ascertain the feelings toward them by the Indians and mixed-bloods of the British territory. Schultz wrote that they claimed to have "taken no part in the late massacre, but had merely come in to make peace with the Hudson['s] Bay company and with the halfbreeds." The local newspaper reported that the Dakotas spent three or four days around the fort "eating, drinking, making peace and making merry and then left." They departed on 31 December 1862. No peace between them and the Métis was secured, for, according to Schultz, the Métis from the White Horse Plains threatened to attack the Dakotas in retaliation for past deaths.[4] In the end no trouble occurred.

In May 1863 at Pembina the Mdewakanton leader Little Crow, a grandson of the Little Crow who fought for the British during the War of 1812, announced his intention of visiting the Red River Settlement: "his ostensible object," wrote the local newspaper, was "to show the Governor some writings which he has had since the war of 1812."[5] He and a group of eighty others arrived at Fort Garry on 29 May and had two meetings with the "Company's big folks" the next day.[6] The first meeting was held in the courtroom, where Little Crow told the British authorities of his people's desire to be at peace with the "English." To demonstrate the truthfulness of this claim, his people produced, and "ostentatiously displayed," medals bearing the likeness of King George III. Little Crow asserted that, at the time of the war, the British had promised that "whenever they [the Sioux] should get into trouble with the Americans they had only to come and the folds of the red flag of the north would wrap them round, and preserve them from their enemies." He and his people "had come to claim the fulfilment of this promise."[7] During the second conference, which was held in a private room at Fort Garry, the Dakotas indicated that they wanted ammunition, which Dallas refused, and provisions. They also asked Dallas to write to General Henry Hastings Sibley of the U.S. Army, telling him that they desired peace, and asking that he release Dakotas taken prisoner during the war. Dallas acceded to writing the letter.[8]

Standing Buffalo returned to the Red River Settlement in August 1864 with his fellow leaders, Turning Thunder, his cousin Wa'ánatan, and The Leaf. Their aim was "to induce the H.B. Company to open a trade with them, so that they might have a market for their furs, &c., and obtain in return some things which they were in need of, and could not now get, owing to their war with the Americans." Governor Mactavish met them at Portage la Prairie and told them not to come to Fort Garry, but they ignored him, arriving in several groups beginning on 27 August. They had a conference with Mactavish at Upper Fort Garry on 30 August at which they said that they had sixteen British medals and spoke of their desire for assistance.[9]

That the Dakotas wished to be allowed to remain on British territory was common knowledge in the Red River Settlement. The newspaper reported that the Sioux had spoken—on various occasions when they had been in the settlement—"of their ancient right to this country, [and] of their desire to get part of it again."[10]

The HBC was reluctant to trade with the Sioux, undoubtedly because it was wary of public sentiment, which was horrified by the events in Minnesota and decidedly anti-Sioux. However, independent Métis traders were willing to open negotiations. The Métis had been in a precarious situation. As the buffalo herds contracted to the south during the 1840s and 1850s, Métis hunters had been forced to follow them. This brought them onto Sioux lands, engendering conflict. Moreover, the American government hoped to prevent British subjects, and especially Métis, from hunting south of the boundary. To circumvent opposition from both the Sioux and the Americans, some Métis elected to trade, rather than hunt, south of the border. The difficulty lay in supplying goods that the Indians wanted: American traders could supply goods via Missouri River steamboats as far as Fort Benton much more cheaply than could Métis traders, who had to rely on overland transportation from Fort Garry or Saint Paul. The only products that Métis could sell profitably to Indians on American territory were those that American traders were prevented (at least in law) from selling: alcohol and munitions.

Sioux and Métis came together to make peace in the aftermath of the Dakota Conflict, just as some groups had in previous years. For the Métis, the purpose of these negotiations was to gain access to the hunt on Sioux lands and to engage in trade. It is clear that the Métis initiated some of these meetings, but there is little documentary information on specific councils, beyond reference to their existence. In a dictation made in 1903, the Métis leader Gabriel Dumont briefly discussed the peace negotiations with the Dakotas held at Devil's Lake in late 1862, at which he was almost killed. "I was going to make peace in a Sioux camp," Dumont said, "and just as I was leaving the tent where I was staying, bending down through the narrow opening that was closed by a hanging skin, a Sioux hit me over the head with his rifle as he pulled the trigger. I was lucky the shot missed but I was left with a bruise. The other Sioux kicked and beat him with sticks. He had dishonoured them and was driven from camp."[11] According to John Andrew Kerr, a Canadian who lived for a time with Dumont's group of Métis and Indians, Gabriel's father (Isidore) and uncle (Jean) were the leaders in these peace negotiations.[12] A peace council mentioned by the mixed-blood trader Norbert Welsh in an interview conducted in 1931 may have been the same one discussed by Dumont. Welsh did not attend the meeting but learned of it from Baptiste La Bombarbe, who had served as the interpreter. According to Welsh the Métis buffalo hunters and Sioux concluded a peace treaty on the plains southwest of the Pembina Hills, "on English territory." Nine Sioux chiefs, including White Cap, Red Dog, and Mapachong, attended, agreeing with the Métis not to fight or to attack each other.[13] The plains southwest of the Pembina Hills are in American, not British, territory, however, and the meeting was probably in the general vicinity of Devil's Lake, although perhaps at some distance. White Cap, who entered Rupert's Land in late 1862, could have attended a meeting somewhere near Devil's Lake in 1862 while he was en route.[14] Although not placed at this meeting by Welsh, Standing Buffalo, who arrived at Fort Garry on 27 December 1862, had probably also come from this council.

Dakota leaders were as eager to initiate peaceful relations with the Métis as the Métis were with them—and for the same reason, to promote trade. In early May 1863 a party of Métis hunters visiting Fort Abercrombie from the Buffalo River (an eastern tributary of the Red River in Minnesota) reported that eight Sioux had come to their camp, smoked the peace pipe, and said that they wanted to live in peace with the mixed-bloods.[15] Little Crow met members of the Métis community of Saint Joseph on his arrival in April 1863, while en route to Fort Garry.[16] Apparently his negotiations were successful, for five Upper Santee representatives, including Standing Buffalo, visited Saint Joseph in early August 1863 to reconfirm the peace that then existed between them and the Red River Métis. They were concerned that the reported deaths of two of General Henry Sibley's mixed-blood scouts during the recent engagements between Sibley and the Sioux would jeopardize the peace. Father Alexis André assisted at the council between the Sioux and Métis, at which peaceful relations were reaffirmed.[17]

From the Métis the Sioux hoped to obtain trade goods, especially arms and ammunition. As the HBC was reluctant to trade with them, they courted peace with independent Métis traders, who usually purchased their outfits from the HBC. Of course, many English-speaking mixed-bloods also worked for the company. For that reason the Sioux also courted the mixed-blood traders, a prominent example being their attempts to cultivate a relationship with the family of William McKay.

William McKay was a member of a large mixed-blood family. Like his grandfather, John, and father, John Richards McKay, William and many of his brothers worked for the HBC. Later most of his sons followed him into the company's employ. In the summer of 1864 he facilitated a peace between Standing Buffalo's Dakotas and the Métis, Crees, and Ojibwas who hunted for Fort Ellice, where he was in charge. This pact also allowed the Dakotas to trade at the post for European goods. Two accounts of these events exist, the first by William's son Angus, the other by his son George. Angus was not yet seven in 1864 and was not a witness to these events. His account was undoubtedly based on stories told to him. George, only ten at the time, did accompany his father to the plains that summer and could tell his story firsthand. However, his account, appearing in his published memoirs, is rather more dramatic and romantic than the more prosaic version offered by Angus in a letter to a historian. Both accounts were written years after the events they describe.[18]

On 1 June 1864 a temporary sales shop at Fort Ellice was destroyed in an accidental gunpowder explosion. Two men were killed outright and another five severely burned, including another of William's sons, Thomas.[19] Because the post was undermanned as a result of the accident, provisions ran low, so William set out to the plains with a party of nine, including his youngest sons, William (then twelve) and the ten-year-old George, hoping to catch the camp of Métis and Crees who supplied the post's provisions.

About seven days out the traders from Fort Ellice encountered some five hundred tents of Dakotas, who at first mistook them for a party of Americans following their trail. William's party, seeing the Dakotas from a distance, in turn mistook them for buffalo. The Dakotas approached the traders, and a parlay was held. According to Angus a Sioux man named Tumma spoke some French, as did William, so these two acted as interpreters. William explained that his party was out looking for the post's hunters, and Standing Buffalo, who knew the location of this camp, agreed to lead William to it if William would help him make peace between the hunters and the Dakotas.

William's party camped with the Dakotas that night, "just outside of the main encampment." The next morning some thirty of the Sioux formed an escort to take the traders to the camp of Métis and Crees, which they reached in three or four days.

William entered the camp alone to prepare the way, leaving the Sioux to bathe and apply various pigments. "Their whole dress," recalled Angus, "was transformed into that of an Indian warrior and brave, ornamented from head to foot, even their horses and firearms were not without decorations and their costumes too were brilliant with decorations." Receiving word from William that they would be received, the Dakotas led the whole party into camp, firing a salvo that was answered by a salvo from the Métis and Crees. The Sioux were welcomed into the camp, where they smoked the peace pipe and were feasted. The following day they were invited into the "council chamber," where a friendship treaty was discussed and accepted, each participant marking an X by his name.

McKay had recognized a good business opportunity. By helping bring peace to the area, not only did he make the plains safer for his hunters, but he also secured the gratitude, loyalty, and trade of Standing Buffalo and his people. Standing Buffalo and 160 lodges of his followers arrived at Fort Ellice in the spring of 1865 to renew ties. Standing Buffalo presented McKay with "a beautifully ornamented pipe of peace and invited us [the traders] to smoke in his lodge."[20] Thereafter Dakota visitors traded regularly at Fort Ellice and occasionally received work doing odd jobs.[21]

According to William Edward Traill, a trader at the post and William McKay's son-in-law, the Dakotas gave McKay the name Wahan (Bear Skin) and considered him "the best friend that they had."[22] Angus noted that trade was the basis of this respect, explaining: "The name of 'Wahannah' by the Sioux Indians was conferred upon him because he traded with them in every thing they had to give; in exchange for something else they needed from him."[23]

The Manitoba Museum in Winnipeg has a grizzly bear–claw necklace in its collection that had once belonged to the McKays. Its exact provenance is unclear. Angus wrote that another of William's sons, Henry, had bought it from the Lakota leader Sitting Bull. Henry's son, Valentine, recorded that Sitting Bull had given it to Henry's fiancée, Ellen Inkster, before their wedding on 29 August 1881 at Fort Qu'Appelle.[24] It seems unlikely, however, that Sitting Bull would have given a bear-claw necklace, an item reserved for men, to a woman. Nevertheless, family history consistently attributes this article to Sitting Bull, who visited Fort Qu'Appelle in May 1881, shortly before surrendering to the American army at Fort Buford in July. It is just as likely that the necklace came from Standing Buffalo, who was at Fort Qu'Appelle only a few days before Henry and Ellen's wedding. Canada's governor-general, the Marquess of Lorne, toured the West in the summer of 1881, arriving at Fort Qu'Appelle on 17 August. Standing Buffalo's people performed a buffalo dance in his honor at the post the following day. "Each brave had a buffalo head and horns, complete, as a head-dress," remarked the policeman Sam Steele, "the appearance of the party being very weird indeed."[25] Whatever its exact provenance, the necklace demonstrates that the link between the Sioux people and the McKay family endured for more than a generation.

William McKay's experiences probably were not unique. Sioux leaders undoubtedly attempted to contact other mixed-blood employees of the HBC. Our knowledge of such contacts is limited by the documentary record, which is all but silent on such matters: the McKay boys' accounts of their father's encounter with Standing Buffalo are exceptional. Other Sioux were apparently confident that the HBC would, in the end, supply them with trade goods. A Métis named Antoine Frenier reported to the Indian agent at Fort Benton in February 1864 that some 150 lodges of Assiniboines, apparently from near Fort Union, had made peace with Dakotas, Yanktonais, and a few Lakotas in the autumn of 1863. In the spring, according to Frenier, the Sioux, and their new Assiniboine allies, would attempt to obtain ammunition from trading posts in the United States. If they failed, they would go north to the HBC posts in Rupert's Land.[26]

A significant amount of trade between the Sioux, the Métis, and mixed-bloods was conducted in the months following the Dakota Conflict. The Métis and mixed-bloods went south to hunt, encountering parties of Sioux, and trade soon flourished. According to White Crane and his party of Yanktonais, the Dakotas under White Lodge and Little Crow had been supplied with ammunition during the winter of 1862–63 by Red River Métis, who said they would join the Dakotas in upcoming raids. A Métis from Devil's Lake named Hancot arrived at the Dakota camp at Painted Wood Creek, an eastern tributary that enters the Missouri River roughly opposite the mouth of Big Knife River, while White Crane was there and counseled against giving up Americans captured during the war in Minnesota; the Yankton and Yanktonai leaders, Struck by the Ree and Wa'ánatan, concurred.[27] In November 1863, Indians informed the commanding officer at Fort Sully that the Sans Arcs had moved from Devil's Lake to Painted Wood (near present-day Bismarck) on account of the scarcity of buffalo at Devil's Lake and that a number of whites or mixed-bloods from Rupert's Land were trading powder, lead, tobacco, and other goods to the hostile Sioux. White Crane arrived at Fort Sully on 1 December and confirmed this report.[28]

During the winter of 1863–64, Métis hunters and traders led by Jean-Baptiste Wilkie Sr. camped at Wood End on the Souris River, where they intended to trade with the Sioux who had also camped along the river. Father Alexis André, now acting in the capacity of peace negotiator for the American government, went to this camp in December and had a meeting with the Sioux, who were not conciliatory.[29]

Many Métis hunters and traders frequented the area around Fort Berthold. Father Pierre-Jean De Smet, who arrived at Fort Berthold in June 1864 on a peace mission to the Sioux on behalf of the American government, encountered Métis hunters at the post almost daily. The Métis were on their summer hunt and came to Fort Berthold to trade. De Smet reported that they were also trading ammunition to the Sioux: "Powder and lead, I fear—and I speak here without positive proof—may be, and will be, plentifully supplied by the half-breeds of the northwest. The temptation is surely great, as I was assured that the Indians exchanged willingly a horse for one hundred balls and powder."[30] Frederic F.

Girard, the trader at Fort Berthold, wrote to De Smet that three British Métis had accompanied the Hidatsa leader Crow's Breast to the Yanktonai and Dakota camps on Heart River to invite them to come to the Métis camp to trade. Girard was certain that they were trading ammunition.[31] De Smet, commenting on Girard's letter, reported: "These half-breeds form large and great camps, consisting from four hundred to a thousand wagons and carts. They are on the most friendly terms with the Sioux, who respect their flag, (British,) wherever they meet them. It is supposed, on reliable authority, that they trade guns and ammunition to these enemies of the country."[32]

In August 1864 the brother of Big Head, a Yanktonai, arrived at Fort Berthold from the Yanktonai camp at the head of Little Knife River with news that the Yanktonais had received seven kegs of powder and balls from a party of British Métis, who had then invited the Yanktonais to go north to trade with them near the British line. General Alfred Sully, who had arrived at Fort Berthold in late August in the course of an expedition to round up hostile Sioux on the Dakota plains, departed in September for the Souris River. Encountering no recent signs of Native peoples, he was convinced that the Yanktonais had, in fact, crossed into British territory.[33] That winter, Colonel Charles Dimon reported from Fort Rice that the Sioux at Fort Berthold under Medicine Bear and Struck by the Ree had rejected all peaceful overtures and were said to have been encouraged by presents and munitions "by certain parties, said to be from the Red River of the North." Scouts at Fort Rice reported in January 1865:

> Half-breed traders from the British lines came into the hostile camp below Berthold with ten sleigh loads of goods. They rode into camp with the British flag at their head and said: "This flag will not be put down for anybody, only for God Almighty. Those who join us will not get hurt. Those who join the Americans will get hurt. We will return the last of the month with more powder, ball and arms, and some Santees, and will take Fort Berthold and then Fort Rice." Then they gave a feast and presented the Indians with five kegs of powder and some sacks of bullets and traded more. At the feast the Man That Strikes the Ree said: "As long as I live I shall never shake hands with the whites." Medicine Bear said: "I am the man to make war with the Americans; kill all you can, I will say nothing against you.["][34]

Active Sioux-American hostilities wound down after 1865, but Métis-Sioux trade continued, much to the annoyance of American army officers. Colonel Philippe Régis de Trobriand, in command at Fort Stevenson, knew that Red River Métis traded whiskey and munitions with impunity to various Lakotas and Cheyennes in the vicinity of Fort Buford on the Knife River during the winter of 1866–67, and he expected them to do the same the following winter.[35] During the summer of 1867 Lieutenant Colonel E. S. Otis reported that Métis were selling ammunition to Sioux intent on attacking the Hidatsas near Fort Berthold, and Lieutenant Colonel E. M. Bartlett, at Fort Sully, offered to destroy Red River traders who, he argued, needed "an example even more than the hostile Siouxs."[36] Troops from Fort Buford raided Métis camps during 1868, but the traders returned the following winter and simply established their posts in different areas.[37] In the autumn of 1869 Major General W. S. Hancock visited the Souris River, where he saw the remains of huts that had been used by Métis traders during the previous winter. Hancock identified the Métis' customers as Dakotas but noted that their leader was "Setting Bull."[38]

While trade was of paramount importance to Sioux-Métis relations and beneficial to both parties, at no time did all Métis support the Sioux. Various camps could be pragmatic and sometimes cooperated with the American army. Indeed, Métis were often the army's major source of information on Sioux movements. In July 1863 a Métis camp under Charles Grant and Jean-Baptiste Wilkie Sr. provided General Sibley with information and three guides, while a camp under Edward Harmon gave news of recent Sioux movements to Captain James Fisk's party of immigrants to the Montana goldfields.[39]

Métis served as guides, scouts, interpreters, and mail carriers for the American army, thus garnering them retribution from the Sioux. For example, Joseph Demerais, the son of the interpreter at Fort Abercrombie, was murdered at Bear's Den Hillock (near the Sheyenne River) by Dakotas, supposedly of Little Crow's band, in May 1867.[40]

Nevertheless, the value that the Sioux placed on peaceful relations with the Métis tempered their actions toward Métis who worked for the American army. In the autumn of 1867 Trobriand, at Fort Stevenson, learned from two of the men who carried the mail between Fort Totten and Fort Stevenson that the Hunkpapas intended to kill anyone who carried mail for the Americans, be they European, mixed-blood, or Indian, but, on at least three separate occasions during the following months, mail carriers who were Métis, or mistaken for Métis, were released unharmed, although with a warning to stop working for the Americans.[41] In November 1867 John George Brown (an Irishman) and another white man were captured by Lakotas and Two Dogs's Yanktonais between Fort Buford and Fort Stevenson. They either pretended to be or were mistaken for Red River mixed-bloods. While the Yanktonais wanted to kill them, a Lakota leader "spoke at length and eloquently, it seems, in favor of the captives, and in the end his opinion carried." The whites were disarmed and set free with a warning not to carry the mail for the Americans. [42] The following month Gardepie (a Red River Métis) and three men were captured by White Cloud's followers. Gardepie and his men were set free, as the Indians said they knew Gardepie, and also told not to carry mail for the Americans. [43] In May 1868, Sitting Bull's Hunkpapas captured and killed Charles MacDonald, Joe Hamelin (both Red River mixed-bloods), and a soldier near Strawberry Lake. A few days later John George Brown and Joe Martin (a Red River mixed-blood) left Fort Stevenson to meet the couriers from Fort Totten halfway. Sitting Bull's Hunkpapas captured them near Middle Strawberry Lake, near Dog Den Butte, and stripped them of their weapons, equipment, clothing, and horses. When questioned, they said that they were mixed-bloods from Red River going to Saint Joseph to hunt. Sitting Bull explained that he would not have allowed the two men from Red River (Charles MacDonald and Joe Hamelin) to be killed, but the young men killed them before they found out who they were. Not knowing that Brown and Martin were couriers, he let them go.[44] Lakotas and Yanktonais who were opposed to the American presence in the region were apparently unwilling to kill Red River mixed-bloods, undoubtedly because they were the source of at least part of their munitions.

American army officers claimed, not only that Métis and British traders supplied Sioux with arms and ammunition, but also that they encouraged further hostilities in an effort to protect their trade. In September 1863 Sully's scouts reported that, while most of the Sioux had fled toward the Missouri River after the Battle at Whitestone Hill on the third of the month, some had gone north to British territory, where they had friends among the Métis. Sibley believed that the Métis would inform the Sioux of any changes in American troop strength.[45] In January 1864 Sibley accused Métis who arrived at Fort Abercrombie of deterring the Sioux from surrendering in order to secure their trade, even though these same Métis had supplied him with information regarding Sioux movements.[46] Sibley was encouraged in this belief by Major Joseph R. Brown, who, along with Father Alexis André, had agreed to serve as a peace commissioner for the U.S. government. Brown had found it almost impossible to find any Sioux to speak to: Sibley's expedition in the summer of 1863 had caused the "hostiles" and many of the "friendly" Sioux to scatter far from Fort Abercrombie. Those he did find were unwilling to surrender, and he blamed this on the Red River Métis, who, he believed, protected their trade with the Sioux by filling them with a fear of the punishments that they would receive if they surrendered. [47] Echoing Sibley's reports, Sully accused British Métis of securing the Sioux trade by keeping the Sioux informed of troop movements and of informing them that American troops could not cross the boundary. [48]

In June 1865 Sully invited the Lakotas, Yanktonais, and Santees to come to Fort Rice to discuss peace. After a poorly attended council on 16 July Sully speculated that the Métis had told the Sioux that it was a trap. [49] Thinking that no more hostiles would come to Fort Rice, Sully left for Devil's Lake in late July, where he encountered a Red River Métis camp and had it searched for contraband; none was found. The Métis swore that they did not sell ammunition to the Sioux, and they told Sully of recent Sioux movements. A second Métis camp was found at Devil's Lake. These Métis claimed to be Americans. Sully believed the information that they supplied but still accused them of passing information about troop movements to the Sioux. To Sully—and he was probably correct—the small size of the second Métis camp was proof that these people were on good terms with the Sioux, for such a small camp could not have defended itself against a hostile force. [50]

Some American officials believed that the British government was responsible for the actions of the Métis, either by actively participating in this trade (through the HBC) or by refusing to do anything to stop it. Major General John Pope, Sibley's and Sully's superior, publicly accused the British of complicity, [51] while Newton Edmunds, the governor of the Dakota Territory, wondered whether the Canadian government could be held responsible. [52] Such claims need to be evaluated critically. Nevertheless, some claims about Métis trading activities were probably true. Although there is no evidence that Métis traders openly fomented war, it is likely that they did little to encourage peace. If conflict ceased on the American plains, the trade in arms and ammunition would be reduced considerably.

In the months following the Dakota Conflict Sioux leaders wasted no time in contacting and attempting to obtain the goodwill of the HBC and the mixed-blood population of Rupert's Land. At the same time they were immediately aware that they had entered an area, not only claimed by a different colonial government, but also occupied and effectively controlled by different aboriginal peoples. Dakota leaders responded quickly by opening discussions with the Ojibwas to allow them rights of temporary access to Ojibwa land. In May 1863, for example, Little Crow arrived with his band at Pembina and spoke of going to Fort Garry. While in Pembina he opened negotiations with the Red Lake,

THE DAKOTA CONFLICT AND MIGRATION

Lake of the Woods, and Pembina Ojibwas.[53] However, the Dakota Conflict also produced refugees who traveled to Red River and wished to remain there permanently. Many leaders, therefore, sought to gain rights of residency from the local aboriginal people: that peace was achieved is demonstrated by the fact that the Dakota peoples were able to continue to live in these areas. The Mdewakanton leader H'damani noted, for instance, that he and his three sons had arrived at Turtle Mountain during late 1862. He gave the local Ojibwas four horses and five sacred pipes, and, in exchange, "[t]he chief warrior of the Ojibeway gave the Turtle Mountain to me and my people."[54] Standing Buffalo, whose people had moved onto the plains between the Qu'Appelle and the Missouri Rivers while most Dakota refugees remained in the parklands, was initially less successful. The Americans at Fort Wadsworth received word from him in August 1864 that his young men were being killed by Plains Crees, Assiniboines, and Blackfeet—all of whom had made war on his people.[55] An American army officer reported that Dakotas in Rupert's Land had attempted to make peace treaties with the Blackfeet and Assiniboines in 1865 but that the Assiniboines had refused and that the negotiations had ended in trouble.[56] In a statement made in March 1870 the Wahpeton leader White Cap asserted that he and his people, however, "have made peace with Half Breeds, Chippawa, Crees, & Assiniboine."[57]

Standing Buffalo, with the assistance of mixed-bloods like William McKay of Fort Ellice, eventually negotiated a successful peace agreement with the Plains Crees. That Standing Buffalo's people remained on British territory indicates that peace was achieved with neighboring groups, but it was not universal. Walter Traill, for example, recorded in his memoirs that Standing Buffalo's people arrived at Fort Ellice from Wood Mountain to trade in July 1868 and that they had had a fight with the local Ojibwas. The next morning the Dakotas were seen "in hasty retreat for the distant plains."[58]

Although difficult to document, conflict between the Dakotas and the Ojibwas continued after the Dakotas negotiated their entry into Rupert's Land. The newspaper in Red River reported early in 1864, for example, that one Dakota had been killed by an Ojibwa and that more trouble was expected.[59] It is noteworthy, however, that much of this conflict was with Ojibwas from Red Lake in Minnesota, not Ojibwas or Crees living in Rupert's Land.[60] The Red River Ojibwas appear to have desired peace with the Dakotas, perhaps because a number of Dakota men had married Ojibwa women. When Ojibwas from Red Lake attacked a Dakota camp on Lake Manitoba, the Dakotas, Métis, and Red River

Ojibwas met in council at Fort Garry, "smoked the pipe of peace; and once again patched up all grievances."[61] Ojibwas, perhaps from Red Lake, killed a number of Standing Buffalo's followers camped near Fort Garry and forced the rest to flee in August 1866, a day after Standing Buffalo had concluded a peace treaty with them and the Crees at the fort. The Métis considered this an unfriendly act on the part of the Ojibwas, and, in retaliation, François Desmarais, who was married or in some other way connected to the Dakotas, killed an Ojibwa man in the HBC store.[62]

Dakota people migrated from Minnesota to the plains of present-day Manitoba and North Dakota during the 1860s and firmly established themselves in the borderlands. The process required delicate negotiations with a host of others—Americans, British, Métis, and other aboriginal peoples. But, by taking advantage of the peace agreements they obtained from other aboriginal groups and of linguistic and cultural ties to the Yanktonais, they generally gained peaceful access to new lands on both sides of the Canada–United States boundary. The Sioux had taken advantage of the boundary, fleeing across it on the approach of American troops, and trading with the Métis. But they had not become "Canadian" Indians. They remained in the borderlands, traveling from one side to the other, and committing themselves to neither the British-Canadian nor the American regime, for a decade longer, before finally settling on Canadian reserves and American reservations.

4. THE MIGRATION OF THE SIOUX
TO THE MILK RIVER COUNTRY

The migration of Dakota peoples out of Minnesota and into the borderlands continued throughout the 1860s. By the end of the decade other Sioux groups were likewise shifting territory. Some were migrating up the Missouri River to its junction with the Yellowstone and, beyond that, the Milk River. Other Dakota groups occupied the country south of Milk River.[1] Several bands of Upper Yanktonais, originally from the area around Fort Rice, migrated up the Missouri to the area surrounding Fort Buford. According to Lieutenant Colonel Henry A. Morrow at Fort Buford, the Yanktonais were interlopers, but, having established themselves north of the Missouri and above the post, they had to be treated as permanent residents.[2] Santees and Yanktons from the southern part of the Dakota Territory joined them in the area.[3] The Santees, Yanktonais, and Yanktons were also joined by northern bands of Lakotas who were, during the same years, moving from the area southwest of the Missouri toward the lower Yellowstone country and from it to the mouth of Milk River.

The various groups communicated and cooperated freely. The Santees, Yanktonais, and Yanktons frequently camped and traveled together, and the Lakotas often crossed the Missouri River and hunted with them. The Santees and Upper Yanktonais also formed ties to Red Stone's Lower Assiniboines, whose agency would later be at Wolf Point. Fellows D. Pease, the American agent to the Crows, reported that many Santees, Cutheads, Yanktonais, and other Sioux were married to Assiniboines and that the Assiniboines usually divided their annuities with them.[4]

Several Dakota groups established themselves north of the Forty-ninth Parallel by mid-decade, although they too remained in contact with Sioux on American territory. Little Crow's Mdewakantons and Little Six's and Medicine Bottle's Mdewakantons and Wahpetons camped from Sturgeon Creek to the White Horse Plains and farther west to Poplar Point and Portage la Prairie.

H'damani's followers lived at Turtle Mountain. Tahampegda's and White Eagle's Wahpetons camped on the Assiniboine River. White Cap's people lived peacefully with the Assiniboines at Moose Mountain (people who had extensive ties to Red Stone's Assiniboines) before moving to the northwest as far as the North Saskatchewan River by the end of the decade. Mahpiyahdinape moved directly to the neighborhood of Fort Ellice (a Hudson's Bay Company [HBC] fort) after the Sioux were attacked by General Alfred Sully's troops at Killdeer Mountain in July 1865.[5] There was a great deal of intercourse between camps, and some groups, notably that of Standing Buffalo, had yet to settle on either side of the boundary. Standing Buffalo's and White Cap's people were invariably mixed with Yanktonais and Yanktons. Indeed, the mixed identify of these camps was often reflected by commentators identifying these leaders and their followers as *Yanktons*.[6]

The migration of various Sioux into the Milk River country has been all but ignored by American and Canadian historians, Raymond DeMallie's extended essay on the Sioux in Dakota and Montana Territories being the only study on the topic.[7] Moreover, historians of both countries have overlooked the transboundary dimension of these events. Studies of the Sioux in Canada, for example, mention only in passing that leaders like Standing Buffalo remained in the borderlands and crossed and recrossed the Canada–United States boundary many times. Such studies give the impression that those Dakotas who entered Rupert's Land after the Dakota Conflict did not return to American soil. Such was not the case. Sioux leaders negotiated with governments on both sides of the boundary to discover which would accord them better treatment, and Sioux who traded with Americans at Fort Peck also tried to open a trade with the HBC. Sioux continued to trade with Métis, whose wintering camps in the Cypress Hills and at Wood Mountain gave them easy access to Sioux camps in the borderlands. The Lakotas had frequently ventured north of the boundary before 1876; in fact, leaders like Sitting Bull traded with the Métis at Wood Mountain at least as early as the winter of 1870–71.

Santee and Yanktonai leaders asked for a treaty with the American government on several occasions during the late 1860s and early 1870s. (They had been left out of the Americans' treaty process in the 1850s.) In September 1869 leaders of the Cuthead and C'an'óna bands of Upper Yanktonais, including Medicine Bear, Thundering Bull, Shoots the Tiger, and Afraid of Bear, and a few Sissetons petitioned the American government to make a treaty of peace and friendship. In return for annuities, a reservation, and farming instruction, the leaders promised on behalf of their followers to be at peace with the Americans and with aboriginal groups friendly to the United States.[8] Lieutenant Colonel Henry Morrow, who received the Yanktonais' and Sissetons' petition at Fort Buford, reported that these and other bands that had no treaty relations with the American government were sources of many recruits to the hostile camps under Sitting Bull, Black Moon, Four Horns, and others. He was fully in favor of their request. Morrow opined that the Yanktonais and Sissetons joined the hostile Lakotas because they were poor and tempted by plunder. He reasoned that, if the Americans gave annuities to these people, they would be less likely to join the hostiles, whose leaders would, therefore, lose influence.[9] A week later the leaders of the Takíni band of Upper Yanktonais—Calumet Man, Afraid of Bull, Long Fox, Eagle Dog, and Standing Bellow—arrived at Fort Buford and signed a similar petition.[10]

A camp of some 260 lodges of Santees, Yanktonais, and some Lakotas arrived in the vicinity of Fort Browning in late April 1871. The Milk River agent, A. J. Simmons, noted that these Sioux were hostile to the Americans and to other Indians and at peace only with the Assiniboines. Told by the Assiniboines that the Sioux planned to attack the agency, Simmons sent them an invitation to come for a council. He, along with Red Stone and Little Bull of the Assiniboines, met Standing Buffalo and others in the Sioux camp on 4 May. After a feast and smoke provided by Simmons, Standing Buffalo explained the reason for his people's presence in the Milk River country:

> Their country below [farther down the Missouri River] was burnt and dead, the game was all gone, they couldn't live in it; they had now come here, they liked this country, here they could make plenty of robes and make plenty of meat. Their country was wherever the buffalo ranged. [H]ere was plenty of buffalo, it was their country . . . and they had come to live in it.

Standing Buffalo repeated his people's request to be at peace with the Americans and to receive annuities. Simmons replied that the Americans also wanted peace and offered to give them the same supplies as were given to the Assiniboines. The Sioux moved closer to the agency the next day, and Standing Buffalo paid a visit to Simmons.

The Santees and Yanktonais departed on 6 April. That same day Struck by the Ree and a group of Yankton men arrived for a meeting with Simmons. Simmons, who believed that his meetings with Standing Buffalo were complete successes, was less sanguine about the Yanktons, whom he described as "renegades from various bands composing a camp of about the worst Indians I ever saw."[11] When in late May Standing Buffalo and Struck by the Ree demanded subsistence and presents as the price of peace, Simmons's superior, J. A. Viall, relented, giving them some goods in the hopes of keeping some control over them.[12]

American officials were well aware that Standing Buffalo's Sissetons and Struck by the Ree's Yanktons and Yanktonais were in close communication with Lakotas under Black Moon, Four Horns, and Sitting Bull, leaders who were opposed to American encroachment on Sioux lands. Viall, the superintendent of Indian affairs in Montana, reported in August 1871 that Sitting Bull's followers occupied the country along the proposed route of the Northern Pacific Railroad and that they intended to oppose the survey and construction of the road. As these people had had no intercourse with the American government, Viall asked permission of the commissioner of Indian affairs to visit them.[13] Viall sent Simmons to Fort Peck in the autumn of 1871 to meet with Black Moon, Iron Dog, Long Dog, Little Wound, Sitting Eagle, and Bear's Rib. Sitting Bull and others had visited Fort Peck in September and October and were not present when Simmons arrived on 4 November.

Simmons was joined on the post by some two hundred lodges of Lakotas on 14 November. Over the course of fifteen interviews, Simmons informed the Lakota leaders that he was a messenger from President Ulysses S. Grant, who wanted to live in peace and wished to learn the Lakotas' disposition. Black Moon stated emphatically that the Lakotas also wanted peace but that to have peace the Americans had to stop construction on the railroad (which would destroy the game), keep American soldiers and settlers out of Sioux lands, and abandon Fort Buford and the trading post on the Musselshell River. Others spoke; their main concern was the railroad. Simmons refused each demand, saying that the railroad would be built regardless of Sioux opinion, that this land was not Sioux land—but Crow and Gros Ventre land—and that Fort Buford and the trading post on the Musselshell were outside the area used by the Sioux. Simmons closed by urging the leaders to consider his words "and make up their minds whether they would make peace and live, or continue hostilities and die like the wolves."

In summarizing the response that Black Moon delivered on the first day of talks, Simmons wrote:

> [Black Moon said] in their way this country belonged to them, they had fought for it and driven the Crows and Gros Ventres back. The whites settled in and drove them out of their country below; they were compelled to come here where they could get some game. They crossed the Yellowstone six

years ago. They had fought for the country they occupied, and it would be difficult to restrain their people from fighting again. Pledged his best efforts for peace: would labor with his people. . . . The rail-road would fill the country with whites and whites' houses: their game would be destroyed. Made a strong appeal for provisions to be furnished them, as a basis for peace and in consideration for their giving up their country to the rail-road.

Black Moon's comments suggest that he was preparing a strategy to address the American threat. Americans would come, build their railroad and trading posts, and drive away the buffalo, thereby destroying the Sioux economy. In exchange for the usurpation of resources Black Moon demanded that the Americans supply his people with the goods that they would need for economic security.[14]

Ultimately, Black Moon and Simmons agreed (according to Simmons) to a list of items. First, the Lakotas would send no war parties against the Americans, pending peace negotiations. Second, Simmons would send Black Moon's statement to the president and ask that the Sioux be given provisions. Third, Black Moon would counsel his people for peace. Simmons was convinced that Black Moon's desire for peace was genuine, so he gave him some provisions to distribute among the people.[15]

In the summer of 1872 the American government sent a larger commission to Fort Peck to meet with Lakota leaders and to persuade them to travel to Washington and meet the president. The commissioners, Assistant Secretary of the Interior Benjamin R. Cowen, N. J. Turney, and J. W. Wham, arrived at Fort Peck in late July and had a council with the Indians in late August. Few Lakotas were present and none of the important Lakota leaders (Sitting Bull, Black Moon and others), although Sitting Bull sent his brother-in-law, His-Horse-Looking. Instead, the Americans found mainly Medicine Bear's Yanktonais. The Indians were concerned about the railroad and the site for an agency, but the commissioners refused to discuss the matter until the Sioux leaders had visited the president in Washington. At first the Indians were opposed to going, but eventually they relented, and a number of Yanktonais leaders, including Medicine Bear, Afraid of Bear, Black Catfish, and others, made the trip.[16]

The American government had hoped that the Cowen Commission would be a first step toward ending Lakota opposition to the construction of the Northern Pacific Railroad, which the Lakotas argued would lead to the destruction of their hunting grounds. However, few nonagency Lakotas had attended talks with either Simmons in June 1872 or Cowen, Turney, and Wham in August.

During this very time some three hundred lodges of Lakotas and Yanktonais had crossed the boundary and gone to the North-West Territories, as the bulk of Rupert's Land became known after it was transferred to Canadian sovereignty in 1870. (A much smaller part of the HBC's former territory became the new province of Manitoba that same year.)

This group's leader was Little Knife, an older man closely associated with the nonreservation Hunkpapas under Four Horns, Black Moon, and Sitting Bull and later described by John F. Finerty, the "war correspondent" of the *Chicago Times*, as "a man for whom high regard was felt by white and red men alike, because he was truthful, honorable, and, for a savage, humane even to his enemies."[17] In the early summer of 1872 Little Knife's delegation sent tobacco to Isaac Cowie, the trader in charge of the HBC's Fort Qu'Appelle, saying that they wished to visit him and make Fort Qu'Appelle their trading post. Cowie replied that the post lay within the Crees' and Ojibwas' country and that it would be dangerous for the Sioux to come, but the Lakotas and Yanktonais were not deterred. They had already been in contact with the Métis and thereby felt some measure of security. They sent one Métis ahead with the message that they were coming anyway and would not hold the company responsible for any attack made against them. Left with little choice, Cowie asked the Ojibwa headmen Pussung, O'Soup, and Chekuk to allow the delegation to visit. The local leaders replied, however, that they would not be able to control their young men. Their people already resented the presence of the Sissetons and Wahpetons under White Cap and Standing Buffalo who had recently begun hunting in the Qu'Appelle district and trading at Fort Qu'Appelle, and they did not wish to share their hunting grounds with even greater numbers of Sioux.[18]

Preparing for the inevitable visit, Cowie asked Alick Fisher, a Métis from the Qu'Appelle Valley, to enlist a force of Métis to escort and guard the Sioux delegation. The Métis force rode out to meet the Sioux, escorted them to the post, guarded them while they were there, and, finally, escorted them from the fort on their departure. The Saulteaux were warned not to approach.

When they arrived at Fort Qu'Appelle, the emissaries cited their long-standing alliance with the British against the Americans and produced a medal bearing the likeness of King George III given to one of their ancestors during the War of 1812. One spokesman said that they wanted to live on British territory, trade with the HBC, and, in the words of his translator, be "good British Indians."

Cowie once again explained that the area was Cree and Ojibwa country. In case this was insufficient discouragement he told them that the HBC did not have the supplies to provide for the Crees and Métis who had been coming into the country in increasing numbers and could hardly supply the Sioux as well. Cowie counseled the Sioux to make peace with the Americans, whose traders could provide goods on the Missouri more cheaply than the British traders could. Nevertheless, the Sioux boasted that, so long as the Métis did not go against them, they could soon subdue the Crees and Ojibwas.

Evidently the Saskatchewan Métis were prepared to aid the Lakotas. According to Edward McKay, a brother of William McKay of Fort Ellice and a former HBC trader who was then farming on Battle Creek in the Cypress Hills: "There is understood to be an alliance defensive and offensive between the Te Tones [Tetons] and the Metis. The Crees and Salteaux are highly displeased with the Metis and Sioux for hunting on their grounds, And only allow them, because they are affraid of them and unable to drive them off."[19]

The Sioux did not expect the Americans to be reasonable. They would come and build their railroad despite Sioux attempts to stop them. Now the Sioux were looking at other options, including possibly moving north. Little Knife had come to lay the groundwork for securing a new supply of European goods and cultivating a relationship with the Métis. The Sioux who met with Cowie told him: "They would never become friendly with the Americans, and they were bound to find safety on the north side of the boundary line. They were highly pleased with our kindness in trying to prevent any trouble with the Saulteaux, though they felt themselves quite able to defend themselves, and they thanked us for our friendly talk and entertainment; but they could not take our refusal as final."[20] This was not what Cowie had hoped to hear.

After their meeting at Fort Qu'Appelle, the Sioux proceeded down the Qu'Appelle River to Fort Ellice, near the junction of the Qu'Appelle and Assiniboine Rivers, and from there continued down the Assiniboine River in the direction of Fort Garry. They met two groups of Canadians during the journey. Sandford Fleming, the chief engineer of the Canadian Pacific Railway, sent west to examine possible railway routes, encountered a group of some sixty to eighty individuals at Rat Creek, some ten miles west of Portage la Prairie, in early August and had a short talk with them. "Ho, Ho; B'jou [*bonjour*], B'jou," said the leader, demonstrating linguistically his contact with the French-speaking Métis, and shook hands with the Europeans. "They had come from Fort Ellice," wrote Fleming's secretary, George Grant, "had recently travelled the long road from Missouri, and were now on their way to Governor Archibald [Adams George Archibald, the lieutenant governor of Manitoba and the North-West Territories] to ask permission to live under the British flag, and that small reserves or allotments of land should be allowed them, as they were determined to live no longer under the rule of 'the long knives.'" The surveyors, however, had little time to talk. The Sioux "would have liked a long *pow wow*, but we had time only for hasty greetings and a few kindly words with them."[21] About a week later Colonel Patrick Robertson-Ross, the Canadian adjutant general who toured the territories in 1872, encountered two separate groups from Little Knife's band near Fort Ellice. Unlike Fleming, he did not stop to talk. He described them only as "bold and wild-looking fellows" but "perfectly friendly in their manner."[22]

Archibald McDonald, the chief factor in charge of the HBC's Swan River District, which included both Fort Qu'Appelle and Fort Ellice, met Lieutenant Governor Archibald on 7 June to discuss the Lakotas and Yanktonais at Fort Ellice, saying that there were three hundred lodges of them at or near the fort and that they were determined to visit Fort Garry. Archibald was mistaken about who these visitors were. He was aware that the "Minnesota Sioux" or "Santees," those Dakotas who came north after the Dakota Conflict and whose presence the Canadian government grudgingly accepted, were distinct from the "Missouri Sioux," the Lakotas, Yanktons, and Yanktonais. However, Archibald and his correspondents, like most outsiders then and since, referred to all Dakota peoples as *Sioux*, thus creating the possibility that one group of Sioux would be confused with another. Archibald mistook the Lakotas and Yanktonais for Dakotas.

William McKay, the chief trader at Fort Ellice, had informed Archibald in May 1872 that Standing Buffalo's Sissetons, who had been trading at Fort Ellice since 1865, would probably visit Red River that summer as they were anxious to obtain a reserve in British territory.[23] Archibald told McKay to ask the Dakotas not to come to Fort Garry, and he instructed Indian Commissioner Simpson to visit the Sioux at Fort Ellice to settle the reserve question.[24] McKay told the Dakotas to wait for the commissioner, and this seemed acceptable to them.[25]

When McDonald informed Archibald in June that the "Sioux" at Fort Ellice wished to pay him a visit, he assumed that these were Standing Buffalo's people and accordingly told McDonald that they must not be allowed to come into the settlement. The arrival of these "half-starved savages," he noted, would be very undesirable. They would all expect provisions, and they might simply take them if they were not freely given. He cautioned, however, that "this [refusal] must be done in a way not to irritate them, or we might, in our efforts to escape depredations here, be surely transferring the scene of trouble to the Upper [Fort Ellice] instead of the Lower [Fort Garry] waters of the Assiniboine."[26]

Archibald's concern was too late. His erstwhile visitors were offended, as James McKay, the president of the Executive Council of Manitoba, soon discovered. McKay recognized that the "Sioux" in question were not Dakotas but "Missouri Sioux." A former HBC trader, McKay spoke Dakota fluently and frequently spoke on behalf of the Dakotas before the government at Red River in the years following the Dakota Conflict.[27] Without any apparent instructions from Archibald, he decided to send a Métis named George Racette Jr., also known as Shaman Racette, with a message for the Lakotas and Yanktonais, who were still camped on Beaver Creek near Fort Ellice. Racette, who had traded with the Sioux on British territory in previous years, was directed to give the Sioux some tobacco, to show them that the "English" authorities wished to maintain friendly relations with them. "The Governor," went the message, "is very sorry he did not see you—he thought you were only the Sioux from the Portage [Portage la Prairie]. You should have stopped and explained to the proper parties where you had come from, and what Tribe you represented."[28] The mission was unsuccessful. Racette reported that the Sioux were upset over Archibald's refusal to meet with them. Racette was also angry. McKay had promised to supply him with presents worth twelve pounds sterling to give to the Sioux. On his arrival at Fort Ellice, however, Archibald McDonald gave him presents worth only six pounds, saying that there was no money from the government to pay for the expenditure. The scantiness of the gifts served to anger the Sioux even more. In the end Racette gave them his own supplies in the hopes that McDonald would reimburse him. McDonald refused.[29] Meanwhile, the Lakota and Yanktonai delegation spent the winter of 1872–73 camped in the vicinity of Fort Ellice.

Adams Archibald left office in December 1872 and was replaced as lieutenant governor of Manitoba and the North-West Territories by Alexander Morris. While Archibald had refused to meet the Sioux encamped near Fort Ellice, Morris readily agreed to see a delegation. Eighteen Sioux arrived, not Lakotas, Yanktons, or Yanktonais, but Dakotas, including White Cap and the son of Standing Buffalo, Standing Buffalo having been killed in June 1871.[30] Morris met them with Indian Commissioner Wemyss Simpson and James McKay, who acted as interpreter. White Cap said that he had come to testify to Sioux's friendship for the English and asked to be given a grant of land to settle on in the spring. Morris, who did not know that the Canadian government had already agreed to provide reserve land to the Dakotas then living in the Canadian Northwest, said that the request would be passed on to the government. Simpson distributed some presents, and the Dakotas went away well satisfied.[31]

The Lakotas, Yanktons, and Yanktonais then at Fort Ellice remained dissatisfied, and news of their dissatisfaction quickly escalated into disturbing rumors by the time it reached Manitoba. One report indicated that Little Knife had sent tobacco to the "Canadian" Dakotas, asking them to join the Lakotas in making war against the Americans, and saying that the "British government" would do nothing for them.[32] Isaac Cowie received information at Fort Qu'Appelle from a Métis trader named Antoine Gladue that a large band of Lakotas was collecting at Frenchman River (a tributary of Milk River) and that Little Knife was said to be in favor of launching a raid against the settlements in Manitoba. Sitting Bull, so the reports went, favored peace and would not agree to a raid, but Cowie's information indicated that Little Knife was supported by the majority. Some reports indicated that the Lakotas would do nothing until they had seen a government representative; another said that they planned to commence hostilities immediately. The latest letters from Father Jean-Marie Lestanc of the Qu'Appelle Mission contained no recent or, in Cowie's estimation, reliable information. Uncertain of the outcome, Cowie advised Archibald McDonald at Fort Ellice "to prepare to send off Mrs. McDonald and the bairns at the packet time."[33]

Settlers in Palestine (now Gladstone, Manitoba) petitioned the Manitoba government in March 1873 to send troops at once. They had heard that the Sioux were concentrating along the Missouri River in preparation for a raid to be launched in the early spring. Palestine, they said, lay on the route from the Northwest. Significantly, they also heard that the Sioux were aggrieved "by the state of matters in the province consequent on the transference of this country to Canada."[34] The transfer of Rupert's Land to the new Dominion of Canada had replaced the old order of the fur trade with a new set of players. The Sioux, no doubt, were concerned about the effect that these changes would have on their trade with the Métis and the HBC.

Archibald McDonald did not understand that Adams Archibald had mistaken the Lakota and Yanktonai delegation for a group of Dakotas from Portage la Prairie. He could not, therefore, understand the governor's instructions—made before he left office in December—not to give the Sioux any aid and to wait until the Indian commissioner arrived. Writing to his superior, Donald Smith, McDonald argued: "It is very easy for a person in his [Archibald's] position at Fort Garry to give orders not to give anything to a lot of wild and starving savages—who have come hundreds of miles to see him,—but I would like to see him carrying out his orders—The Indians could never have gone back with out some assistance in provisions and ammunition." McDonald gave the Lakotas provisions and ammunition in February 1873 to enable them to start back for the Missouri.[35]

Alexander Morris, the new lieutenant governor, knew almost nothing of the winter's events until March 1873, when James McKay informed him "that a party of American Sioux headed by '*Little Knife*' left here last Fall in a very dissatisfied spirit, and made sundry threats." Morris decided at once to send two trusted emissaries to gather information. John Norquay, an English mixed-blood, was sent to Palestine to ascertain if the threats were serious and, in case the reports proved correct, make arrangements to form two companies of mounted "half breeds of both races." Pascal Breland, a Métis member of both the Legislative Assembly of Manitoba and the North-West Council (the governing body of the North-West Territories), was dispatched to the plains to meet the Lakotas. Morris also suggested to the Canadian government in Ottawa that it open communications with the American authorities as the Lakotas and Yanktonais were from the Missouri River in American territory.[36]

In Palestine Norquay attended a public meeting called on 14 March 1873 at which he learned that the village had received information about the Sioux from the HBC trader Thomas McKay (one of William McKay's sons), who had come in sometime before from Fort Ellice. McKay reported that the Sioux who had wintered at Fort Ellice intended making a spring raid on the province and that their "quiet deportment" was being replaced by a "more arrogant tone." Norquay made his own inquiries about the Sioux "and found out that a considerable amount of uneasiness prevails among them and that they are holding Councils very frequently and some have been heard to say that in the spring they would do whatever they pleased as they expected large numbers of themselves in from the plains." While in Palestine Norquay was shown two letters sent by traders to their friends at Portage la Prairie. One had written from the Red Ochre Hills to a Mr. Whiteway that "Ooosoop or Back Fat [the Ojibwa headman O'Soup] states the Sioux are going in to the Settlement and I hear it is for no good." Abraham Spence wrote his mother from the Qu'Appelle Lakes that "[t]he Sioux are gathering at Wood Mountain and are going down to the Settlement but I dont know what is their intention." A man from High Bluff, one Mr. "Pocha" (perhaps Poitras), told Norquay that the Dakotas at that place had said that many more "Sioux" were expected in the spring.[37]

Meanwhile, Pascal Breland was heading west in the general direction of Wood Mountain with instructions "to say all he could to reassure the minds of the Sioux in that vicinity, and having obtained all the information possible as to the actual position of affairs to return and, if he found any cause for alarm[,] to send a trusty courier in advance to report to the authorities here."[38] Breland arrived at Fort Qu'Appelle in early April 1873 but was unable to gather any new information about the Lakotas' and Yanktonais' movements. He spoke to a number of HBC men at the post, including Isaac Cowie.[39] They strongly believed that the Sioux would go to Manitoba in the early spring or summer, and he gave "every credence to this view." From these discussions, Breland concluded:

> Whether they will actually levy war is only slightly doubtful, but they are very certain to levy a heavy "black mail" on the inhabitants of any place they may appear at. I consider Fort Ellice to be in great danger and the arms and ammunition stored there in the hands of the Sioux would not only furnish them with the means, but also enbolden them and incite them to use these means, for waging war on Manitoba.[40]

As winter receded, the traders at Fort Ellice were beginning to receive fresh, if wildly inaccurate, information. The latest news from the Indians of the plains, said McDonald, was that both Little Knife and Sitting Bull had been poisoned by American traders operating in the Cypress Hills.[41] The Sioux, so the rumor went, had subsequently attacked the American posts and killed all the traders. As it turned out, neither Little Knife nor Sitting Bull was dead, and no American traders had been killed, but the HBC men did not know this.[42]

Breland continued his journey to Wood Mountain, where, he had learned, Little Knife and his delegation were now camped. Arriving on 19 April, he found the Yanktonais encamped with a group of Métis from Wood Mountain under the leadership of Pierre Berger. The Lakotas had departed. Breland called a meeting for 23 April, which was attended by the Yanktonai leaders Struck by the Ree, Two Dogs, Ehannaienke, Napitchota, Matoienke, and Pananikoupi and by two Dakota chiefs, Wakiendota and White Cap. Joseph Mitchel and Jacques Hamelin, both Métis, served as interpreters, and Father Lestanc attended at Breland's invitation. Breland shook the leaders' hands and then, following his instructions, told them that Queen Victoria regarded all the inhabitants of the North-West with "love and kindness." The Yanktonais were not about to let slip the opportunity to herald their historic ties to the British crown. They "received this message of Peace with transports of joy and gratitude," Breland reported.

> By the mouth of their speakers, they on their side recalled to mind their old friendship for the English, and as evidence of their friendship, they showed some old medals with the arms of England, medals which their grandfathers had bequeathed to them and which they preserved as life

tokens. They saluted the English Flag, & thanked the Queen *for sending them such kind words. The Sioux loudly declared that they had never injured the English, and wished always to live at peace with them.*

They asked that the queen take pity on "her Sioux children" and especially on the Dakotas living at Portage la Prairie who had requested a reserve in Canada and, finally, that they be allowed to visit the governor at Red River.

In response to Breland's questions about the supposed invasion of Manitoba, they explained that the rumors were untrue. Little Knife had been disgruntled but had spoken only for himself. In fact the rest of the camp were ashamed of his actions. "That which all the Sioux wished," wrote Breland, "was peace with everyone, and above all with the English."[43] Breland returned to Manitoba confident that hostilities with the Sioux would not erupt.

Despite all their travails, no one from Little Knife's delegation met with Morris that summer. Manitoba officials lacked any desire to accommodate the Yanktonais or Lakotas, whom they viewed as "American" Sioux. The Canadian government was, however, prepared to offer each Dakota family of five eighty acres of land in Manitoba on which to settle and farm. The followers of Standing Buffalo and White Cap had maintained a buffalo-hunting economy on the western plains on both sides of the Canada–United States boundary and did not want to relocate to the Manitoba sites proposed by the Canadian government as their reserve. A series of discussions followed over the next few years between Dakota leaders and Canadian officials during which these Sioux also cited historic ties to British territory to bolster their requests for a reserve in the North-West Territories.

A deputation of Dakotas, including the younger Standing Buffalo, visited Morris at Winnipeg in July 1873, close on the heels of his failure to meet Little Knife. After an older man presented a George III medal for Morris to inspect, several men spoke, "the great object of the visit being to ascertain from the Governor where the reserve which is to be given to them outside the Province will be situated and to find out whether it is likely to suit the purpose."[44] The Sioux did not receive a satisfactory answer.

The Canadian government sent Alexander Morris, Minister of the Interior David Laird, and a retired HBC chief factor, W. J. Christie, to the Qu'Appelle Valley in the autumn of 1874 to negotiate a treaty (Treaty Four) with the Crees and Ojibwas. This move prompted concern among the Standing Buffalo and White Cap bands as it was unknown how the treaty might affect their status. On 16 September 1874, the day after the negotiations concluded, Morris and

Laird met with "a party of Sioux from the Woody Mountains" led by White Cap, the younger Standing Buffalo, and the Crow. White Cap had heard that the country was being sold and wanted advice on how to live. He had lived on British territory for twelve years and "wishe[d] to remain under protection of the English." The younger Standing Buffalo explained that he, like his father before him, was not afraid to travel anywhere in the country as he was at peace with the Crees and the whites. He, like his father, would die "in the English Country." Morris could not promise them any land on the plains and hoped, instead, that they would visit the site on the Assiniboine River in Manitoba that the Canadian government was prepared to grant as a reserve to the Dakotas of Portage la Prairie. The Dakotas did not favor this site, there being no room for horses and no buffalo to hunt there, and the meeting ended without a satisfactory conclusion.[45]

The next year, White Cap, the younger Standing Buffalo, and other leaders met W. J. Christie and M. G. Dickieson at Fort Qu'Appelle, after the Canadians had taken the adhesion of some Ojibwas and Assiniboines to Treaty Four. The Sioux, wrote the two commissioners, "assure us of their friendly feeling towards the subjects of the Queen, and as they had been now 13 years on this territory they wished to be left as they were, and have the privilege of hunting with the half-breeds of the Qu'Appelle Lakes. They did not wish to settle on the reserve set apart for the other Sioux at the Little Saskatchewan, saying that they did not like the place. They wished that some decision should be come to regarding them."[46] Christie could promise nothing; Morris had not expected that Christie would meet the Dakotas and had not given him any instructions.[47] Informed of Christie's meeting with White Cap and Standing Buffalo, Morris wrote to the two leaders to tell them to select lands for a reserve—but not lands close to the boundary, which might attract more Sioux from the United States.[48]

In the fall of 1876, Dickieson found White Cap and the younger Standing Buffalo at Fort Qu'Appelle when he returned there to make treaty payments. White Cap had not yet chosen lands for a reserve, but the younger Standing Buffalo had selected lands in the Qu'Appelle Valley.[49] The Canadian government did not understand that the White Cap and Standing Buffalo groups were separate bands. It agreed in the spring of 1877 to a single grant land in the Qu'Appelle Valley for both groups, although the formal allotment and surveying of the reserve did not occur for several years. White Cap's followers moved north in 1878 and were granted a reserve on the South Saskatchewan River the following year.[50]

In the aftermath of the Dakota Conflict, Dakota leaders had developed trade ties with Métis from British territory. Such trading relationships were replicated farther west as Sioux peoples migrated to the Milk River country in northern Montana. Trade established by Dakotas and Yanktonais in the 1860s continued in the 1870s; increasingly, Métis traders also encountered Lakotas.

Winter counts made by Jaw (a Sans Arc/Hunkpapa) and an unidentified Hunkpapa individual indicate that Métis traded with Lakotas during the winter of 1870–71.[51] Other documentary sources confirm the date of this event and elaborate on the details. Father Lestanc of the Qu'Appelle Mission reported that in the autumn of 1870 Sitting Bull had gone to Wood Mountain, where he traded with Antoine Ouellette (frequently known as Irretty), an independent Métis trader who purchased his goods in Saint Paul, and Joseph McKay, one of William McKay's brothers, who worked for the HBC. According to Lestanc, McKay gave Sitting Bull gifts in the name of the HBC. Sitting Bull invited the traders to come to his camp on Milk River, and McKay sent Baptiste Bourassa and Shaman Racette, who traded for the company and on his own account.[52] Lestanc mentioned no trouble in his report on this trading expedition. However, McKay told Isaac Cowie at Fort Qu'Appelle a decidedly different story. McKay informed Cowie that "a party of his men, under Baptiste Bourassa, when on their way to trade at Milk River with a camp of Sioux, who had sent for them, had been robbed of their whole trading outfit and arms by other Sioux under Sitting Bull."[53] Because the HBC did not condone trading with American Sioux, McKay undoubtedly offered this explanation to cover his trade.

Father Lestanc garnered more information about Sioux-Métis trade during the winter of 1870–71. He and a guide became lost while traveling to a Métis wintering camp on Porcupine Creek. They were found by some Sioux (probably Dakotas), who gave them food and directed them to the village, at which Lestanc found abundant liquor destined for the Indian trade.[54]

Authorities in Montana, whose attempts to regulate the Indian trade on American territory met repeated opposition from liquor traders from Fort Benton, saw that their work was complicated by mixed-blood traders who engaged in clandestine trading activities in the north.[55] Indian Agent A. J. Simmons remarked that the Dakotas, Yanktonais, and Lakotas whom he met at Fort Browning in the spring of 1871 "keep constantly on hand a large supply of am[m]unition which they can always procure from the Half-breeds of the British possessions."[56] Lieutenant William Quinton, in command of the military escort at Fort Browning, added: "A constant traffic is kept up between the half-breeds from British Territory and all the Indians of the North West. The half-breeds supply them with powder, lead and an unlimited supply of rum, in exchange for robes and peltries."[57] Reports from Fort Buford indicated that Hunkpapas and other Sioux wintering on the Yellowstone were trading with the Métis for ammunition and liquor.[58] White Bull, Sitting Bull's nephew, also recalled during two interviews with Walter Campbell, his uncle's biographer, that three Métis traded at Sitting Bull's camp, possibly at the mouth of the Powder River, in the winter of 1870–71 or perhaps the winter of 1869–70. They arrived in a one-horse sleigh bringing groceries, breech-loading guns, and powder.[59]

As in the 1860s, trade was made possible by the annual renewal of peace between the Sioux and the Métis. Sitting Bull traveled to the north in the autumn of 1872 to negotiate with the Métis camped on Frenchman River to trade for ammunition and other goods. After an absence of nearly a month, he returned with a promise that the Métis would come to trade at the Hunkpapa camp at the head of the Dry Fork. They arrived about two months later, bringing five sleighloads of whisky, but not the desired trade goods. Tensions in the camp mounted as people got drunk, and the Métis departed.[60] Relations between the Lakotas and the Métis endured, however, despite this disturbance. In the spring of 1873, when the Yanktonais at Fort Peck tried, on behalf of the American traders, to encourage Sitting Bull to trade at the post, Sitting Bull refused, noting his "treaty" with the Métis.[61] Lakotas returned to Canada on a large scale the following winter. Isaac Cowie recorded in December 1873 that eight hundred lodges of Lakotas were then in the Cypress Hills.[62] This represented an aggregate of several thousand individuals—an extraordinary number for a winter camp. They were lured to the area, no doubt, by the game, timber, and shelter found in the hills, but also by the proximity of Métis traders.

American officials were determined to oppose this clandestine trade on American territory. American traders completely supported their government's use of troops against illegal trade, as this eliminated their competition. For example, Abel Farwell, an American trader who operated an illegal trading post near the Sweet Grass Hills in Canadian territory, alerted American authorities in the winter of 1871–72 that John Kerler, an independent Canadian trader, and a party of Métis were trading illegally near Frenchman River on American territory.[63] J. A. Viall, the superintendent of Indian affairs in Montana, informed General John Gibbon: "The Oncpapa and Teton Sioux under chief 'Sitting Bull' receive supplies of ammunition from this source and are encouraged by these outlaws to make war upon the Government of the United States and its citizens and particularly to oppose the construction of the North Pacific Rail Road." He asked that military force be used to seize the traders' goods and suppress the trade. [64] As a result, two companies from Fort Browning under Captain H. B. Freeman arrived at the camp of some sixty Métis and twenty Dakota families early on the morning of 2 November and captured two trading outfits and John Kerler. The other trader, a Métis named François, was absent. The troops confiscated those trade goods, consisting of blankets, ammunition, alcohol, and other items, for which they had transportation. Nine buildings and the remaining goods were burned. [65] The Métis claimed that their village was on British territory, but to no avail. [66]

In May 1874 trading outfits belonging to several Métis, including Antoine Ouellette, and to Jean-Louis Légaré, a Canadian from Québec, were confiscated on Frenchman River by American officials led by Charles D. Hard, the sheriff of Fort Benton, and Fred O'Donnell, a clerk at Fort Peck. Légaré was arrested for trading with the Sioux on American territory and held for three hours, after which he and his party were released. Hard and O'Donnell "did then distribute among the Sioux Indians present all the Tobacco[,] Sugar and matches which he had in his outfit and did take away all the rest of his [Légaré's] goods and Furs to Fort Peck." [67]

Légaré had been involved in the Métis-Sioux trade for four years. He arrived at Wood Mountain in the fall of 1870 to work for Antoine Ouellette. That winter he traded at Little Woody Mountain, south of Talle de Saules—possibly with Sioux, but this is unknown—while Ouellette traded at Wood Mountain with Sitting Bull. Although he soon became an independent trader, Légaré still worked alongside Ouellette. [68] Even after his arrest in May 1874 he remained near the Sioux for at least another month—near enough to report on their movements to the British contingent of the North American Boundary Commission in early June. [69]

Those involved in the Sioux trade resented the actions of the Americans and tried to gain the support of the Canadian government in their dispute. Kerler, Légaré, and Ouellette all claimed that their camps were located on Canadian territory and, therefore, that the Americans had acted illegally. Alexandre Marion, who had been trading ammunition to the Sioux in Légaré's and Ouellette's camp shortly before the arrival of Hard and O'Donnell, argued that the Americans' position—that the Métis were operating on American territory—was only a pretext for plundering the Métis of their goods. He accused Hard and O'Donnell of being "freebooters." [70] These attempts to counter the Americans' actions were unsuccessful, and the Americans were able, in large measure, to curb Métis-Sioux trade on the American side of the boundary. Viall did not find this outcome completely satisfactory. The suppression of the whisky trade on American soil had only prompted traders—American, Canadian, and Métis—to move their operations to the "Whoop-Up Country," an area well north of the boundary, where, Viall complained, they could sell liquor to the Indians beyond the reach of American authorities.[71] The Sioux were not the only ones to use the boundary to their own advantage.

According to the elder Standing Buffalo and the other Sioux who spoke to Indian Agent A. J. Simmons in May 1871, the arrival of Americans and the depletion of game on the lower reaches of the Missouri River had forced the Sioux to move higher up the river. By the mid-1870s they were firmly entrenched in their new homes in the Milk River country. There, in the borderlands, they had obtained provisions and expressions of a desire for peace from the Americans and promises of reserves from the Canadian government. From Métis traders, who had founded their communities in the Cypress Hills and at Wood Mountain at the end of the 1860s, they received arms and ammunition that, in part, helped them expel the Crows and Gros Ventres from the lands they now occupied. Yet, if Canadians were slow to enter the country north of the boundary, Americans, to the south, were not. They threatened to build a railroad through the region, destroying the game and claiming the territory of this emerging borderlands community.

5. THE SIOUX, THE SURVEYORS, AND THE NORTH-WEST MOUNTED POLICE, 1872-1874

Between 1872 and 1874, the boundary between Canadian and American territory on the Northern Plains was finally surveyed and demarcated on the ground. British and American teams from the North American Boundary Commission surveyed the frontier from the Northwest Angle of the Lake of the Woods to the Red River over the winter of 1872–73, while the often-swampy ground was frozen. The border running from the Red River to Wood Mountain was surveyed during the summer and early autumn of 1873 and the remainder from Wood Mountain to the Rockies in the summer and early autumn of 1874. The boundary commissioners were joined in the field in 1874 by the North-West Mounted Police (NWMP), which had been established by the Canadian government in 1873 to administer justice in the newly acquired North-West Territories. The force made its historic March West in the summer of 1874 over the trail cleared by the boundary commission the year before.

The arrival on the plains of the boundary commissions and the police co-incided with a period of instability and disquiet among the aboriginal people of the region. The Canadian government acquired sovereignty over Rupert's Land, the vast territorial holdings of the Hudson's Bay Company, in 1870. The change in government and news of the arrival in Red River of soldiers following the Red River Resistance of 1869–70 made Native leaders on the plains wary of Canadian intentions. The Cree leader Sweetgrass sent a message to Lieutenant Governor Archibald in April 1871 telling him: "We heard our Lands were sold and we did not like it, we dont want to sell our Lands, it is our property, and no one has a right to sell them."[1] According to the missionized Crees of Whitefish Lake (who also contacted Archibald to demand that their privileges and land rights be respected by the new government), the nonmission Plains Crees "think that their lands and hunting ground shall be taken from them without any enumeration."[2] On the plains between the Qu'Appelle and South Saskatchewan Rivers, aboriginal attempts to halt Canadian encroachment led to tension and, ultimately, confrontation. In 1873 news reached Alexander Morris that the Crees, Ojibwas, and Assiniboines were suspicious of the settlements of whites and mixed-bloods along the South Saskatchewan River.[3] When Pascal Breland was sent to the plains in the autumn of 1873, one of his tasks was to assure the Indians that they would be visited in the summer of 1874 by Canadian treaty commissioners, who would respect their rights and settle all land questions to their satisfaction. When met by Breland in late September, the Crees and Assiniboines refused to accept gifts, fearing that to do so would be to relinquish lands.[4] In October Robert Bell of the Geological Survey reported that the Crees and Ojibwas were "generally full of anxiety and uneasiness respecting the intentions of the 'English' and Canadians towards them." The surveyors were made to feel completely unwelcome. "On several occasions," wrote Bell, "these Indians threatened to steal our horses and outfit and even to kill us all; and finally ordered us to turn back, saying at the same time that 'we might thank God if we got home safely.' They sometimes refused to shake hands with members of our party, which, among the Indians, is considered a declaration of enmity. On one occasion when they were present in great numbers, they were dissuaded from killing us by Mr Charles Pratt, a native missionary of the Church of England, who appealed to their honor as 'braves' and thus shamed them from committing the deed; on another occasion by telling them positively that if they murdered us Her Majesty the Queen would avenge our deaths if it should take twenty years to do it."[5] During the following spring the Plains Crees did, in fact, bully the surveyors into temporarily halting their work on the Bow River.[6]

The British and American boundary commissions and the NWMP were new intrusions on the Northern Plains, and it is apparent that aboriginal peoples, including the Sioux, did not understand, at first, what they represented. The Sioux were familiar with railroad surveys: surveyors working for the Northern Pacific Railroad, along with their military escorts, had entered the valley of the Yellowstone River in the autumn of 1871. Black Moon had made it clear to Indian Agent A. J. Simmons, during their meetings at Fort Peck in November 1871, that his people were opposed to the railroad because it would destroy the game. In the spring of 1872 Spotted Eagle of the Sans Arcs informed Colonel David S. Stanley at the Cheyenne River Agency that the Lakotas had not given their consent to the surveyors and that they would fight them. In mid-August a group of Lakotas and Cheyennes skirmished with troops under the command of Major Eugene M. Baker, and a few days later Hunkpapas skirmished with Stanley's command.[7] The Lakotas and other Sioux in the borderlands were distrustful of the boundary commission. However, they soon realized that the "stone heaps" left behind by the surveyors represented a territorial divide to correspond to the social one between the Americans to the south and the British and Canadians to the north. The marking of the boundary was a development that they supported.

Although the Canadians were unsure how the Sioux would respond to the presence of the boundary surveyors and the NWMP, Alexander Morris, the new lieutenant governor of Manitoba and the North-West Territories, anticipated difficulties. Writing in mid-December 1872 to his liaison in Ottawa, the secretary of state for the provinces, he observed: "There is a movement of some kind among the Indian Tribes in the North West Territories and the American States. I believe it to be in part created by the Boundary Commission. They do not understand it and think the two nations are uniting against them."[8] While Morris did not specifically mention the Sioux in this dispatch, he was well aware of Lakota hostility to railroad surveys in the United States.

Morris was not the only official who was concerned about the Sioux. Donald R. Cameron, the British boundary commissioner, received reports from hunters and traders in early 1873 that the Lakotas were committed to resisting the construction of the Northern Pacific Railroad through their lands because its construction would destroy the buffalo herds. In addition the traders were convinced that the American commission on the boundary survey would be obstructed as soon as it arrived in Lakota territory. One "old hunter" remarked that, in the event of an attack, the Lakotas would not be able to distinguish between the British and the American portions of the commission, although most of Cameron's informants believed that the British commission would not be molested.[9]

Cameron wanted to avoid difficulties between his men and the Lakotas. To encourage better relations with the Sioux, and to obtain intelligence about their intentions, he established a trading post at Turtle Mountain in the winter of 1873–74 for the benefit of the Mdewakantons and Wahpetons who had lived in the area since 1862 and whose leader was H'damani.[10] He also suggested to the Canadian government that H'damani's people be granted a reserve at Oak Lake, a request that the Dakotas had asked him to make to the British authorities on their behalf.[11] Cameron knew that these people were Dakotas, but he hoped that, if they were treated well, they would send favorable reports about the British commission to the Lakotas and Yanktonais living farther west.

Encounters between British survey teams and the Sioux in 1873 were rare and, contrary to the predictions and fears of Britons and Canadians, passed without incident. Sioux, probably Dakotas met at Wood End in early August, were "very friendly" and allowed Captain Samuel Anderson, the chief astronomer of the British commission, to take a photograph of them and their camp. [12] Others, most certainly Yanktonais or Lakotas, camped on Frenchman River, exchanged visits with the commission, which they met late in the season. While exploring the creek one day several commission members had sighted the camp and entered it out of curiosity. They were ignored for a few minutes; then half a dozen young men came out to greet them. The young men could not speak English, but one of them was able to ask if the whites were "King George's men." The surveyors responded positively, after which there was much handshaking and the leader of the camp invited them into his lodge. One of the surveyors, L. F. Hewgill, wrote: "Here we were treated with the utmost courtesy and hospitality, buffalo tongues were cooked for, and eaten by us, with an especial relish. . . . Of course the proverbial pipe was passed around after which we shook hands with our friends and returned to camp, meeting on our way numerous Indians who had evidently been paying our camp a visit from the number of articles they were carrying back with them. ([W]e had a large stock of presents for the Indians.)" Later that day the camp leader and a number of his young men rode over to see the leader of the surveying party. On their departure they were given provisions and some clothing. [13]

Captain Anderson had another friendly encounter with a group of Sioux in October 1873, soon after that year's field operations had come to a close. He had gone out on a reconnaissance to locate the Métis village at Wood Mountain that the British commission hoped to use as a base camp the following year. After some futile searching he happened on a party of Sioux who had just come from the settlement and who directed him to it. [14] Were it not for the "happy accident" of meeting these people, he later wrote, "this site would not have been discovered that season, for it lay 25 miles north of the boundary-line, concealed among the ravines on the reverse or north side of the plateau." [15] The Sioux clearly knew this area well.

The 1874 season began much more ominously, with renewed reports of Sioux dissatisfaction with the boundary survey. Alexander Morris had an interview on 26 May with a trader named Whiteford, a cousin of James McKay, who told him that three Lakota leaders had had a meeting with a Métis named Poitras at Wood Mountain. According to Poitras, the Lakotas "had summoned the Metis to consult and ask their opinion as to stopping the Boundary survey as they believed that the Americans 'had got the English with them to form a rampart for them against the Sioux.'" The Métis of Wood Mountain refused to interfere, saying that this was a matter for the government, but the Lakotas were said to be crossing the Missouri River in large numbers—supposedly as many as fifteen hundred lodges—so that they would be ready to stop the survey if their leaders decided that they should do so. Whiteford felt that there would be no trouble if the purpose of the boundary survey was clearly explained to the aboriginal people, "as the Indians would prefer to have the boundary between the two countries clearly defined."[16]

Alarmed by such a menacing—albeit hearsay—report, Morris decided to canvass the opinion of other people who traded on the plains. On 28 May he interviewed William Gosselin, a Métis scout who had worked for the British boundary commission in 1873. Gosselin said that none of the scouts from 1873 would accompany the party in 1874 because they anticipated trouble from the Native people—and from the Lakotas in particular. "They are very hostile to the Americans," he said, "& did not understand the object of the Survey."[17] Joseph Tanner, a part-Ojibwa trader also known as "Kissoway," feared that the Americans' military escort might provoke hostility from the Lakotas, and he corroborated Whiteford's report that some of the Lakotas had asked the Métis to join them in stopping the survey. However, he felt that there would be no trouble if the British force accompanied the Americans and if it explained the purpose of the survey to the Lakotas. Tanner was aware that the newly established NWMP were also scheduled to enter the plains that summer. He informed Morris that many aboriginal people had heard of the police but that they did not fully understand who they were. Clearly, some confused the police with the Americans' military escort. According to Tanner: "The Indians had been told that a party of soldiers had gone & scattered through the country, & that the object was for the Americans to take away their country against their will."[18]

Jean-Louis Légaré, who had just returned from trading with the Sioux and whose camp had been raided by American officials, reported that some 250 Sioux lodges were on Frenchman River and that they had told an American trader who carried English and American goods that they would not allow the survey to be conducted in their lands. Although an American, the trader had not been harmed.[19] A note of optimism was sounded by Michael Klyne, who had lived on Frenchman River since 1867. He told Morris that the British surveyors would have no difficulties with the Lakotas because "[t]he Sioux respect the English." However, he warned that there might be some trouble between the Lakotas and the Americans as the Lakotas "steal from or kill Americans when they have a chance."[20]

Donald Cameron heard similar warnings. Charles Grant of Point Michel on the Pembina River reported: "Indians have assembled one hundred miles west of Wood Mountain Settlement to stop the Boundary survey until [the] government has declared a satisfactory policy."[21] And Alexandre Marion, the Pembina-area Métis who had been in Légaré's camp when it was raided, told Cameron that numerous Lakotas were collecting at Wood Mountain to meet him. However, George Arthur Hill, in charge of the boundary commission's trading post at Turtle Mountain, had heard that aboriginal people had planned to attack the American commission and then the British but that the Lakotas had objected, "expressing a desire not to interrupt the friendliness which has hitherto prevailed between the British and Indians."[22] Although Samuel Anderson, in charge of the British expedition at Wood Mountain, had reported no hostile action on the part of the Lakotas, Cameron instructed him in June not to retaliate if the Lakotas made any attempt to obstruct the survey operations but simply to collect any of his party who might be detached and to withdraw.[23]

The NWMP arrived at the border settlement of Dufferin in June 1874 in the midst of these rumors concerning the Sioux. The force's fears regarding Sioux intentions were augmented in early July when reports arrived that a party of Yanktonais had murdered three Métis men and wounded two of their wives at nearby St Joseph, in the Dakota Territory.[24] To prevent any of the murderers from fleeing to Canada, Commissioner George Arthur French deployed the force along the boundary, but no Sioux were found. More telling than this bravado was the fact that French returned to Winnipeg in mid-July to consult with Morris and two Métis about changing the force's route from Dufferin to the Bow River. The hope was to "pass through a favorable country and avoid much of the Indian country, evading the Sioux altogether."[25]

Tension between the American boundary surveyors and the Sioux was more common in 1874 than in the previous year. When Captain W. J. Twining, the chief astronomer and surveyor of the American commission, arrived at Fort N. J. Turney on Frenchman River in the first week of July, he learned that a party of Yanktonais from Fort Peck had stolen nine of the traders' eleven horses the day before. The Yanktonais did not challenge Twining's military escort, but on 17 July, when his men were camped between Wood Mountain and the Cypress Hills, a party of Yanktonais chased a mail carrier nearly into his camp.[26] Americans interpreted subsequent visits by small groups of Yanktonais as potentially hostile encounters. Writing of a visit from Deer Tail and twenty-five others west of the Cypress Hills on 25 July, Dr Valentine T. McGillycuddy implied that only recent reinforcements to his camp's numbers spared it from molestation.[27]

During the 1874 season the British component of the boundary survey encountered numerous groups of Sioux people, mostly Dakotas, but also some Yanktonais and Lakotas. Reports of trouble between the Sioux and the British surveyors exist, but they are difficult to corroborate and provide only the most superficial information about the Sioux participants. For example, Henri Julien, a journalist who traveled west with the NWMP, reported in late July that a party of Sioux had visited the British commission's depot near the junction of North and South Antler Creeks and had "levied black mail in the way of crackers, pork and other eatables."[28] Julien's language obscures much about this encounter: had the Sioux actually "levied black mail" (and, if so, how), or was this interpretation based on his stereotypes about Indians? Whatever happened, this episode was evidently not significant. Donald Cameron did not mention the incident in his year-end reports, and a policeman whose party traveled through the area at about the same time noted in his memoirs that reports of hostile Sioux being in the area proved to be false.[29]

A few other incidents occurred. Policeman James Finlayson recorded in his diary that "Indians" raided a British boundary commission camp on Frenchman River in late August and "went off with Three thousand dollars worth of stuff." Julien also noted the event and identified the Indians as Sioux.[30] Lieutenant Francis V. Greene, an assistant astronomer with the American boundary commission, recorded that a band of Yanktonais pillaged the British depot on the East Fork of Milk River, also in late August. According to his account, a chief and his son approached the depot and asked for food, whereupon the Britons forced them to leave. The following day the two returned with their band of about a hundred people, "tied up the two Englishmen, divided the supplies at the depot into two parts, took one part and went off."[31] Samuel Anderson of the British commission also recorded the incident, noting that, in addition to taking half the provisions stored at the depot, the Sioux "broke open a box of candles and lit 26 of them and danced all night for the ediciation [edification?] of the unfortunate depot keeper."[32] To Finlayson, Greene, Anderson, and Julien, the

Sioux participants in these events were untrustworthy savages; their accounts are silent on how the Sioux viewed these events.

However, in 1874, as in 1873, the majority of encounters between the Sioux and the British surveyors were peaceful, even cordial. In mid-July, for example, the mail carrier from the British boundary commission visited a Sioux camp west of Saint Joseph, where he "dined with the Sioux and was even welcomed by them."[33] That same month, in the badlands south of Wood Mountain, Albany Featherstonhaugh met Sioux and Assiniboines "who asked numerous questions about the objects of the expedition, and appeared relieved to hear that no idea of a railway lay at the bottom of it." They knew of the railroad surveys in the United States and perhaps knew that Little Knife's band had encountered Sandford Fleming's Canadian Pacific Railway survey party in the North-West Territories in 1872. They were pleased when told that the object of the commission was to mark the boundary between American and Canadian territory. Indeed, he noted, "it is said that they were rather disappointed that a wall or continuous bank was not set up across the plains, a thing which they had been led to expect."[34]

Valentine Francis Rowe, a member of the Royal Engineers, had the most sustained contact with the Sioux in 1874. In anticipation of meeting Sioux people in the following season, Rowe had spent the winter of 1873–74 learning all the Sioux he could, and, although he remained far from fluent, the various Sioux whom he met in the early part of the 1874 season were delighted to meet a white man who could say a few words "they could recognise." Rowe was thrown from his horse on 11 June near the commission's camp at Wood End, hitting the ground on the left side of his head and face, and fracturing the base of his skull. A tent was erected over him where he fell, and he remained there for nearly six weeks before he was strong enough to be moved to the camp at Wood Mountain.[35] During his recovery he was the object of great concern to the Sioux people who visited the area.

Rowe's first visitors were a Dakota family headed by a man named the Elk. The Elk spoke to Rowe about buffalo, hunting, and the rattlesnakes found along the Missouri River. The Elk's wife was pleased by Rowe's gifts of a few needles, buttons, and thimbles. The Elk and his family departed, however, on the approach of a large band of Yanktonais—that of Struck by the Ree and Two Dogs, the same band that had met Breland at Wood Mountain the previous year.

The Yanktonais had just had a fight near the Cypress Hills with some Blackfoot, who had been obtaining alcohol from American traders and stealing horses from the Métis. The Yanktonais had joined the Métis and successfully repelled the Blackfoot.[36] British surveyors working farther west where Milk River crosses the boundary encountered the Métis camp involved in this fight.[37]

The Yanktonais pitched their camp about three hundred yards from Rowe's tent, and the leaders "would not allow the very noisy ones of the party to come near me reserving the 'sick English Chief' for their own visiting." Some of the young men who had been involved in the fight with the Blackfoot came to look in on Rowe, but the leaders sent them away so as not to disturb him.

Rowe was visited by the Yanktonais leaders nearly every day, but his most involved conversations were with Two Dogs. Two Dogs wished to impress on Rowe the impact that Europeans had had on the Sioux peoples. Before the Europeans arrived, he reflected, the Sioux were powerful and had lived on the buffalo; while they were glad to accept goods from the traders, the Americans now came from all directions and took Sioux land. Echoing earlier comments by Black Moon and Standing Buffalo on the speed and impact of American encroachment, Two Dogs pointed out that the Sioux "slept and when we woke up there were roads, roads everywhere—the Buffalo was driven back to these Plains and the Dacotahs hunt today only between the swift river and the muddy river. (Saskatchewan & Missouri) Where now is our Land? our earth our water, our trees? it was all ours—I look, but where can our children pitch their tepis?" Two Dogs complained that the American government had promised the Sioux much but had delivered nothing. He was pleased, however, to see the British: "The Great Mystery has spoken—my heart is not bad, my heart is glad to see the English, the English are good, but the Big Knife [the Americans] is bad, they kill our children. The Big Knife & the Dacotah fight: the children of the Great Good Mother have good hearts & are friendly to the Dacotah and the Dacotahs' hearts are good toward the English." He explained, as Struck by the Ree and other Yanktonai leaders had explained to Pascal Breland in 1873, that the Sioux had never fought against the British. Asked how he and his people could distinguish between the British and the Americans, Two Dogs explained that the American soldiers killed not only men but women and children but that "[t]he English comes in the midst of our people all by himself—alone—he does not bring warriors or many guns, he comes alone & he walks here, there, among our people, he does not fear the Dacotah People." This, surely, was mysterious. Two Dogs expressed the peace that existed between the Sioux and the British in spiritual terms, saying: "The Great Spirit takes care of the English, we do not touch him!"[38]

Commissioner Cameron was delighted by Rowe's good rapport with the Yanktonais and equally pleased with Two Dogs, whose pacific disposition boded well for the safety of the British commission. To help Two Dogs introduce himself when he encountered other Europeans, Cameron gave him a paper noting that he was the "Executive Chief of the Ihuktawanah [Yanktonai] of which Padinapap [Pananiapapi, or Struck by the Ree] is head" and commenting on his friendly behavior toward the members of the British commission. A note of good conduct, it was a passport that gave this particular "American" Indian safe passage to the British side of the line. Two Dogs kept the paper for at least seventeen years, showing it to a Canadian Indian agent in 1891.[39]

Meanwhile, the NWMP arrived in the neighborhood of Wood Mountain in August, having encountered no Native people since leaving Manitoba. At Wood Mountain they encountered fifty lodges of Struck by the Ree's and Two Dogs's Yanktonais who were returning from a buffalo hunt farther west.[40] On 12 August a Yanktonai scout entered the police camp on Old Wives Creek, telling the police of his people's recent fight with the Blackfoot. French gave him some tobacco and invited his camp to a "pow-wow" the next day.[41] The scout and his party arrived for a formal visit at ten o'clock the following morning. According to Policeman John H. McIllrie, the council began poorly. "It was not at all an interesting affair," he wrote. "There were no big Chiefs, and the speakers were poor and our interpreter was poor. We sat and looked at each other for about half an hour and smoked, when one of the braves got up and shook hands all round, saying *how-how* or something like it." The "brave" then asked why the police were coming through "their country." McIllrie complained in his diary that the question was "a beastly piece of cheek as they are Sioux that have been driven out of the States" and not Indians from Canada.[42] Commissioner French, however, calmly replied that "the White Mother had heard that the American outlaws had killed some of her red children [at the Cypress Hills Massacre in 1873], and that she had sent me, with these braves to capture the men who did it." French then "impressed upon them the fact that we did not want their land."[43] The Yanktonais listened approvingly to French's speech, and then, according to McIllrie, two or three made speeches in which they "professed great love and esteem" for the police.[44] To cement peaceful relations, French gave the Yanktonais generous presents of tobacco, powder, balls, flints and steels, cloth, and flour.[45]

The police and the Yanktonais remained camped on Old Wives Creek for several days, the police to establish a cripple camp, the Sioux, no doubt, to learn

THE SIOUX, SURVEYORS, AND MOUNTED POLICE

more about the newcomers. A number of the policemen visited the Yanktonai camp and, as the police were poorly equipped, did some trading. F. A. Bagley, for example, reported that he "[g]ot a couple of pairs of buffalo hide soled mocassins from the Sioux."[46] Likewise, the Yanktonais went to trade at the police camp, prompting McIllrie to comment: "They are a nasty begging lot and will sell anything they have got."[47] On the evening of 14 August several Yanktonais around the police camp performed a dance, saying that "the Blackfoot would be crying at night": the singer had been in the recent fight and had killed a Blackfoot.[48] The surgeon J. G. Kittson visited the Yanktonais' camp and, having been given permission by its leader, presumably Struck by the Ree, but perhaps Two Dogs, and its "Pa-ge-we-chas-ta," gave everyone a physical examination. Kittson eagerly doled out his medicines but found that the Yanktonais had little interest in them. [49] The Yanktonais were joined by a small group of Dakotas under Raising Bull (a son of the elder Standing Buffalo) on 17 August, after which the combined Sioux camp departed.[50]

Following the departure of the Yanktonais and Dakotas, the police encountered no more Sioux until early September, when they reached a point west of the Cypress Hills. During the evening of 4 September seven Sioux approached the police camp with loaded guns. The police extended a skirmish line, but a Sioux who could speak French came forward unarmed and explained that they had been with some Métis when the police advance guard had passed and, seeing no carts, had thought that they were Blackfoot. The police gave them tea, buffalo meat, biscuits, and ammunition, which pleased them.[51] After the meal they performed a dance for the police.[52]

The arrival on the plains of the boundary commission and the NWMP offered the Lakotas and Yanktonais new information about Europeans and generally improved Anglo-Sioux relations. When Santees had traveled to Rupert's Land in 1862, they did so knowing that American troops would not follow them across the boundary. The Western Sioux had no such prior experience. Thus, in 1872, just as Morris had suspected, they did not understand the purpose of the boundary survey that the British and Americans were then beginning. Many, like the Sioux encountered by Featherstonhaugh in 1874, must have feared that the surveys were preparatory to a railway. Moreover, the Sioux may have likened the arrival of the Canadian police force to the arrival of American troops on Sioux lands farther south in the 1850s. Leaders such as Two Dogs—just as much as Black Moon and Four Horns—were concerned about the impact of new railways and disillusioned by American encroachment on Sioux lands.

It was these concerns that prompted the curiosity that such leaders showed the North American Boundary Commission and the NWMP. Encounters between the Sioux and the surveyors and the police not only allayed the fears of the Sioux, and thereby reduced the threat of conflict, but, more important, gave the Sioux an opportunity to voice their grievances against the Americans. The Sioux expressed their support for the boundary survey and clearly wished to establish peaceful relations with the British, whom they viewed as potential allies. Given the limited intrusion on the plains by Britons and Canadians in the 1870s, it is not surprising that the Sioux saw them as less threatening than the Americans. For this reason they were willing to adopt them as friends instead of viewing them as foes.

6. THE GREAT SIOUX WAR, 1876-1877

The historiography of the American West usually presents the Great Sioux War of 1876–77 as the final chapter in the conflict between Lakotas and Americans over land in the Black Hills. The fact that, as a result of this conflict, some northern Lakota bands fled to Canada is of peripheral concern; since the Sioux were "American" Indians, the lens of Lakota-American relations is the only one trained on these events. Similarly, histories of the Lakotas in Canada usually leave the impression that it was only after the Battle of the Little Bighorn that Lakota bands began crossing the border. In fact, however, Lakotas, along with Yanktonais and Santees from the Milk River country, were in contact with aboriginal peoples and Métis traders in the Cypress Hills/Wood Mountain region throughout the conflict. A different picture emerges if the Lakotas are seen as a people of the borderlands. In the aftermath of the Custer fight, the Lakotas strove to renew and strengthen their ties both to the Yanktonais at Fort Peck and to representatives of the Hudson's Bay Company (HBC) at Fort Qu'Appelle. Once in Canada, the Sioux willingly manipulated their identity, telling Canadian officials that they were "British" and that they had been so since their peoples' involvement in the War of 1812.

In the spring of 1876 the Lakotas called a council that was to be held at the western end of the Cypress Hills and to which they invited Native peoples from throughout the Northern Plains. A mixed-blood trader who had passed by Wood Mountain in the spring claimed that Sitting Bull had sent messengers with tobacco to the Métis at Wood Mountain to tell them "[t]hat the Sioux were likely to come into the Mountains [meaning the Cypress Hills], that they wished to be at peace with the Half Breeds, when they came in, but that if it was to be otherwise, the Sioux would fight to the death." The Métis made no reply as most were out on the plains.[1]

In May several local aboriginal leaders asked North-West Mounted Police

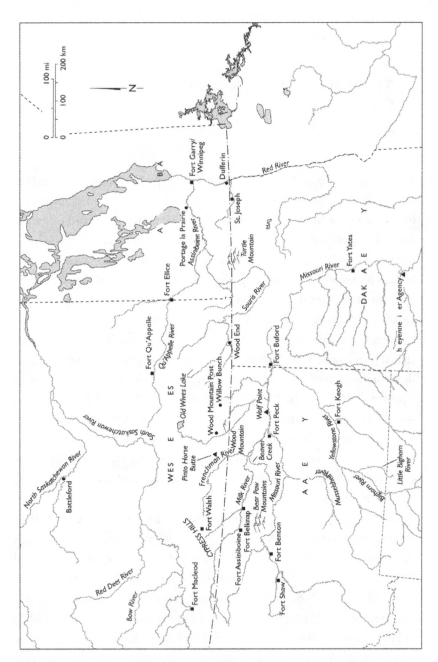

The Northern Plains in the 1870s

(NWMP) Assistant Commissioner A. G. Irvine at Fort Walsh to attend the meeting. They were prompted by fears that violence would break out as many groups who had never met before would be at the meeting. Irvine, who believed that the event would be a sun dance where "the different tribes pledge friendship to one another," said he would try to attend. If he could not, he would send someone.[2]

L. N. F. Crozier, the policeman in command at Fort Walsh, reported that he had "had a number of *Pow Wows* with Indian Chiefs, who come every day to tell some news about the Sioux or get advice." He wrote in mid-June that there were "all sorts of rumours of hostile Sioux, from the American side, Crossing over here . . . in one instance a Saulteux chief came to inform me, that he had received information that a large party were already on this side, and that they had informed the Crees, that they did not wish to do any harm to any Indian or half-breed, that they intended to attack the Fort, and Kill all the soldiers, and take all the ammunition and provisions." Many in the aboriginal and mixed-blood community believed the report and left the vicinity of Fort Walsh for the Qu'Appelle Valley.[3]

On the American side of the boundary Fort Peck Indian Agent Thomas J. Mitchell noted the departure of many of his agency's Indians in late May. He believed that they had left to go hunting, most heading north of Milk River and near the Canadian border.[4] One camp of some 140 lodges of Yanktonais, probably from Medicine Bear's or Afraid of Bear's bands, split away from the hunting parties, however, and traveled to Fort Walsh, arriving in mid-June. Once at Fort Walsh they belatedly celebrated Queen Victoria's birthday by firing a "feu de joie" at noon, having races in the afternoon, and having a bonfire and lantern slides in the evening. Crozier gave a feast to those at the post in the evening, and "some of them danced all night in honor of the Great Mother." They departed on the morning of 19 June to join the "general gathering" taking place nearby.[5]

The documentary record says little of substance about the meeting. A Canadian source, undoubtedly a policeman, reported that it was attended by some three thousand lodges of Peigans, Blackfoot, Bloods, and Assiniboines from Canada, besides Gros Ventres, Crows, and Lakotas from the United States.[6] John S. Wood, of the Blackfeet Agency in Montana, added that Dakota, Yanktonai, Ojibwa, Cree, and Mandan representatives also attended.[7] As Lakota-American hostilities were then in full swing (the battle on the Little Bighorn River had taken place on 25 June), the Lakotas had called the meeting to garner aboriginal support for a Lakota migration into Canada if it became necessary. According to Agent Wood, who obtained his information from the Peigan leader Little Plume, many of the Sioux, but especially the Santees and Yanktonais, were willing to use force if the Canadians tried to prevent their entry. The aboriginal peoples of the area were unsympathetic: the Blackfoot, Bloods, and Peigans under Little Plume withdrew from the council, declaring, said Wood, that "the Sioux were their enemies, and that they would fight them if ever they came to this country [Canada], and that the whites were their friends, and they would help them whip the Sioux."[8]

The Lakotas may also have used the occasion to tell Native leaders on the Canadian side of the boundary of Sioux treaty relations with the Americans. It is clear that the Cree leaders who negotiated Treaty Six at Fort Pitt and Carlton House a few months later, in August and September 1876, were aware of the provisions previously granted to the Sioux in the United States. When the Canadian minister of the interior informed Morris in 1877 that the government was unhappy with the emergency aid provision included in Treaty Six, Morris replied that "Our Canadian Indians" were fully aware of events in the United States and pointed out that "It was the knowledge that similar terms had been previously granted to the American Sioux Indians, that led to the demands of the Crees for food and clothing, carpenters and blacksmiths &c" during the negotiations for the treaty.[9]

Irvine and eleven men left Fort Walsh on 22 June to attend the meeting but arrived too late. They found one thousand lodges, one hundred of which were from Sitting Bull's band, and distributed some rations and tobacco before departing.[10] To Irvine the encounter had been a complete success. Arriving at Fort Macleod on the evening of 27 June, Irvine sat in the room of his fellow policeman Richard Nevitt "and talked until daylight this morning." "He told me," wrote Nevitt, "the same things over two or three times and altogether was a little tiresome but I behaved politely and sat him out."[11]

The Blackfoot followers of Crowfoot and other "British" leaders did not attend the Cypress Hills council, but the Lakotas contacted them. The Methodist missionary to the Blackfoot, the Reverend John McDougall, informed Morris that Sioux messengers had sent tobacco to the Blackfoot with an invitation "to join them in war against the Whites, and if not against all, against the Americans."[12] When the Blackfoot declined the Sioux proposal, the Sioux threatened continued warfare between the Blackfoot and the Sioux. The Blackfoot leaders were debating this latest message when the NWMP policeman Cecil Denny arrived in Crowfoot's camp on the Red Deer River in July. Denny assured Crowfoot that the police would support the Blackfoot in the event of a Sioux attack, while Crowfoot noted that his people could send two thousand warriors against the Sioux. [13] Whether the Sioux actually proposed attacking the Blackfoot or only hoped to gain access to Blackfoot lands is unclear from the European documentary record. Just what support the police proposed to offer the Blackfoot is equally unclear.

While Sioux representatives were venturing north of the Canada–United States boundary in the spring and early summer of 1876, Métis traders were traveling south of it. That spring the post interpreter at the Cheyenne River Agency reported that a party of Red River Métis had been camped for over a month north of Bear Butte in the Black Hills and that they had been conducting an extensive trade in ammunition with the Lakotas. [14] It is not certain that any Métis were at the fight on the Little Bighorn in June. He Dog, an Oglala, told the Western history enthusiast Walter Camp: "In my camp there was a Canadian half breed who spoke very good English as well as Sioux." [15] However, when Camp asked if any Europeans or mixed-bloods were with Sitting Bull on 25 June, One Bull, one of Sitting Bull's nephews, said that he had "[n]ever heard of any." [16]

The Lakota-Métis arms trade may have had some impact on the course of the Sioux war. It is impossible, however, to determine whether artifacts recovered from battle sites (bullets, cartridges, etc.) came from American or Canadian sources because the Métis from Wood Mountain and the Cypress Hills traded the same kinds of ammunition (generally Henry and Winchester cartridges) as American traders. [17] A single Enfield bullet (FS1781) was recovered during an archaeological survey of the Custer site conducted in the mid-1980s: although of British manufacture, it could easily have come from an American source. [18]

The Lakotas scattered after the fight on the Little Bighorn. Many northern bands—those of Sitting Bull and others—moved around eastern Montana, eventually arriving in the neighborhood of Fort Peck. This was not by chance as the Yanktonais and Santees at Fort Peck were the same people with whom these northern Lakotas had been associated since the 1860s. Fort Peck and its environs were also close to Wood Mountain and the Métis traders with whom the Fort Peck Sioux had traded for the previous decade. The Lakotas were unable to remain among the Yanktonais and, over the course of the autumn, migrated into British territory.

The first indication that Lakotas would cross into Canada came in August, when two Crees reported to Crozier that a Sioux camp was on Frenchman River in Canadian territory. Crozier sent Sub-Inspector W. D. Antrobus to find it, but he returned four days later without success. Crozier then received information about the Lakotas from a Métis named Gabriel Solomon. Solomon had met a Métis named Laframboise at Old Wives Lake, north of Wood Mountain, who had just come from Sitting Bull's camp: there he had attended a council during which Sitting Bull had said that

> he found himself surrounded [by American troops]—in his own words— "like an island in the middle of the sea;" there were only two ways of escape—one to the country of the Great Mother, the other to the Span- iards. . . . Sitting Bull was undecided whether he would go to the Spanish country (meaning, I suppose, Mexico) or to Canada. Sitting Bull calls a council every day to talk about which way they will go. In a speech at the council, the other day, he said: "We can go nowhere without seeing the head of an American. Our land is small, it is like an island. We have two ways to go—to the land of the Great Mother, or to the land of the Spaniards."

Solomon had also met a scout from Sitting Bull's camp in the Qu'Appelle Valley who said that he had come to learn what the "English" had to say about Sitting Bull. The scout did not talk to any Canadians as Solomon turned him back. Crozier reported—undoubtedly on the basis of statements from Solomon not included in the latter's affidavit—that the Lakotas had told the Métis not to winter at Wood Mountain or along Milk River as they intended going to those places. Crozier did not know who these Sioux were in particular or even if the rumor was true.[19]

The decision to winter at Wood Mountain was not made by chance. Notwith- standing Crozier's information, the Lakotas likely hoped to meet and trade with the Métis at Wood Mountain rather than avoid them. Long Dog, a Hunkpapa, and twenty-three families and Inkpaduta, a Wahpekute, and another five lodges crossed the Missouri at Wolf Point on 6 September and remained several days before departing for the north, saying that they were going to Wood Mountain. Agent Thomas Mitchell spoke to Long Dog and Inkpaduta on 11 September at the crossing of Porcupine Creek on the road between Fort Peck and Wolf Point. They spoke freely, telling him that, in their haste to get away from the soldiers, they had abandoned their lodges, travois, and other possessions and that they were going to Wood Mountain to gather supplies and equipment for the winter.[20] Mitchell did not say that the Sioux would trade with the Métis, but this was probably the case. George Boyd, a scout at Fort Peck, informed Walter B. Jordan, a trader at Fort Buford, in early October that Sitting Bull was planning to send a delegation to Fort Peck to trade. "They want ammunition," reported Boyd, "and if they do not get it, it will be bad. They will go to Wood Mountain to trade and get it from the half-breeds."[21] General John Gibbon, the commanding officer of the District of Montana, informed Inspector James Morrow Walsh of the NWMP in November "that half breeds are building posts in the Woody Mountains, north of the line, and have invited these hostile Indians there, to trade for ammunition."[22]

The Lakotas were also eager to renew trade ties to the HBC. When the Canadian treaty commissioner M. G. Dickieson visited Fort Qu'Appelle in September 1876 to make payments under Treaty Four, he met, in addition to White Cap and the younger Standing Buffalo, "a delegation of Sioux from the United States." They had made a peace with Little Black Bear's Crees during the Cypress Hills council in June and had now come to discuss matters with the Canadians:

> They represented that they found it difficult to live on the American side and wished to come to ours, where they heard the means of subsistence could be obtained. (They had on a previous occasion had a "talk" with Mr. [W. J.] McLean of the Hudson's Bay Company and wanted to procure from him repeating rifles and ammunition.)

Dickieson did not comment on their request for arms but assured them that traders on Canadian territory would provide them with subsistence items in trade.[23]

Equally important to Lakota leaders was maintaining their ties to the people—Yanktonais, other Sioux, and Assiniboines—then living peacefully near Fort Peck. In mid-September, Agent Mitchell learned from his interpreter, Joseph Lambert, whom he had sent to the Yanktonai and Assiniboine camps, that Sitting Bull had sent messengers to both telling them that he wished to be friendly with all neighboring groups and that he would give a gift of one hundred horses to each group that became friendly with him and admitted him to their camps on friendly terms. Both the Yanktonais and the Assiniboines had supposedly rejected Sitting Bull's offer and sent word back through his messengers that he was the enemy of their friends, the whites, and that they wanted nothing to do with him.[24] Such remarks were likely made for Mitchell's benefit. One hundred nineteen lodges of Hunkpapas, the followers of Iron Dog, Hawk, Crow, Little Knife, Long Dog, Iron Buck, and Elk Horn, arrived at Fort Peck on 30 October and sought refuge in the Yanktonai camps north of the Missouri River. Iron Dog and Crow went to the post and gave Mitchell four government horses and one mule that had been captured during engagements with U.S.

troops. Messengers from Wolf Point then told the Hunkpapas that troops were approaching, and, on hearing this, they all fled. (Colonel W. B. Hazen arrived on 1 November.) Mitchell believed that the Yanktonais and Assiniboines refused to cooperate with the Hunkpapas; however, the Yanktonais gave Mitchell ten more horses after the Hunkpapas had left, suggesting that there was communication between the camps. [25]

Sitting Bull was not among those who arrived in the vicinity of Fort Peck in October. He did send word to Mitchell, however, that he wanted peace and to be allowed to trade for ammunition. If Mitchell did not permit this, he would go north to Canada, where, he claimed, he had been promised that he could trade for "plenty." [26] It is tempting to think that this statement was the result of Dickieson's offhand assurances made to Sioux delegates at Fort Qu'Appelle in September.

At the same time as he was negotiating with Mitchell, Sitting Bull sent Long Wolf and Red Hand to Fort Walsh to arrange an interview with James Walsh. Walsh declined the request but said that, if Sitting Bull or any of his people came across the line, they would be treated the same as any other peaceable people, so long as they obeyed Canadian law. [27]

Lakotas began crossing into Canada as early as October 1876. Lieutenant R. H. Day, who had been left with a detachment at Fort Peck after Hazen's departure on 4 November, reported that Long Dog and Iron Dog had remained near Fort Peck after the troops had left but that the followers of Iron Dog, Long Dog, Little Knife, White Guts, Crow, Hawk, and, perhaps, Inkpaduta were then hunting near Wood Mountain. [28]

Once in Canada, the Lakotas quickly approached the traders. A scouting party of twelve, led by Little Knife and Crow, arrived at Jean-Louis Légaré's trading post at Wood Mountain on 17 November 1876. Saying that they had heard he had a store and that they were in need, they proposed that Légaré give them tobacco, sugar, and tea and that they would come to him to trade their furs when they were ready to trade. A speaker, not identified but apparently Crow, explained that they had heard that "the Great Mother (the Queen) was good for her children. That they came across to sleep quiet in Canada." Légaré gave them what they asked for as this was the "Indian fashion." Seventy lodges came and camped close to Légaré's store the next day. When he traded with them, they generally ordered dry goods—cotton and print cloth, tea and sugar. Légaré noted that the Sioux "used to talk to the scale to be solid and Strong, to get more by that in it." Years later he wrote of this meeting that the Sioux had never seen white people before as "they had no idea how to buy or Sell." Apparently, he considered it better not to mention his own trade with the Sioux during the 1870s.[29]

The Lakotas who remained on American territory were also looking for traders. By mid-November Iron Dog had summoned the Yanktonais from Fort Peck to join him at the head of Porcupine Creek, where he and others had gone to trade with the Métis for ammunition.[30] The Yanktonai leaders Medicine Bear and Black Tiger met Agent Mitchell at Wolf Point on 6 December with the news that they had met Sitting Bull, Black Moon, Four Horns, Red Horn, The Man that Wants the Breast, and a prominent Sans Arc leader (not named in the source), and their followers, at a crossing on Milk River between Wolf Point and Fort Peck. They told Mitchell that Sitting Bull and his followers were out of ammunition and spirits but that they were on their way to British territory "to procure a supply of the former which in itself, Sitting Bull says, will produce the latter."[31] Two Minneconjous who had left Crazy Horse's camp on Tongue River and gone into the Cheyenne River Agency in late December reported that Sitting Bull and sixty lodges were heading north when they had seen them some forty miles from Fort Peck and that they had undoubtedly crossed the boundary since.[32] Hearing that Sitting Bull was so close, U.S. Army Lieutenant Frank D. Baldwin, who had arrived at Fort Peck on 6 December, took his command to find him. Sitting Bull intended to go to British territory—and the two Minneconjous assumed that he had done so—but he seems to have changed his mind and doubled back. Baldwin encountered Sitting Bull's camp near the head of Red Water Creek on 18 December and a skirmish resulted.[33]

While in the vicinity of Fort Peck, Sitting Bull's people were in contact with the Yanktonais. Baldwin had noted, while preparing to go after Sitting Bull, that the Fort Peck Yanktonais were "affording aid and assistance to [the] Hostiles in many ways."[34] Items found in Sitting Bull's camp after the engagement on 18 December—sugar, coffee, tobacco, tea, and other articles—convinced Baldwin that the Sioux had either drawn these things from Mitchell or been trading with the Yanktonais.[35]

Having heard from Lieutenant Day in November that Sioux camps were moving north, James Walsh sent Sub-Inspector Edmund Fréchette, six policemen, and two scouts from Fort Walsh to Wood Mountain to investigate. Arriving at Légaré's trading post in early December, Fréchette counted fifty-seven lodges, the followers of Iron Dog, Long Dog, Little Knife, and Lodge Pole. Walsh arrived at Wood Mountain on 21 December and found that Black Moon and an additional fifty-two lodges had arrived on 19 December. Walsh had a council that evening with Black Moon, Little Knife, Iron Dog, Long Dog, The Man that Crawls, White Guts, The Drag, Inkpaduta, and the "Canadian" Dakota leader White Eagle, who had assembled the Lakota leaders.[36] "Do you know that you are in the Queen's country?" Walsh asked.

> *Their answer was that they did[.] I [Walsh] asked What have you come for? They replied that they had been driven from their homes by the Americans and had come to look for peace. They had been told by their Grand Fathers that they would find peace in the land of the British. Their Brothers the Santees had found it years ago and they had followed them. They had not slept sound for years and were anxious to find a place where they could lie down and feel safe. They were tired of living in such a disturbed state.*

"[I] [e]xplained the laws of the country to them," Walsh continued, "as has been our custom in Explaining to other Indians and further told them they would have to obey them as the Santees and other Indians do. The several Chiefs then made speeches in which they implored the Queen to have pity on them & that they would obey her laws." Black Moon's remarks differed little in substance from those of the Yanktonais and Lakotas who parlayed with Pascal Breland at Wood Mountain in 1874. Like those earlier visitors, Black Moon hoped diplomacy would secure the goodwill and aid of the Canadians.

A second meeting was held the following day, at which the Lakotas asked permission to purchase ammunition to be used for hunting.[37] Walsh relented, although he was concerned—at least officially—that ammunition might be sent south to Sioux who were still in conflict with American troops. In the report that he sent to his superiors Walsh mentioned having instructed Légaré, whom he met on his return to Fort Walsh, to trade only two and a half rounds of fixed ammunition to each family, thus ensuring that little, if any, surplus would be sent south. Joseph Langer, a Métis trader from Wood Mountain who attended the council, told a different story, stating that Walsh had told the Sioux that they could have two traders at Wood Mountain and from twenty to thirty rounds of loose ammunition per man for hunting.[38]

Walsh returned to the vicinity on 3 March 1877, arriving at Medicine Bear's camp of Yanktonais on Frenchman River (and very close to the boundary) just as Four Horns arrived with fifty-seven lodges of Hunkpapas. At Walsh's request Medicine Bear called a council at which he addressed the Lakotas and then the Yanktonais. "I put the same questions [to Four Horns that] I did to Black Moon," wrote Walsh:

Do you know that you are now in the Queen's country? Their answer was
that they did. I asked What have you come for? They replied that they had
been driven from their several homes by the Americans and had come to
look for peace. They had been told by their fathers that they would find
peace in the land of the British. They had not slept sound for years and
were anxious to find a place where they could lie down and feel safe.

The Lakota leaders stressed their historic ties to the British and how they refused
to acknowledge the changes brought about by the War of 1812:

They claim that the Sioux are British Indians, that 65 years ago was the first
their father's knew of being under the Americans. Their fathers were told at
that time by a chief of their British father (it was a father they say they had
at that time) that if they did not wish to live under the Americans they could
move northward, & there they would again find the land of the British.
Why the White Father gave them and their country to the Americans they
could not tell.

From childhood they were instructed by their fathers that properly they
were children of the British. They were living with strangers but their home
was to the North. That in their tribes can be seen the medals of their White
Father given to their fathers for fighting the Americans & although the
British gave them & their country to the Americans they never made peace
with them. That they always intend[ed] moving to the country of their
fathers. [39]

These remarks outline a considerable Sioux diplomatic strategy: They and
the British were, and had always been, allies. That the British had abandoned
them to the Americans was incomprehensible but had not changed the fact
of their alliance and the obligations each had to the other. The British had
promised continued support, and the Sioux expected to find it still. They would
never be at peace with the Americans, who fell outside this alliance. Surely the
Canadians would honor their obligations to the Sioux, just as the Sioux had
always honored their own obligations.

Walsh was surprised to see the Yanktonais on Canadian territory and asked
Medicine Bear why he and his people had come: Medicine Bear said that his
people had also become dissatisfied because the Americans had refused to supply them with ammunition. Before leaving Fort Peck Medicine Bear and his
band had "held a Council & decided to leave the Americans for Ever. The camps
divided into small parties & started north to meet again on the British side of
the line. That he was now waiting for them & on their arrival a council would be

held & a final decision made what they should do." Walsh suspected that they would return to the Fort Peck Agency. Four Horns had not decided whether to remain with the Yanktonais on Frenchman River or to join Black Moon at Wood Mountain.

Over the winter of 1876–77 northern Lakota bands spread out along the borderlands but within reach of Métis traders. A Métis, Pierre Charbonneau, reported in mid-January 1877 that Long Dog's camp was on Cart Creek, about thirty miles south of the boundary. Information from Métis and Indians at Fort Peck suggested that the camp was still there in February and that it was supplied with plenty of ball and powder by traders from Canada.[40] George Boyd believed that several runners had passed by Fort Peck that winter carrying word to Sitting Bull and the other Indians of the ammunition trade in the north. Sitting Bull's camp was on the move. Boyd did not know where it was going but suspected that Crazy Horse's camp would strike north to Milk River and then go up either Frenchman River or Rocky Creek to get to the Métis at "Mountain De Baugh" (Montagne de Bois, or Wood Mountain) to trade ammunition.[41]

Ammunition from the north did make its way through to Lakota camps on American territory. Eagle Shield and Swelled Face, Minneconjous who had left Crazy Horse's camp on Tongue River on separate occasions and surrendered at the Cheyenne River Agency in February, both reported that Sitting Bull, or runners from his camp, had arrived at Crazy Horse's camp with ammunition received from Métis traders on Frenchman River. "Sitting Bull," said Eagle Shield, "brought plenty of ammunition with him which he got from the Red River Half-breeds. I got some of the Cartridges and also some tobacco and I saw others get some the same. They were needle cartridges. I got about thirty. Others got more than I did. . . . I understood fifty boxes [of ammunition] were brought in. . . . The trade was mostly in ammunition, tobacco and blankets."[42] Swelled Face added that Sitting Bull planned to go north again to trade with the Métis and to meet Black Moon, No Neck, and White Eagle, whom he had sent to Canada to get ammunition and to get the Red River Métis to join them.[43]

Sitting Bull did make his way north over the next few months. His followers had left those of Crazy Horse south of the Yellowstone River in February 1877 and, in early April, met in council on Beaver Creek with the Fort Peck Yanktonais. Black Tiger, a Yanktonai leader who was present at the council, told Day that Sitting Bull said that he was going to go to Fort Garry, where he would wait to learn what happened to the Indians. If the United States disarmed and dismounted the Indians, Sitting Bull said that he would not return. Sitting Bull

2. The presence of a Red River cart in this Dakota camp, photographed in the Red River valley in about 1880, suggests intercourse with Métis. (William H. Jacoby, Minnesota Historical Society E91.31/P52, neg. 7267-A.)

1. This watercolor, by William Armstrong, depicts a Dakota buffalo hunter on the White Horse Plains, just west of Fort Garry, during the mid-eighteenth century. He may well have come to the Métis settlement to trade as well. (William Armstrong, *Sioux Buffalo Hunter, White Horse Plains, Red River* [55.17.2], Collection of Glenbow Museum, Calgary, Alberta.)

3. Stanley J. Morrow photographed this council at Yankton, Dakota Territory, between Yanktonai and American representatives in the 1870s. The speaker is wearing a Hudson's Bay Company trade blanket. (National Anthropological Archives, Smithsonian Institution, 2004-50438.)

4. British and American boundary surveys marked the border on the Northern Plains with these mounds of earth between 1873 and 1874. These "sappers" were members of the British commission. (Provincial Archives of Manitoba, Boundary Commission, N11937.)

5. This Sioux burial was photographed by the British boundary commission in 1873 or 1874. (Provincial Archives of Manitoba, Boundary Commission, N11945.)

6. These two Métis families, photographed by the British boundary commission in 1874, were among those who went west to the Cypress Hills and Wood Mountain to hunt and trade. (Provincial Archives of Manitoba, Boundary Commission, N11932.)

7. Struck by the Ree's and Two Dogs's camp, photographed by the British boundary commission in 1874, also received visits from the North-West Mounted Police that year. (Provincial Archives of Manitoba, Boundary Commission, N14129.)

8. An engraving after a sketch by Henri Julien depicts the council between the North-West Mounted Police and members of a Yanktonai camp on 13 August 1874. (Henri Julien, *The Great Pow Wow with the Sioux on the 13th Aug, 1874* [59.40.8], Collection of Glenbow Museum, Calgary, Canada.)

9. Standing Buffalo led his people to Canada following the Dakota Conflict. His son, the younger Standing Buffalo, photographed here in 1875, succeeded in negotiating a reserve for his people in Canada. (Glenbow Archives, NA-2791-6.)

SITTING BULL ON DOMINION TERRITORY.

U. S. SOLDIER :—Send him over to our side of the line and we'll take care of him.
N. W. MOUNTED POLICE OFFICER :—So long as he behaves himself, the British right of asylum is as sacred for this poor Indian as for any royal refugee.

10. In this crassly nationalistic cartoon (originally published as the cover of the *Canadian Illustrated News* for 22 September 1877), Henri Julien depicts Sitting Bull sitting with his back against a boundary marker and listening while a North-West Mounted Police officer extols the superiority of Canadian Indian policy to an American soldier. (National Archives of Canada, c-066055.)

BARRACKS SQUARE   FORT WALSH   1878

11. Sioux men, women, and children mix freely with members of the North-West Mounted Police inside Fort Walsh in 1878. The man seated to the right of the central flagpole is purported to be Sitting Bull. It is interesting that the police allowed some of the Sioux to enter the fort on horseback. (T. G. N. Anderton, National Archives of Canada, c-19024c.)

12. This sketch, by Sydney Prior Hall, depicts the dance performed by members of Standing Buffalo's band at Fort Qu'Appelle on 18 August 1881, on the occasion of the governor-general's visit to the post. (National Archives of Canada, c-148592.)

13. In this studio portrait taken at Sioux Falls, South Dakota, in the early 1880s, Sitting Bull dons his Hudson's Bay Company trade blanket, a last vestige of his time in Canada. (Palmquist and Jurgens, Minnesota Historical Society E93.1s/r8, neg. 12139.)

had sent word to Iron Dog and Four Horns, then at Wood Mountain, to meet him in council at Little Wild Horse Lake. [44] John Culbertson, who had been camped with some Métis at the junction of Frenchman River and Milk River, reported to Day that Sitting Bull's camp arrived in the vicinity of the Métis camp on 16 April, crossed Milk River on 23 April, and planned to leave for the north to join Four Horns's camp on 27 April. [45] Medicine Bear's band joined Sitting Bull near Milk River and traveled north with them. One hundred thirty-five lodges—followers of Sitting Bull, Bear's Cap, No Neck, and Spotted Eagle—crossed into Canada on 30 April and moved up Frenchman River, where they rendezvoused with camps led by Four Horns and Struck by the Ree. [46]

Learning that Sitting Bull had crossed the border and had made camp at Pinto Horse Butte, Walsh set out to meet him, which he did in mid-May. During Walsh's council with Sitting Bull the Sioux "claim[ed] that their grandfathers were English, and that they had been raised on the fruit of English soil." Walsh warned Sitting Bull that the Sioux would not be allowed to continue the war against the Americans from the Canadian side of the border, and Sitting Bull replied that "he had buried his arms on the American side of the line before crossing to the country of the White Mother." Walsh was not convinced of Sitting Bull's sincerity and told Assistant Commissioner Irvine that Sitting Bull was "of a revengeful disposition, and that if he could get the necessary support he would recross the line and make war on the Americans." [47] On his return to Fort Walsh, Walsh told his fellow policeman John McIllrie that he "saw Sitting Bull, but says he hardly knows what to make of him." [48]

It is difficult to determine how many Lakotas sought sanctuary in Canada in the months following the fight on the Little Bighorn. Contemporary commentators were apt to exaggerate. Canada's governor-general, the Earl of Dufferin, reported to the British colonial secretary on 1 June 1877 that ten thousand Sioux were in British territory, although he later reduced that figure to eight thousand. [49] The American consul in Winnipeg, James Wickes Taylor, informed the State Department that, although he believed that there were some five thousand Sioux in Canada, some parties recently returned from the plains estimated that there were as many as nine thousand. [50]

Although many writers noted the number of individuals or lodges in the camps they encountered during the Lakotas' stay in Canada, camp populations were not stable as family groups and individuals repeatedly combined and separated, and at no time was a comprehensive census made. A plausible estimate of the number of Lakotas who crossed into Canada might be derived from records made in the months immediately following the Bighorn fight, when observers in the field were eager to report new arrivals to their superiors. Such commentators sometimes counted individuals but usually chose the easier task of counting lodges.

Proceeding in this way, the documentary record suggests that the number of Lakota refugees was closer to three thousand. James Walsh of the NWMP counted 109 lodges in Little Knife's and Black Moon's combined camp when he met them for the first time in December 1876 and 57 in Four Horns's camp when he met that leader in March 1877. According to Assistant Commissioner Irvine, Sitting Bull brought 135 lodges to Canada. The records of the NWMP are less clear about how many followers of Little Hawk and Big Road (the "Crazy Horse Band") arrived over the winter of 1877–78. An American scout, John Howard, noted in January 1878 that 205 lodges of Oglalas, Minneconjous, and Sans Arcs had crossed the Missouri River heading north. This figure accords well with estimates of the size of the Crazy Horse band in Canada.[51] These records give a total of 506 lodges: at six people per lodge, the population could be estimated at 3,036 people.

This figure compares well to population counts made by American military officials when the Sioux who had surrendered at Fort Buford and Fort Keogh were shipped to Fort Yates on the Standing Rock Reservation in 1881. These records indicate that 1,149 people at Fort Buford and 1,620 at Fort Keogh were placed on steamers to be shipped to Fort Yates on 26 May and 12 June, respectively. Another 59 people left Fort Keogh on an overland journey to Fort Yates on 14 June. Finally, Sitting Bull's following numbered 185 people.[52] These records provide a total of 3,013 people, a number very close to those estimated to have arrived in Canada.

The refugees were drawn from all seven constituent groups of the Lakota people. In addition, at least 11 Yanktons and Yanktonais, 4 Cheyennes, 3 Eastern Sioux, 1 Assiniboine, and 1 Arikara were among those who headed north and lived in Lakota camps in Canada. Many authors have stated that the majority of the migrants were Hunkpapas, but the evidence suggests that less than half of the Lakotas who entered Canada were, in fact, from that group.

The records are far from conclusive. Commentators often wrote about the composition of camps they happened on, but no record of the overall distribution of people exists. However, the names of 333 individuals were recorded in the documents examined for this study. It is hardly surprising, given the patriarchal views of those documents' European authors, that of these 300 individuals all but 23 were men. Of these individuals, 112 (34 percent) were Hunkpapas, 52 (16 percent) were Minneconjous, 52 (10 percent) were Oglalas, 38 were members of other groups, and 99 had no band affiliation recorded. Although this sample cannot be considered reliable (the amount of missing data leaves a wide margin of error, the total number of individuals from which the sample is drawn can only be estimated, and the sample is not random), it may be suggestive of the overall band composition.

The Lakotas who crossed the boundary in 1876 and after clearly expected to be allowed to stay in Canada, and they said as much to the Canadians whom they encountered. On no less than four documented occasions Sioux leaders explained that their rights in Canada had existed since the days of their grandfathers. Black Moon, Little Knife, Iron Dog, Long Dog, and others told Walsh at Wood Mountain in December 1876 that "their Grand Fathers had told them that they would find peace in the land of the British." Four Horns and Medicine Bear told Walsh the same thing at Wood Mountain in March 1877, adding that "[f]rom childhood they were instructed by their fathers that properly they were children of the British." Finally, Sitting Bull told Walsh at Pinto Horse Butte in mid-May 1877 that the Sioux "claim[ed] that their grandfathers were English, and that they had been raised on the fruit of English soil." He reiterated this belief during the Terry Commission in October. During a private interview with James F. Macleod he recounted: "The first time our nation learned to shoot with the gun, to kill meat for our children and women, it was by the English we were taught."[53] Sitting Bull maintained his position to the end. In the spring of 1881—just weeks before he surrendered at Fort Buford—he told the policeman S. B. Steele at Fort Qu'Appelle: "Canada was . . . his country, and the Mela Hoska (Long Knives) had no claim upon him. His friends were the Shaga Lasha (British), and always had been; the revolution did not give the Mela Hoska the right to govern him and his people."[54]

Such expectations were not hollow assertions; they were grounded in a larger pattern of borderlands interactions over a longer period. Northern Lakota bands took time and effort to renew and solidify support from other borderlands communities during the Great Sioux War—especially the Métis from British territory and the Yanktonais at Fort Peck, with whom they had been associated in the past. These steps, coupled with diplomatic initiatives directed toward the Canadians, gave the Lakotas some reason to believe that their movement over the boundary would be permanent.

7. THE LAKOTAS AND MÉTIS
AT WOOD MOUNTAIN, 1876–1881

In his refusal to listen to what American General Alfred H. Terry had to say during their meeting at Fort Walsh in October 1877, Sitting Bull made a remarkable comment about his people's long-standing relationship with the Métis. "I was born and raised in this country with the Red River Half-Breeds," he said, "and I intend to stop with them. I was raised hand in hand with the Red River Half-Breeds . . . and that is the reason why I have come over here."[1]

Relationships between Lakota and Métis people ranging from trade to marriage have gone largely unrecognized in Lakota historiography, especially after the Lakotas' flight to Canada in 1876. The history of the Lakota people in Canada emphasizes encounters with the North-West Mounted Police (NWMP) and the U.S. Army and concludes when Lakotas surrendered at American military posts. Yet the Métis at Wood Mountain were ubiquitous in the fabric of Lakota relationships with others. They were the traders in the Sioux camps and the employees of the Canadian and American traders at Wood Mountain. They were scouts and interpreters for both the Canadian police and the U.S. Army. When important events occurred at Fort Walsh or the Wood Mountain Post, the Métis were there, serving as facilitators and interpreters.[2] So common was it for Métis to serve as cultural mediators between aboriginals and Europeans that the word that Lakotas used to denote them, *slota*, has taken on the additional meaning of "interpreter."[3]

Shortly after Sitting Bull arrived in Canada, an American priest, the Benedictine Abbott Martin Marty, visited his camp near Pinto Horse Butte. Marty, a missionary on the Standing Rock Reservation, had come to Canada intent on convincing the Hunkpapa leader to return to the United States. Marty's reception, and that of his two mixed-blood guides, William Halsey, the interpreter from the Poplar River Agency, and John Howard, one of Colonel Nelson A.

Miles's scouts, was cool. Sitting Bull suspected Marty of being a spy. The Métis in Sitting Bull's camp played an important role in averting trouble.

Marty wrote of his visit in glowing terms, noting that he had been "received there with great ceremony"[4] and that his tent had been crowded with visitors during his stay. The young men had come, laughed, told stories, and sung, while the women had "made him welcome."[5] On the other hand, the police surgeon Richard Nevitt noted that Sitting Bull had asked the police what to do with the three Americans, noting that "if he was on the American side he would know very well—which meant that their scalps would adorn some lodge pole."[6] A council was held on 2 June 1877, attended by Assistant Commissioner A. G. Irvine, Inspector James Walsh, a number of policemen, Marty, and several Lakota leaders, among them Sitting Bull, Pretty Bear, Bear's Cap, The Eagle Sitting Down, Spotted Eagle, Sweet Bird and The Minneconjou. Motioning to Walsh, Sitting Bull said: "You told me if any one came into camp 'Let me know.' Some Americans came. I did let you know."[7] Always the astute politician, Sitting Bull wanted the police to understand that he had heeded their directive to obey the law and had spared the lives of the Americans. However, he also told Father Jean Baptiste Marie Genin, whom he met near the Cypress Hills in the autumn of 1877, that it was the intervention of Métis traders that had convinced him to spare the lives of Marty and Howard. He had suspected Marty of being a "disguised Yankee" who had come to tell lies. His young men had wanted to kill Marty and Howard (whom Miles had, in fact, described as a "scout and spy"), and it had been Antoine Ouellette and André Larivée who had saved the two men's lives.[8] Antoine Ouellette had been trading with the Sioux since the early 1870s, while Larivée, an interpreter at the Wood Mountain Post, lived in the Lakota camp with his two Sioux wives.[9] Both men had ties to the Lakota camps and had influence.

The participation of Ouellette and Larivée as facilitators was also evident when the NWMP were attempting to set up the Sitting Bull, or Terry, Commission at Fort Walsh in October 1877. Before the commission met, Walsh had sent one of the force's interpreters at Wood Mountain, Joseph "Caillou" Morin, to the Hunkpapa camp to convince Sitting Bull to meet General Alfred H. Terry, the commanding officer of the Department of Dakota (an administrative unit of the American army), who was coming north on behalf of the American government to meet the Lakota leaders and convince them to return to the United States; although of part Sioux descent, Morin was unsuccessful despite five attempts. Walsh then sent Louis Leveillé, a Métis who had accompanied him as an interpreter during his very first meeting with Sitting Bull, but also to no avail. Walsh then went to meet Sitting Bull himself, taking with him Antoine Ouellette and André Larivée. According to Genin, it was these two Métis who were responsible for convincing Sitting Bull to meet Terry. [10] Reflecting the Eurocentric bias typical of the time, Walsh's own account of his attempts to convince Sitting Bull to meet Terry makes no reference to Métis participation; nor does that of Walsh's superior, NWMP Commissioner James F. Macleod. [11]

That the Métis were important to the Lakotas is evident in the actions of the Lakotas themselves. The night after the Marty council concluded, Sitting Bull told Assistant Commission A. G. Irvine in a private talk that he had robbed a trading post on the Missouri River some years before and that he had made restitution to the trader, a Métis, by way of horses and gold dust. The Métis was now in his camp and was demanding more horses. Sitting Bull was now too poor to give him more but was willing to do so when he was better off. Irvine told Sitting Bull: "[T]he trader I knew to be a good man and if he [Sitting Bull] could do anything towards paying him something in return for what they [the Sioux] had stolen, I would be glad, but not to let it trouble him." [12] But the affair did trouble Sitting Bull, who clearly wanted to remain on friendly terms with the Métis.

During the summer of 1878, Sitting Bull again made clear his desire to promote friendly relations with the Métis. The Hunkpapas held their sun dance that summer near the Métis village at Wood Mountain. During the dance Grey Eagle, White Cow Walking, White Bird, and Good Crow stole some one hundred horses belonging to the Métis. According to Louis Goulet, a Métis who was then carrying the mail between Wood Mountain and Fort Walsh for the NWMP, the owners, led by Joseph Poitras (known also as Beaucasque or Bocase), went to the Sioux camp to reclaim the horses but were rebuffed; the horse raiders offered to keep the best horses and give back the rest. The Métis then made a complaint to the NWMP. Walsh, "Caillou" Morin, and a number of policemen went to the Sioux camp and threatened the Sioux with expulsion from Canada. Sitting Bull was eager to cooperate. According to Goulet, Sitting Bull told the assembled Sioux:

> Our only protection . . . is in Canada where the Americans can't come after us as they'd like to. Right now, our only allies are the Métis, who are also our relatives through their Indian mothers. If we get them on our backs, we'll be caught in a cross-fire with the Americans on one side and the Métis on the other, not to mention the Red Coats [NWMP]. [13]

Sitting Bull sent his *akicita* (the camp police) after the thieves—who included his brother-in-law, Grey Eagle—and forced them to return the horses. As not all the missing animals could be found, the Hunkpapa leaders were forced to make up the deficit.[14]

White Cow Walking, White Bird, and Good Crow were punished by being stripped naked and tied up night and day for about a week. After they were released the three were invited to a feast and were given gifts of leggings, otter robes, new moccasins with porcupine quillwork, and necklaces. Grey Eagle, who was not punished because he was Sitting Bull's brother-in-law and because his two sisters (Sitting Bull's wives) cried for leniency, received nothing. "[It] [w]as a good lesson for [the] whole tribe," concluded Morris Bob-Tailed Bull, one of the *akicita* involved in the affair: "[N]o more laws [were] broken."[15]

Sitting Bull was deeply troubled by the affair—not just the theft and its implications for Sioux-Métis relations, but also Walsh's threat to expel his people. Two weeks later he and Long Dog with a large camp visited Walsh at the Wood Mountain Post and demanded an explanation. A scuffle broke out that almost ended in bloodshed, but Morin, Goulet, and two other Métis pushed between Walsh and the two Sioux leaders to help prevent a fight.[16]

The Sioux leaders valued the friendship of the Métis because the latter remained important trading partners. American officials, who did not have first-hand information in their possession, were certain that this trade was largely in ammunition that would be used against American troops. Colonel Miles wrote in September 1877, for instance, that he had received several trustworthy reports that the Lakotas had received large amounts of ammunition since taking refuge in British territory. One such report had said that the Métis brought a train of some eighty Red River carts to Sitting Bull's camp in mid-August and traded Henry and Winchester ammunition in exchange for American horses, mules, robes, and other articles.[17] Father Genin, who arrived at Wood Mountain on 10 August 1877, noted, however, that the Sioux had not received their ammunition, of which they had a great amount, through trade. Although the Sioux often hunted with the Métis, to the best of Genin's knowledge the Métis had not furnished them with any cartridges. Instead, the Sioux had become proficient at refilling spent cartridges.[18]

Métis traders and their families were in the area of Beaver Creek when Miles's scouts and troops engaged Sioux hunting parties on 17 July 1879. Convinced that the Métis were selling arms and ammunition to the Sioux, Miles began arresting the Métis he encountered. The Métis, he wrote, *were in close communication with the hostile Sioux under Sitting Bull, and it was reported to me that they were supplying those Indians with ammunition. I, therefore, determined to break up the traffic, and to that end sent out bodies of troops, surrounded their camps, and gathered them together on one field to the number of over a thousand people, together with their eight hundred carts, herds of horses, tents and other property before mentioned. These were all sent out of the country after being kept for some time, thus breaking up one of the means of supply to the camp of Sitting Bull.*[19]

The Métis were more important to the Sioux as suppliers of food, not cartridges. Miles was much closer to the truth when he reported on 31 July 1879 that the Sioux traveled south of the boundary to hunt and steal stock, which they took to their camp and eventually traded to the Métis.[20] Buffalo herds north of the boundary became increasingly scarce and by the autumn of 1879 had completely failed. The Lakotas' trade with the Métis had turned to subsistence items. Major George Gibson had reported from Fort Keogh in January that the Sioux were starving and often had had to trade ponies to the Métis for meat, and W. L. Lincoln of the Fort Belknap Indian Agency complained in his year-end report that Lakotas were responsible for stealing from the Yellowstone and elsewhere hundreds of horses that either ended up in the Hunkpapa camp or were traded to the Métis.[21]

The Lakotas relied on the Métis for food when the hunt was unsuccessful or insufficient, and the Métis were willing to fill this need. However, the Sioux traded for food as a last resort. When the herds were at hand, they preferred to control the hunt and restrict the access of others, including the Métis. John F. Finerty of the *Chicago Times* noted, while visiting the Sioux camp at the Wood Mountain Post in late July 1879, that the Métis were distrustful of the Sioux—and with some reason. During a council between the Sioux and Walsh held while Finerty was present the followers of the Hunkpapa leader Bad Soup threatened to cut up the tents of any Métis who went hunting and, in so doing, interfered with the Sioux hunt.[22]

Despite the difficulties that arose, the Métis at Wood Mountain profited from their relationship with the Sioux. The Métis had been drawn to Wood Mountain in the first place because it offered ready access to the herds. The arrival of the Sioux caused Métis hunts to suffer, but the Métis overcame these losses through trade. Métis living elsewhere, but especially those from the Missouri River in Montana, had fewer opportunities to trade with the Sioux and were more likely to compete with them for food. As a result they actively opposed the Sioux presence in the region.

Among those who opposed the Sioux was Louis Riel, the leader of the Red River Resistance of 1869–70 who, having gone into exile after the end of his provisional government, lived for a time in the Eastern United States. Riel eventually returned to the West, arriving on the Missouri River in the autumn of 1879, and was welcomed into the local Métis community. [23] His actions over the next several years indicate that he had thrown his lot in with these people and was acting as their advocate. This is very apparent when one examines his interactions with the Sioux, then encamped just north of the boundary. Because Sioux hunts south of the boundary encroached on lands used by the Métis, Riel worked to remove the Sioux from the region by trying to convince them that life would be better if they surrendered to American military authorities.

It is not clear whether Riel crossed into Canada on his arrival in Montana and visited the Métis settlement at Wood Mountain. James Walsh believed that he had and that it was the intention of most of the Métis of the Wood Mountain district to winter at the Big Bend of Milk River, where Riel planned to be. [24] It is possible that Riel intended to contact Sitting Bull. Such a meeting may have occurred at Wood Mountain or south of the boundary, but, as the historian George Woodcock has argued, Riel had no ties to the Plains Indians at this time, and, if any Métis messenger went to Wood Mountain, it was probably the better-connected Gabriel Dumont. [25]

By mid-October 1879, Riel was traveling with a Métis camp on Beaver Creek. If not in communication with the Sioux, he certainly was aware of them. Thomas O'Hanlon, a merchant from Fort Belknap who was then transporting a herd of seven hundred cattle to the Poplar River Agency (formerly the Fort Peck Agency), wrote to Riel asking him for information about the Sioux, thus suggesting that Riel had intelligence about them even if he had not met any himself; and, at the end of the month, Gabriel Hamelin wrote from Wood Mountain to tell Riel of the second visit of Abbot Martin Marty that month. [26]

The fear of Canadians surrounding Riel's appearance in Montana can be attributed, in part, to people like Jean L'Heureux, an enigmatic Canadian who lived with Crowfoot's Blackfoot band in the 1860s and 1870s and who was on the government payroll as an interpreter in the 1880s. Many aboriginal peoples and Métis did cross the border from Canada and spent the winter of 1879–80 along Milk River. According to L'Heureux, Riel attempted to foment dissatisfaction toward the Canadian government among these Indians. The Métis, he wrote, told "all sorts of falsehood to the Indians, viz:—'That the presence of the Mounted Police Force in their country was the cause of the Buffalo desertion, that the Canadian Government was to take no more care of them, [and] that their Indian Treaty stipulations were not to be fulfilled." [27] Writing to Prime Minister John A. Macdonald in the wake of the North-West Rebellion of 1885, L'Heureux related that Riel and four of his counselors had had a long visit with him in Crowfoot's camp in the winter of 1879–80, during which they had propounded a plan to capture the Wood Mountain Post, Fort Walsh, Battleford (the capital of the North-West Territories), and, with the aid of the Blackfoot, Fort Macleod. After this, Riel was to proclaim a provisional government and argue the aboriginal peoples' case before the Canadian government at Ottawa. A general peace between the tribes was to be enforced, and "'Sitting Bull' and all American hostile Indians were to be invited to join, with promises of plunder and horses."[28]

L'Heureux's story was undoubtedly embellished, if not apocryphal. The reports from Father Joseph Hugonnard, the missionary in charge of the Qu'Appelle Mission during that winter, made no mention of such plots. Hugonnard wrote from Wood Mountain in the spring of 1880 simply that Riel had had frequent councils with the Métis.[29] A letter to Riel from none other than Jean L'Heureux—undated but undoubtedly written in the winter of 1879–80—noted that the Blackfoot had many "robes faites," suggesting that Riel was more interested in trade than in political agitation.[30]

Although Riel may have made provocative speeches, he was much more concerned with improving the condition of the Montana Métis and of the Métis families from Canadian territory who had been forced south to hunt than he was with inciting hostility against the Canadian government. Many of these Métis were related through marriage to the Gros Ventres and Upper Assiniboines of the Fort Belknap Reservation, on which they were then squatting.[31] By cultivating these relationships Riel hoped to persuade the Fort Belknap Indians to allow Canadian Indians and the Métis to hunt in the area. Commissioner James Macleod learned of Riel's activities from an NWMP mail carrier—and also that the proposed agreement did not include the Sioux.[32] The Gros Ventres and Assiniboines were hostile to the Lakotas and would have rejected any attempt by Riel to include the Sioux in this accord. Consequently, Riel was not concerned for the Sioux.

Although James Walsh reported that Sitting Bull camped near the Wood Mountain Post throughout the winter of 1879–80, the Hunkpapa leader did also travel to the Sioux camps on Milk River and met Louis Riel in late January.[33] Crozier learned from Edward Lambert, who had just returned to Fort Walsh from a trading expedition among the Sioux, that Riel had offered to intercede on Sitting Bull's behalf with the American government. "Keep the peace and do not get yourselves between two fires until Spring at any rate," Riel had supposedly told Sitting Bull. "If you want then to go back and live in peace with the Americans I will see the President and arrange everything for you."[34]

No documentary record exists of Sitting Bull's reply to Riel's offer. It is possible that Sitting Bull told Riel that he would prefer to communicate with the Americans through Walsh—and not Riel—for, after his meeting with Sitting Bull, Riel went to Fort Assinniboine and gave Lieutenant Colonel Henry Moore Black a memorandum blaming the unwillingness of the Lakotas to surrender on the "the underworking influence of the Canadian Mounted Police."[35] Riel received word in April 1880 from a man at Wood Mountain who had spoken to Sitting Bull regarding the latter's intentions. Sitting Bull had said that he was going to go to "Canada" to find out from the Canadian government if the Lakotas would be allowed to remain on "English" territory.[36] Sitting Bull, Spotted Eagle, and several other leaders did meet Walsh at Wood Mountain in May. At that time Sitting Bull told Walsh to tell the queen and the American president that he was ready to make peace with the Americans and that he wanted to go to Ottawa to meet the White Mother's daughter (one of Queen Victoria's daughters, Princess Louise, was married to the Marquess of Lorne, the Canadian governor-general) and then go to Washington to meet the president.[37]

When Riel spoke to Lieutenant Colonel Black in February, he intimated that the Lakota leaders were discussing peace and might send a deputation to the post. No deputation arrived, but Riel returned to Fort Assinniboine on 18 March 1880 and informed Black that the Métis had endeavored to convince the Sioux to return to the United States. Riel explained that Bull Dog and Red Elk, representing fifty-seven lodges of Brulés, had asked him to intercede on their behalf to find out what terms the Americans would grant the Sioux if they surrendered. Riel pleaded for American leniency, arguing against dehorsing and disarming the Sioux, and claiming that "the moral effect" of such a policy "would enivitably be to bring in all the Titons and Sitting Bull himself in the course of a few weeks."[38]

In his biography of Riel, the political scientist Thomas Flanagan wrote that Riel left Pembina in mid-August 1879 and arrived in the vicinity of Wood Mountain in mid-September: he intended to meet Sitting Bull there, but it is unclear whether he did. Riel's hope was to form a confederation of Métis and Indians and to use Montana as a base from which to invade Western Canada and establish a Native republic. Sitting Bull went to see Riel on Milk River in January 1880, but the meeting produced no results: without the aid of the Sioux, Riel's plans could not succeed. Riel thanked Black in the spring of 1880 for his kindness in allowing the Métis to remain on the reservation and appeared willing to try to persuade the Sioux to surrender, but Flanagan claims that this was "disingenuous"—Riel was trying to get the Sioux into the Americans' good books while simultaneously hoping to use them in his invasion of Western Canada. With the collapse of his Native confederacy, Riel turned to other issues.

During this entire period, however, Riel was instead trying to look after the interests of the Métis people in Montana with whom he lived. They were squatters on an American Indian reservation: Riel's discussions with Black were an attempt to allow the Métis to remain on the reservation during the winter. His conversations with aboriginal leaders were attempts to gain their permission to allow the Métis to remain on their lands. Riel may have made other more inflammatory, anti-Canadian speeches, but these appear to have been of more concern to Canadian officials than to him. Finally, Riel was not attempting to incite the Lakotas to join him in any hostile action in Canada. The Lakotas were competitors for the same resources as the Métis for whom Riel acted as spokesman. Riel's discussions with Black indicated that he was attempting to induce the Sioux to surrender: such an outcome would have removed the Sioux from the area and freed resources for the Métis and their Gros Ventre and Assiniboine kin. Riel purposefully excluded the Sioux from the agreement (reported by Macleod) that he hoped to make with the American Indians. Riel's later actions—his attempts to secure land grants for the Métis from Miles in August 1880 and his marriage in 1881 to a Montana Métisse—indicate that he had thrown his lot in with this community.[39] This was not a fallback position adopted by Riel when his attempts at a Native confederacy failed: it was what these years were all about for him. When Riel accepted the invitation of the Saskatchewan Métis to come to Canada in June 1884, he said that he hoped to return to the United States by September.[40] He did not intend remaining long, and there is no reason to doubt his word.

The Métis at Wood Mountain served as facilitators, interpreters, and traders during the Lakotas' sojourn in Canada. Significantly, their trade with the Sioux depended on the protection provided by the boundary. When they traded arms, ammunition, or alcohol to Sioux on American territory, the Métis relied on their boundary-crossing options to protect themselves from prosecution. Later, when Métis purchased horses stolen by the Sioux on American territory, they knew that the boundary still protected them from American prosecution. Métis living in the Cypress Hills and at Wood Mountain took advantage of their position in the borderlands to develop an amicable, mutually beneficial trading relationship with the Sioux.

8. THE FAILURE OF PEACE
IN CANADA, 1878-1881

Northern Lakota groups encroached on the lands of other aboriginal groups—Gros Ventres, Assiniboines, and Crows—as they moved northwest toward the Forty-ninth Parallel in the decade before the Great Sioux War. Their position as invaders, interlopers, and, after 1876, refugees was made even more precarious by the failure of the buffalo herds on the Northern Plains. To gain access to the hunt, the Lakotas had little choice but to seek peace with their neighbors on both sides of the border.

The Lakotas were successful in gaining peace with Native peoples living mainly in Canada before 1879 but not with those living in the United States. The food crisis, beginning in the autumn of 1879, forced Lakota hunters back into the United States, where they came into increasing conflict with "American" Indians and with "Canadian" Indians who were also forced south to hunt. Scholars have intimated that it was the Canadian government's refusal to provide food aid that was the main factor forcing the Lakotas out of both Canada and the borderlands.[1] But, in the end, it was really opposition from other aboriginal peoples.

The arrival of the Lakotas on the Canadian side of the boundary heightened the potential for conflict between them and the resident Native peoples. However, very little violence occurred before the food crisis in the autumn of 1879, much to the credit of the diplomatic efforts of Lakota leaders. Following their arrival in Canada, Lakota leaders like Sitting Bull met the leaders of Blackfoot, Cree, and other groups that spent most, but not all, of their time on Canadian territory.

It is exceptionally difficult to document these meetings specifically. Officers of the North-West Mounted Police (NWMP) or the U.S. Army often reported rumors of meetings and usually did not provide an exact chronology. Moreover, since none of these writers attended any meetings, they could say nothing of what was discussed. Interviews given by participants to white academics years later provide a little information on the topics discussed, but such accounts are invariably undated. As a result it is difficult to link the various nineteenth- and twentieth-century accounts or to know for certain if two accounts that seem to refer to a single meeting actually do. In addition, because Sitting Bull was, for Americans, the most famous Sioux leader of the era, white commentators wrote more about his movements than about those of any other leader. The activities of other important leaders remain obscure. Any reconstruction of Sioux diplomacy must remain tentative at best.

The purpose of peace negotiations was to gain access to land and—more important—the buffalo hunt. Once in the Cypress Hills/Wood Mountain area in the spring of 1877, Sitting Bull quickly approached an Assiniboine camp. An Assiniboine living in the Hunkpapa camp, a man who had been captured as a child in 1857, eased Sitting Bull's introduction. Sitting Bull had adopted this man as a brother some time before 1870 and had named him Jumping Bull, after his father. Jumping Bull claimed that his relatives, including a cousin named Big Darkness, lived in the Assiniboine camp that the Hunkpapas encountered in Canada. Taking advantage of these kin ties, Jumping Bull introduced Sitting Bull to his relatives, and "all went smoothly." To cement the new relationship the Lakota leader gave the Assiniboines many horses.[2]

The noted Blackfoot leader Crowfoot led his people on a hunt nearly to the Cypress Hills in the spring of 1877. Learning of Crowfoot's whereabouts, Sitting Bull sent him tobacco, but Crowfoot refused to smoke it until he knew more of Sitting Bull's intentions. That summer Sitting Bull and a peace mission approached Crowfoot's camp, located in the Sand Hills, north of the Cypress Hills. High Eagle, a relative of Crowfoot, was present at the meeting and remembered that Crowfoot and Sitting Bull shook hands and exchanged tobacco. After they had smoked, Crowfoot agreed to speak to Sitting Bull. They had a long conversation, which was followed by a dance. The Hunkpapas departed later that day. The two camps continued to hunt together before Crowfoot's people returned to the west.[3]

Sitting Bull met Crowfoot, Good Eagle, and other Blackfoot leaders in the Sand Hills after the Terry Commission had ended in October. Sitting Bull's nephew One Bull told Walter Campbell that the Blackfoot leaders had alluded to the Montana gold rush of the early 1860s and implied that the Sioux had somehow given the Americans permission to travel to the goldfields. Since miners had to travel to Montana up the Missouri River and through Sioux-held lands, the upstream Blackfoot may well have blamed the Sioux for American incursions into Blackfoot territory. Nevertheless, the Lakotas and Blackfoot made peace.[4] James F. Macleod, the commissioner of the NWMP, heard of the meeting from Crowfoot. "'Crow Foot,' the leading chief of the Blackfoot," he wrote, "told me that he had been visited by 'Sitting Bull,' who told him he wished for peace. 'Crow Foot' replied that he wanted peace; that he was glad to meet him on a friendly visit, but that he did not wish to camp near him, or that their people should mix much together in the hunt, and it was better for them to keep apart."[5] There was peace but little trust or cooperation. Crowfoot did not want his people to come into collision with the Sioux over food.

Crowfoot was still in the Sand Hills in the spring of 1878. The Bloods under Red Crow and Hind Bull were nearby, and the Lakotas were camped in the eastern part of the Sand Hills and south to the boundary. Peace with Crow-foot's people did not, however, guarantee peace with Crowfoot's own allies. Any expansion of peace had to be worked out individually with each new group. Sitting Bull sent tobacco to the Bloods in May 1878, but this only angered the Blood warriors. When Crowfoot arrived at the Blood camp, he and the Blood leader Medicine Calf managed to prevent the warriors from leaving camp and attacking the Lakotas.[6] There is no evidence that the Bloods ever supported the Lakotas' presence north of the boundary.

It appears that Sitting Bull also sent messages to the Peigans in the spring of 1878. The Peigan leader White Calf told Lieutenant Colonel John R. Brooke at Fort Shaw later that year that he had received entreaties from Sitting Bull but that he had declined them.[7] White Calf's band encountered Sioux from Canada in the Bear Paw Mountains in the fall of 1878. The two groups agreed to camp near each other (probably to prevent the two groups from working at cross-purposes and spooking the herds) and not to allow horse stealing. When the camps broke up in the spring of 1879, however, the Sioux stole thirty horses from the Peigans and headed toward the boundary. The Peigans pursued, and a battle ensued in which one Peigan and six Sioux were killed.[8]

Sitting Bull, meanwhile, had visited a Blackfoot camp on the Bow River in the spring of 1879. He was likely unaware of hostilities between other Sioux and the Peigans further south that were occurring at the same time. Having talked to Sitting Bull and held a dance, the Blackfoot moved to Fort Macleod, where, the NWMP policeman Simon John Clarke noted, Sitting Bull "is trying to Make friendship with them."[9] Hostility between the Sioux and various Blackfoot-speaking people was by no means universal.

Sitting Bull and Crowfoot met for the last time in the summer of 1880. Lakota and Blackfoot camps were hunting north of the Missouri River, on American territory, and, to ensure that conflict would not erupt between hunting parties, Sitting Bull invited Crowfoot's band to visit. Morris Bob-Tailed Bull, a Hunkpapa, related to Walter Campbell that Sitting Bull had told Crowfoot that their two peoples were now friends and that there would be no more war or horse stealing. Their children could sleep soundly and be healthy. Crowfoot had stood and said the same. Sitting Bull announced that he had named his eight-year-old son Crowfoot after the Blackfoot leader.[10] Sitting Bull's actions were probably an attempt to extend his kinship network to include Crowfoot by offering him this opportunity to assume a personal kin relationship. High Eagle, a Blackfoot participant, told the story to Blackfeet Indian Agent G. H. Gooderham in nearly identical words.[11] Such a bond, to the Sioux, was as real as that between biological relatives. Yet a few days after the ceremony a Lakota war party raided the Blackfoot camp and stole a number of horses. Crowfoot denounced Sitting Bull and said that the Sioux were now his enemies.[12]

The Lakotas were competitors for the dwindling herds of buffalo, not only with the Blackfoot, but also with the Crees, and it was the nontreaty Crees under Big Bear who initiated peaceful contact with the Sioux. Peace made sense for both peoples, however. If the Crees and Sioux were at peace, they could spend their time hunting instead of fighting one another. In July 1878 Big Bear explained during an interview at Fort Walsh to Frederick White, the comptroller of the NWMP, that he and his followers—some eight hundred lodges—had all camped near the mouth of the Red Deer River to allow the buffalo to pass north. So that the Crees could hunt without fear of Lakota attack Big Bear had then attempted to arrange for the Sioux and his band of Crees to hold their annual medicine lodges together. Concerned that Canadian officials were suspicious of his motives, Big Bear later changed his mind and decided that only he and one headman would represent his band at the Lakota sun dance.[13] Big Bear passed along the same information to Commissioner Macleod, who noted that Sitting Bull was also expected to be one of the guests at the gathering. Macleod sent his confidential scout, Andie Larivière, to the sun dance with instructions to report every few days to Assistant Commissioner Irvine.[14]

Big Bear probably also attended the Sioux sun dance in 1879, but this is unclear. In July Inspector L. N. F. Crozier was informed at Fort Walsh by a brother of the Cree leader Big Sky that Big Bear and seventy Cree lodges had visited Sitting Bull's camp, then located south of the boundary. According to Big Sky's brother, Big Bear complained to the Sioux that "[t]he people on the other side of the Line [the Canadians] only give us a handful when they give anything to us, I am afraid myself and people will starve." When Big Bear had finished, a Lakota spokesman agreed that, to ensure the survival of everyone, the Sioux would share the hunt with the Crees. At first, Crozier was disinclined to believe the story. He was more uncertain after questioning Big Sky's brother more closely.[15] Eventually, he concluded that the story was, in fact, false. It was, he wrote in his year-end report, "an instance of the many stories one hears, and of the difficulty in believing even those upon whom you might imagine reliance could be placed."[16] In the end it is unclear whether Big Bear and Sitting Bull met in the summer of 1879. Such a meeting is possible. The Sioux did hold a sun dance in early July—precisely the time when visitors might choose to meet them. Frederick Cadd, a Briton who operated a trading post at Wood Mountain for the American firm of William Emery and Company, noted, for example, that a number of agency Yanktonais from Many Horns' and Struck by the Ree's bands attended this sun dance—without, however, mentioning any Crees.[17]

Relations between the Lakotas and the aboriginal peoples of the Canadian plains became strained once the buffalo failed in Canada in the autumn of 1879. The disappearance of the bison forced aboriginal peoples who lived in close proximity to the international boundary—and even more northern groups— to travel south to hunt on American territory. Thousands of northern Native peoples migrated to the last of the herds in the United States. Eventually, the increasing number of hunting parties bound for the United States attracted the attention of government officials. Edgar Dewdney, the Indian commissioner for the North-West Territories, estimated that somewhere between seven and eight thousand Crees, Assiniboines, Bloods, Blackfoot, and Peigans left for the United States in 1879.[18] That large numbers were involved in this migration was also indicated by Norman T. Macleod, the elder brother of James F. Macleod and newly appointed Indian agent for Treaty Seven, who reported that "only the old and helpless" remained behind in the Blackfoot camp near Fort Macleod.[19] W. L. Lincoln, the American Indian agent at Fort Belknap, estimated that between three and five thousand "British" Indians were in the neighborhood of the Bear Paws and Little Rockies alone.[20] Jean L'Heureux reported to Dewdney that the close proximity of Assiniboines, Gros Ventres, Crees, Saulteaux, Métis, and Lakotas in the Milk River country and competition for the same food source resulted in a revival of "tribal animosties of old and ancient feuds" during the winter of 1879–80.[21] L'Heureux noted that the Sioux had stolen some 300 horses from the Blackfoot and Crees and that some 160 horses had been taken from the Sioux: Blackfoot had killed eight Sioux, and Crees had killed four. [22]

Aboriginal peoples in Canada were certain that it was the presence of the Lakotas along the boundary that had prevented the herds from returning to Canada during their annual migration. Crowfoot implored Dewdney and Macleod in the summer of 1879 to "drive away the Sioux, and make a hole so that the Buffalo can come in." Dewdney concluded that it was "the same story from one end of the Country to the other; the Sioux are preventing the Buffalo from crossing the line." [23] Tension among Blackfoot, Cree, and Lakota hunting parties, especially those hunting in the Milk River country, became endemic.

American Blackfeet Agent John Young reported that the Sioux stole many horses from the Peigans during the winter of 1879–80. The Peigans had pursued the raiders, resulting in the deaths of six Peigans and one Sioux. Warfare, Young concluded, consisted of cyclic raiding and retaliation. [24] The records are filled with fragmentary accounts of such encounters. An unidentified party of Sioux fought with an unidentified group of Peigans in the Bear Paw Mountains in January 1880. [25] The Oglala holy man Black Elk recalled in 1931 spotting Blackfoot scouts near Poplar River in the spring of 1880. He alerted his camp, followers of Big Road, and the people fled. They heard the Blackfoot firing into their abandoned tipis. [26] Some 160 lodges of Peigans (under Double Runner and Bull in the Middle), Bloods (under Running Rabbit and Wolf Collar), and a few Blackfoot and Gros Ventres were camped near Fort Maginnis in the autumn of 1880 when a party of Sioux stole forty horses from the Bloods; the Bloods pursued the Sioux, killing one. [27] A mixed Blood/Blackfoot camp south of the Missouri River was raided by some of Sitting Bull's Sioux after the first snow of 1880. The pursuit party exchanged shots with the Sioux but was unable to recapture any horses, and no one was killed. [28] Blackfoot raided Sitting Bull's camp (then at the mouth of Frenchman River) on two successive nights in late October; a day after the second attack, a hunter named Scarlet Plume was ambushed and killed by Blackfoot. That night three Blackfoot crept into camp but were detected. They escaped after a pursuit. [29] Major Guido Ilges of the U.S. Army reported from Fort Benton that over two hundred Blackfoot lodges camped on the Missouri River were at war with the Sioux. [30] Two Crows (a Hunkpapa scout working for Colonel Nelson A. Miles) reported in December that Hunkpapas had had an engagement with Bloods near the Little Rockies and that one Hunkpapa had been killed. [31] Over the winter of 1880–81 some three hundred horses were stolen from Crowfoot's Blackfoot and Big Bear's Cree camps and some twenty Blackfoot and Crees and eight Sioux killed.[32]

Lakota relations with the Crees and their allies were equally strained. Sioux raiding parties stole thirty-nine horses from the Ojibwas at the farm run by the Department of Indian Affairs on Maple Creek, some thirty miles northeast of Fort Walsh, and an unreported number from the Crees at Fort Walsh during the autumn of 1880. According to Canadian Indian Agent Edwin Allen, such raids made the Crees afraid to settle on a reserve for fear that their settled state would allow the Sioux to come and steal all their horses.[33] An American scout, William Everette, reported to Miles that the Crees had sent a letter to Sitting Bull, who was then on American territory, telling him not to return to Canada unless he wanted a fight.[34] Crees retaliated on the night of 17–18 April 1881, when a party stole a number of horses from the Sioux at the Wood Mountain Post. The next day a Sioux woman saw one of the Crees in the bushes behind the post. The Sioux searched but could not find him—he had managed to get to the post and was admitted. Sitting Bull demanded that the Cree be handed over. Crozier refused, creating tension between the Sioux and the police.[35] A Cree camp on Beaver Creek had a fight with the Sioux in June in which one person on each side was killed.[36]

The Lakotas often returned to American territory to hunt following their arrival in Canada. Such hunts were carefully planned: to protect the women and children camps were pitched on the Canadian side of the boundary, only the hunters traveling south, rarely more than an easy day's ride. If the camps were located on the American side of the border, they were placed close enough to it that they could be moved quickly to Canadian territory.[37] As the herds diminished and then failed, this strategy became unworkable. James Morrow Walsh of the NWMP reported from Wood Mountain in October 1878 that the scarcity of food had caused the Lakotas to talk of wintering across the border on Porcupine Creek or at the mouth of Frenchman River. "The women of the camp I believe," Walsh wrote, "are urging the men to cross and save their children from starving."[38] Sitting Bull explained to Walsh during a council at the Wood Mountain Post on 23 March 1879 that

> I am and most of my people are at present camped on the South side of the line, but my camp is close to the line, we have been forced to this move to get food for our children, while our horses were strong we hunted from the North side of the line, but when they became poor and could not make the long journey to Buffalo, we were obliged to move our camp, but I will not

remain South of the line one day longer than I can help for I wish to be as far away from the Americans as I can get and live.[39]

The Lakotas attempted to negotiate peace with those groups who controlled the lands where buffalo could still be found and into which they had been forced to venture for game. The Gros Ventres and Upper Assiniboines of Fort Belknap and the Crows were long-standing enemies of the Sioux, and they, unlike the peoples who lived for the most part on Canadian territory, remained unrelenting in their hostility to Sioux hunts south of the boundary.

American military authorities learned in July 1877 that Sitting Bull had sent two emissaries to talk with Big Beaver, the chief soldier of White Eagle's Gros Ventre band. Major Guido Ilges was certain, after talking with the principal men of the Gros Ventres at their camp at the mouth of the Marias River on the morning of 18 July, that some Gros Ventres would join the Sioux if the American government failed to provide more rations and annuity goods to them.[40] The scout John Howard reported to Miles in September that the Gros Ventres had gone up the forks of Milk River to meet the Sioux and to talk over their grievances against the American government. The Lakotas also wanted to come to an agreement with the Gros Ventres to reduce horse stealing. This mission was a failure: the Lakota delegates were received coldly, and the Gros Ventres gave no definite answer.[41]

Ilges reported from Fort Benton that Sitting Bull had sent tobacco at the end of March 1878 to all the neighboring tribes and invited them to a council to be held in early May. As of mid-April, sixty lodges of Assiniboines and nearly all the Gros Ventres had crossed into Canada to attend this meeting.[42] Ilges made a tour of inspection in May and failed to find any Gros Ventres or Assiniboines. He learned from "Milk river people" better acquainted with them than he that most of the Gros Ventres and Assiniboines had gone to the Cypress Hills to attend the meeting.[43]

By the winter of 1878–79, the Lakotas had turned their attention increasingly toward the Upper Assiniboines, those Assiniboines who lived further up the Missouri River and whose agency was at Fort Belknap. Indian Agent W. L. Lincoln reported in December 1878 that the Sioux had made peaceful overtures to the Assiniboines at the agency. So far these had been without success, but Lincoln was concerned that the Assiniboines might, in the end, become more friendly and familiar with the Sioux.[44] Lincoln was also concerned that the disposition of the Fort Belknap Assiniboines might be swayed by relatives from

Canadian territory, who, he feared, were on friendly terms with the Lakotas, and who were then encamped with those from the American agency.[45]

Lakota attempts to establish peaceful relations with the Gros Ventres and Upper Assiniboines were unsuccessful, and strife between members of these groups was common. A party of Assiniboines surprised a group of Sioux south of the Cypress Hills on about 10 October 1878, killing eight.[46] A group of Assiniboines or Gros Ventres stole fifty-nine horses from a Sioux camp forty-five miles from the NWMP's East End Post in January 1879.[47] Assiniboines attacked a party of six Sioux on Milk River in February, killing five of them and stealing a number of horses. This prompted a retaliatory raid by the Sioux on the Gros Ventres and Assiniboines. By mid-May four Gros Ventres and two Assiniboines had been killed and a number of horses stolen.[48] Sioux raids apparently achieved their aim: the Gros Ventres, Assiniboines, and Crows came into Fort Belknap in June, having been frightened away from the hunt by the Sioux.[49] Still, Sioux camps remained subject to devastating retaliatory raids. Assiniboines under Little Mountain attacked a camp of fifteen Sioux a few miles south of the boundary on 14 March 1881, killing twelve, and wounding the other three, one of whom later died. At Wood Mountain Crozier concluded that the Sioux were beginning to realize that they would be safer if they returned to the United States and surrendered.[50]

Peace with the Gros Ventres and Assiniboines was very important, but, of all their diplomatic efforts with the aboriginal peoples of the Missouri River, the Lakotas were most concerned that peace be achieved with their long-standing enemies the Crows. Crow territory was a last refuge for the buffalo, and the Crows, having battled the Sioux for years, would not share.

Overtures to the Crows were initiated, not by the Sioux, but by guests in the Oglala camp—the Nez Percés. The Nez Percés had participated in the Walla Walla council in 1855 and had received a reservation of five thousand square miles, only to have ten thousand gold miners inundate a portion of it by 1860 and American stock raisers encroach on it in the 1870s. The Nez Percés resisted government plans to relocate them, thus precipitating the Nez Percé War of 1877.[51] The Nez Percés fled east and then turned north, heading for the "Old Woman's Country."[52] For most the epic flight ended fifty miles from the border when Chief Joseph surrendered to Miles and General Oliver O. Howard on 6 October. About three hundred, led by White Bird, slipped away and reached Canada.[53] For the first months after reaching safety they camped with the

Hunkpapas, but they later formed their own camps while associating more closely with the Oglalas after the latter's arrival.

The Nez Percés had had historic ties to the Crows, so they took the opportunity in 1878 to open discussions. In November Walsh reported the return to Wood Mountain of six Nez Percés who had left the Oglala camp, apparently in September, to visit the Crows in the United States. The Oglalas had been wary of the mission, having told the six that "if they crossed the line they could never return to the Ogallalla camp."[54] Yet the endeavor was seemingly a success. The Nez Percés reported that "they were kindly treated by both the 'Crows' and the 'Gros Ventres' whom they also visited, and that the 'Crows' asked them to return to the Teton camp as messengers of Peace."[55] The Crows were willing to send a peace delegation to the Lakota camp, as were the Gros Ventres, but they were not willing to make peace with the Yanktons.

Sitting Bull heard of these events from the Oglalas and wanted to be involved. Discussions were held in the Sioux camps in December to determine what to do. At the first council, held on about 16 December, the Nez Percé leader, White Bird, reported that the Crows had asked whether Sitting Bull had made peace with all the Indians north of the boundary, whether the buffalo were numerous, and whether guns and ammunition were sold to Indians in Canada. The Nez Percé delegates answered affirmatively to all three questions. The Crows then explained to the Nez Percés that the Americans talked of taking away their guns and horses and that, if this were true, the Crows would move into Canadian territory. Those present at the council debated how safe the Lakotas and Nez Percés were in Canada. Could the Crows become allies? They decided to hold a council of all the headmen to discuss the issue.

At a second council, held two days later, the headmen decided that the Sioux would not be strong enough if the Canadians permitted the Americans to send their troops across the boundary, whereas peace with the Crows would give them the ability to face both the Canadians and the Americans if necessary. A delegation was selected to visit the Crows to make the peace.[56] Walsh learned in January 1879, however, that Sitting Bull's and White Bird's messengers had failed. The Crows had stolen a number of horses from Sitting Bull's camp, which was then on Frenchman River and two and a half miles inside American territory, and the Lakotas were planning a retaliatory raid.[57]

The failure to secure peace with the Crows in the winter of 1878–79 signaled the beginning of a new round of raids between the two groups. On one occasion that winter Crows stole fifty-nine horses from the Sioux at a place thirty miles north of the boundary.[58] On another Crows attacked an Oglala camp on Frenchman River, killing several Sioux.[59] In January 1879 a party of thirteen Lakotas stole fifty horses from the Crow camp on the Bighorn River in retaliation for thefts committed by Crows. The Crows pursued the fleeing Sioux and, after an all-day battle, killed the Lakotas' horses and mortally wounded a boy.[60] A party of Sioux hunters was attacked by Crows some fifteen miles south of the boundary in mid-February 1879: one Lakota, Hairy Bear, was killed and then hacked into pieces, three others were wounded, and nineteen horses were stolen.[61] It took a large, well-armed party of some fifty Lakotas, nineteen Santees, and five Métis to cross the boundary and recover Hairy Bear's body.[62]

The war with the Crows went very poorly for the Lakotas. According to Frederick Cadd, who traded with the Sioux that winter, more than thirty Sioux were killed, although some may have been killed by Assiniboines or Gros Ventres, while not one Crow died. Sitting Bull was very disappointed at not having been able to make a peace with the Crows; Cadd noted that he "had set his heart on it."[63]

Lakota-Crow raiding continued in 1879. This was a better year for the Sioux, who were, at least at times, successful in driving the Crows from hunting grounds on the lower Milk River. "The Crows," reported Agent Lincoln in June, "are badly demoralized and desire to get back across the Mo. River."[64] Nevertheless, Crow raids against the Lakotas were equally vigorous. Walsh told Miles in July, during their meetings at Miles's camp just south of the border, that the Crows were responsible for twice as many thefts north of the boundary as the Sioux were south of it.[65] The fact that Crow raiding was a tremendous concern to the Lakotas is underscored by the fact that three winter counts and their variants made by Lakotas who lived in Canada during this period (the Swift Dog/High Dog, Jaw/Jaw Variant, and Walter Campbell's unattributed Hunkpapa counts) employed glyphs representing deaths at the hands of Crows to mark the years between 1878 and 1880.[66]

Largely in response to Walsh's reports in early 1879 about the Lakotas' attempts to negotiate peace with the Crows, the Canadian government instructed NWMP Assistant Commissioner Irvine to tell the Lakota leaders that they and their followers were not to cross the boundary. Replying to this message during a visit to Fort Walsh in May 1879, the Sans Arc leader Spotted Eagle remarked that the difficulties were really the fault of the Americans, who, he charged, had encouraged the Crows to make raids against the Sioux. Spotted Eagle countered with an admonition to the police to "keep the Boundary Line good and strong."

The Crows wanted only to fight, so he had turned away from them, but, if the Canadians did not prevent the Crows from crossing the border, "there will be fighting."[67]

The American government periodically sent its troops across its boundary with Mexico during the 1870s and 1880s to curb resistance from aboriginal peoples in the southwest. Only once had it employed the same strategy to the north. On either 17 or 18 January 1864 a small detachment of American troops under Lieutenant Cochrane of the Pembina garrison crossed the boundary and abducted the Dakota leaders Shak'pay and Wakanozhan.[68] But Canada was not Mexico, and, given the tense relationship between the United States and Great Britain following the American Civil War, the American government could not afford to use this strategy again without a harsh, possibly dangerous, reply from Britain. John F. Finerty of the *Chicago Times* noted the American reluctance to violate Canadian territory when he wrote of his visit to Sitting Bull's camp in July 1879: "Were Sitting Bull at that time protected by Senor Diaz' government instead of by that of Queen Victoria's son-in-law, McKenzie would have been allowed to 'whoop him up.' . . . Such is the difference between our affection for England and for Mexico."[69]

If the American military was reluctant to create an international incident by crossing the boundary, it was less scrupulous about using Native auxiliaries to do what it could not do itself. The Lakotas knew this all too well. In making his charges against the American government Spotted Eagle was echoing claims made earlier by Sitting Bull. Sitting Bull had told Walsh in early 1879 that his desire in opening negotiations with the Crows had been to make his people strong enough to repel an attack from the Americans if the latter chose to attack them. It was then that the Americans had sent the Crows to steal his horses. "The Americans have beat me," Sitting Bull said. "There is no man in the American country that wears trowsers that is not a rascal. I said I would not commence war first. I have been waiting for them to attack me. They have done it."[70] He told Walsh during a council at the Wood Mountain Post in March that he had sent his young men, not to fight the Crows, but rather to form a defensive alliance with them: he blamed, not the Crows, but the Americans.[71] Sitting Bull repeated this charge in June when he was interviewed by the *Chicago Tribune* reporter Stanley Huntley, explaining to Huntley that he had tried to make peace with the Crows but that the Americans had sent them to steal his horses. Long Dog, speaking after Sitting Bull, added that the Crows killed Sioux hunters and that the Americans had sent the Crows to fight his people. Huntley disagreed, saying that he did not think this was so, to which Long Dog replied: "I think you lie. But we are not afraid of the Crows, and we do not want any war with your people."[72]

The Lakotas responded to Crow raids on behalf of the U.S. Army by launching a series of counterraids against these scouts. Raids were made against Crazy Head's band near Fort Keogh on several occasions in February 1880 and against the Crow scouts at Fort Custer in March.[73]

The Lakotas were not alone while they battled the Crows, Gros Ventres, and Assiniboines. They had maintained their ties to the Yanktonais throughout their sojourn in Canada. Struck by the Ree's Yanktons and Yanktonais were present at Fort Walsh in October 1877 when General Alfred Terry traveled to the post to meet with Sitting Bull and other Lakota leaders and to convince them to return to the United States. In fact Struck by the Ree and a member of his band named Nine spoke during the council.[74] Terry conceded on his return to Saint Paul in November that the Yanktonais of Fort Peck were indeed "in close contact with the hostile Sioux, who are encamped just across the frontier."[75] Some two hundred lodges of Yanktonais arrived at Sitting Bull's camp on Frenchman River in January 1878 to join the Lakotas on their hunt,[76] and about one hundred lodges of Cutheads and Yanktons, probably belonging to Thunder Bull's band, were camped near Wood Mountain in August 1878, probably on their way to attend a sun dance then being organized by the Oglalas.[77] Hunkpapas and Oglalas were in frequent communication with Black Catfish's Yanktonais and the Wolf Point Assiniboines during the winter of 1878–79. Walsh reported from Wood Mountain that "parties are arriving almost daily from the above two places [Poplar Creek and Wolf Point], with flour corn potatoes &c which are either given by the Yanktons and Assiniboines to hostiles or exchanged with them for skins robes &c."[78] Lieutenant Colonel George P. Buell reported from Fort Custer, on the basis of reports from the scouts Fleury and Cross, that the Yanktonais were trading ammunition obtained from American traders to the hostile Sioux, and the scouts Cyprian Matt and Murray Nicholson informed Lieutenant A. M. Henry at Fort Benton that the hostile Sioux had been "running with" the Yanktonais all winter.[79]

Not only did the Yanktonais harbor and supply the Lakotas, but they also fought the latter's enemies. The Yanktonais had their own reasons for fighting the Gros Ventres, Upper Assiniboines, and Crows—they, like the Lakotas, were encroaching on the territories of these people—but these actions complemented those of the Lakotas. In early January 1878 four Yanktonais from the Man That Owns the Horn's camp at the Poplar River Agency (the former

Fort Peck Agency) enlisted the aid of a group of Métis to make peace with the Gros Ventres and Upper Assiniboines of the Fort Belknap Agency. The attempt failed, and the following night the Yanktonais stole eleven horses and refused to give them up. Raiding between the Fort Belknap Indians and the Yanktonais was soon widespread. White Dog and Medicine Stone, both Assiniboines, stole twenty-three horses from the Man That Owns the Horn's camp in March in retaliation for the eleven stolen by the Yanktonais.[80] White Dog brought ten of these horses to Fort Belknap and claimed to have killed two Yanktonais.[81] In February Yanktonais belonging to Many Horns's band stole twelve horses from a Gros Ventre camp and eleven from Little Chief's Assiniboines. Many Horns refused to return the horses when scouts from Fort Belknap arrived at his camp on the Big Bend of Milk River.[82]

On 26 June 1878 the Gros Ventres and Assiniboines clashed near Fort Belknap with the Yanktonais from Black Catfish's band. Agents W. L. Lincoln (of Fort Belknap) and Wellington Bird (of Poplar River) had quite different interpretations of the skirmish's causes. To Lincoln, the Yanktonais—with some "hostile" Lakotas—were to blame for provoking the fight. To Bird, the Yanktonai leaders were opposed to hostilities, and the fight had been caused by the threatening behavior of White Dog of the Assiniboines.[83] While the agents disagreed, the raiding continued. The Yanktonais stole twenty-one horses from the Gros Ventres and Assiniboines near Fort Belknap on the night of 2 October; the next night they stole twenty more. This was followed later that month by a retaliatory raid led by White Dog and others during which the Assiniboines stole thirty-five horses.[84] In April 1879 engagements between the Yanktonais, Gros Ventres, and Assiniboines resulted in the deaths of two Gros Ventres and two Assiniboines.[85] A clash in February 1880 resulted in the death of at least one Assiniboine and one Yanktonais.[86]

Yanktonais were also in conflict with the Crows, Blackfoot, and Crees, thus supporting the Lakotas on these fronts. In the spring of 1879 Yanktonais belonging to the bands of Black Catfish, Black Tiger, and one or two others were stealing horses from the Crows, although Joseph Culbertson, a scout at the Poplar River Agency, believed that they had been stolen from Americans.[87] A year later, in June 1880, a combined Yanktonai and Lakota camp on Red Water Creek destroyed a party of twelve Crow horse raiders.[88] During the summer of 1880 James Walsh noted in a newspaper interview that the Blackfoot and the Yanktonais came into frequent conflict. A few Blackfoot had been killed by Yanktonais, and some Crees whose murders had been blamed on Lakotas had probably been killed by Yanktonais. [89] Joseph Culbertson, the son-in-law of the Yanktonai leader Black Horn reported in October of that year that the Milk River country above Poplar River was full of war parties and that the Blackfoot had killed three Yanktonais. [90] Captain Ogden B. Read, in command at Camp Poplar River, reported that one Blackfoot, possibly from a combined Blackfoot/Cree camp under Crowfoot and Big Bear then at Black Butte, had been killed by the Yanktonais six miles below Poplar River in early June 1881. Read noted that the Crees and Yanktonais were also at war but that the Crees under Little Pine had expressed a desire to visit the Yanktonais before winter, thus holding out the possibility of peace. [91]

Studies of the Lakota experience in Canada commonly note that, when food became scarce in Canada and Lakotas returned to the United States to hunt, individuals and family groups took the opportunity to surrender themselves to American military authorities. Yet this view skips over complex Lakota-Yanktonais relationships. [92] When Lakota people returned to the United States, they did not simply surrender; they chose instead to join the Yanktonais at the Poplar River Agency with whom they had been in contact since the late 1860s and had developed numerous kin ties. In fact, the existence of such ties created controversy in 1881 when American military authorities arrested "peaceful" Yanktonais along with "hostile" Lakotas on the latter's return to the United States. A heated exchange between Poplar River Agent N. S. Porter and Major D. H. Brotherton erupted in April when troops arrested a number of agency Indians found in a camp led by the war leader Gall on the Big Muddy and took them to Fort Buford. Many were married to hostiles but had not taken part in any hostilities, and Porter wanted them released. Porter had tried to separate the hostiles from the agency Indians when they were all at Poplar River, but this had proved impossible for they all claimed to be agency Indians. [93]

The Yanktonais' actions indicated not only that they considered the Lakotas to be kinspeople but also that they were eager to have the Lakotas remain with them. The American Army scout E. H. Allison complained in December 1880, for example, that many Lakotas had returned to the United States fully determined to surrender, but they were met at Poplar River by Yanktonais who gave them food and persuaded them to remain there. [94] Others were willing to share goods at the agency with the Lakotas. After Porter refused to give ration tickets to Lakotas who met him in council at the agency in August 1880, the Yanktonai leader Black Horn, whose wife was Hunkpapa, told them that the agent lied and that he could give them ration tickets if he wanted. Shortly after this Black

Horn arrived at the agency with about one hundred mounted and armed men and demanded provisions; he was "partially successful."[95] In November 1880 Black Horn again sent messengers to the Lakotas, telling them that they should not believe the Americans' threat of military action against them and that they could go to the agency and get supplies from the Yanktonais.[96]

Lakota groups who ventured into the United States hoped to remain in the borderlands. They believed that they had every right to remain in the area as it had been their home before their flight to Canada. Their leaders repeated this theme many times during discussions with American military officials.

Spotted Eagle and Rain in the Face arrived in the vicinity of Fort Keogh in October 1880. Miles sent Captain E. L. Huggins to escort them and their followers to the post. During several conversations, Spotted Eagle told Huggins "the woes of the indians; their poverty; the injustice of the whites; the indians had never harmed the whites except in self defence; all they asked for was to be left alone." Rain in the Face told him that aboriginal people were always treated poorly by the Americans and asked whether his people, the Hunkpapas, would be given the same terms of surrender as Spotted Eagle's Sans Arcs. Huggins assured him that they would, that no exceptions would be made, as Miles always kept his promises. To this Rain in the Face replied: "Gen. Miles promised [Nez Percé Chief] Joseph that if he would surrender he and his people would be taken to Idaho near the old home but they were taken to the sickliest place in the Indian Territory. They are dying there yet." Rain in the Face wanted his people to be allowed to return to their homes in this part of the country—and not be shipped off to some sickly place.[97]

Captain Read reported the arrival of Gall and twenty-three lodges at the Poplar River Agency in late November 1880. Gall, he wrote, "is [as] impudent as usual; says he will answer no questions; the country belongs to him, and he will go and do as he pleases, and neither he nor Sitting Bull has any idea of surrendering." Read had no choice, essentially, but to agree. He had no orders to remove the Lakotas and admitted that they could do whatever they wanted except draw rations.[98] Gall was less strident at a second council held on 1 December. He explained to Read that he knew the entire country and that he liked this area best because it held plenty of buffalo and wood. If allowed to remain, he would surrender his arms and ponies and go or send for Sitting Bull and the rest of the Lakotas. Neither he nor Sitting Bull would go to Fort Buford or Fort Keogh. Read believed that granting Gall permission to remain at the Poplar River Agency would ensure the surrender of all the Lakotas. Otherwise, they would not surrender and, instead, would receive during the winter what they needed from the Yanktonais, many of whom, complained Read, "are as bad as any of the hostile."[99]

During a council held at Fort Keogh in April 1881, Big Road, Hump, Rain in the Face, Bull Dog, Spotted Eagle, and Horse Road made it clear to Lieutenant Colonel J. N. G. Whistler that they did not wish to be moved to the agencies on the lower Missouri River. Hump explained: "The great Spirit raised us in the Country. . . . The agencies down below have no business with us." Spotted Eagle stated definitively: "God raised me in this Country and this land is mine." While Rain in the Face argued: "We all came back here and want to raise our children here and we don't want to go away from this Country."[100]

Except for those few who remained at Wood Mountain or, later, the new town of Moose Jaw and those who joined the Poplar River Yanktonai community, the Lakotas were removed from the borderlands by the end of the 1880s. When confronted with food shortages, the Lakotas formulated a new strategy of gaining access to the hunt by making peace with the aboriginal peoples of the borderlands. NWMP Commissioner Macleod noted this strategy in 1879, writing that councils between Sitting Bull and other aboriginal leaders were intended to secure peace, not forge hostile alliances. Canadian Indians, he continued, "have visited and mixed with the Sioux, and the Sioux with them, and I have no reason to think those visits have meant anything more than a desire to make peace with one another, as they had been enemies for years before."[101] The strategy failed, and with its failure came the Lakotas' removal from the region.

After being transported downriver to Fort Yates, Big Road, Rain in the Face, Bull Dog, Spotted Eagle, and others addressed a letter to American President James Garfield, telling him that they wanted nothing to do with the streams around Fort Yates and that they wanted to see him to discuss their future.[102] Their future, however it unfolded, would be out of their control.

9. OVERVIEW:
THE NORTHERN BORDERLANDS

A great deal of the historiography of the United States and Canada has focused on nation building. Looking back, the frontier thesis of Frederick Jackson Turner served to explain the presumed distinctive character of the American people and American democracy. Likewise, the staples thesis of Harold Innis explained the very existence of the Canadian state.[1] Aboriginal peoples were obstacles to and not participants in the nation-building process. Aboriginal peoples and their histories have been left out of the mainstream. As Bruce Trigger has noted, most historians have viewed aboriginal history as an adjunct to European colonial history.[2] The history of the colonial and early national periods of the United States and Canada has provided a framework onto which the histories of aboriginal peoples have been grafted.

In recent years, and especially with the rise of ethnohistory as a methodology for understanding the history of Native peoples, historians have shown a genuine interest in the study of aboriginal history in its own right, and their views on that history have been transformed. Yet the nationalist perspectives of historians remain largely unchanged and unchallenged. Canadian historians are concerned with the history of Canada, American historians with that of the United States. For this reason historians today, like their non-Native predecessors, carelessly slot Native peoples into these nationalist frameworks. In Canadian history one sees "Canadian" Indians responding to Canadian actions and "American" Indians responding to American ones. Borderlands people, living on the interface between two societies, political jurisdictions, or economic regimes, have found that their history has been written in very one-sided ways. Historically speaking they have been marginalized, just as academics have often marginalized individuals who lived on the borders of ethnic or racial categories.[3] In reality borderlands groups, like individuals living on cultural borders, are given more options—not fewer—by their position on the "edge."[4]

Indigenous peoples throughout the colonial world made tactical use of European colonial boundaries. In Africa, for example, where European boundary making throughout the continent partitioned indigenous societies, people crossed colonial boundaries to evade taxes or labor conscription (especially when it was military conscription), sell goods or find employment in neighboring colonies whose economies were stronger, and avoid warfare with European troops.[5] In Asia pastoralists moved their herds across boundaries to find shelter, pasture, and water. In one case along the boundary between what was then the Ottoman Empire and Persia, surveyors found boundary pillars three miles out of place. The local Kurdish inhabitants explained: "[O]ur grazing grounds had been given to the Afghan village and their irrigation-water had been given to us, so we made an exchange, had our own little boundary commission, and re-erected the pillar where it now stands in its proper place."[6]

The position of colonial boundaries often had little impact on indigenous identities. In 1965, for example, the king of Ketu, a Yoruba state located within modern-day Nigeria, told an interviewer: "We regard the boundary as separating the French and the English not the Yoruba." Despite a century of foreign rule and countless border crossings, the king of Ketu and his people had remained *Yoruba*.[7] Twenty years later a former chief of the Tobacco Plains Band of Kootenays in British Columbia stated the point bluntly: "We shouldn't be classified as Canadian or American. We are the same people; we're all Kootenays."[8] Clearly, the history of the borderlands Sioux is but one chapter within a larger volume of indigenous peoples' history in border areas around the world.

In 1818, when Great Britain and the United States agreed on the Forty-ninth Parallel as the border between their respective territorial possessions on the Northern Plains, they ignored or overlooked the fact that their new boundary ran through territories occupied by many aboriginal societies, cutting them in two. Suddenly, lands used by the Blackfoot, Assiniboines, and Ojibwas, among others, were split between the jurisdictions of two colonial governments, despite the countless economic, political, and kinship linkages that spanned the border.

Historians in the field of Native-white relations often write of "Canadian" and "American" Indians as if these national labels had some special explanatory power or have been as meaningful to aboriginal peoples as they have been to European newcomers. In doing so they have continued a tradition established more than a century ago by Indian agents on the Northern Plains. Canadian Indian Department officials and their American counterparts wrote in the 1870s and 1880s of the North and South Assiniboines, not in an effort to recognize divisions acknowledged by the Assiniboines, but simply to distinguish those who lived in Canada from those who lived in the United States. Assiniboines from Moose Mountain and Wood Mountain in Canada had extensive ties with those at Wolf Point in the United States, but to Canadian and American officials they were simply "British" Indians.

It is a testament to the process of partition that the very names by which aboriginal peoples of the Northern Plains have come to be known vary on each side of the border. The Blackfoot, Peigans (usually), and Ojibwas of Canada are the Blackfeet, Piegans, and Chippewas of the United States. This phenomenon has occurred throughout the colonial world.

A full history of the partition of aboriginal groups in the region has not been written, but a cursory examination of the documentary record suffices to show that all borderlands people, not only the Sioux, had a complex relation to the line that the Europeans had drawn. Like the Sioux, aboriginal peoples from across the Northern Plains did not hesitate to cross the boundary if they believed that advantages could be had in doing so. This was readily apparent when aboriginal peoples crossed the boundary to escape warfare. Eastern Sioux fled to Rupert's Land in the 1860s. Western Sioux arrived in Canada in 1876. Nez Percés joined them in 1877. By the time the Bannocks fled their Idaho reservation in 1878 one army officer was prompted to write his wife: "I have no idea where this thing will end, but rather think we will have another chase to the British line."[9] The flow of people was reversed after the North-West Rebellion of 1885, when many Métis and Crees fled Canada for the United States.

Periods of warfare punctuated a history of cross-border migration that was much more mundane. All groups freely crossed the border when hunting. American General William T. Sherman, for example, noted correctly: "The British Indians always follow the buffalo, ignorant of the Boundary line."[10] Moreover, it was not just the Sioux who engaged in clandestine trading. When they were refused arms and ammunition pursuant to presidential order in the 1870s, Blackfoot peoples from Montana "at once proceeded to the Trading Posts in the Dominion of Canada, where they obtained all the ammunition they desired without question."[11]

Transboundary migration was readily apparent during treaty making. When aboriginal land was sold in one country, its owners—even those who resided in the other country—expected their share of the proceeds. In the decades following the negotiation of American treaties Native people from British territory repeatedly presented themselves to American Indian agents for rations and annuities.

Nowhere was the presence of "British" Indians at American Indian agencies noted more frequently than among the Blackfoot. Lieutenant Colonel Alfred Sully of the U.S. Army advised the American commissioner of Indian affairs in the 1870s that these people claimed land stretching from the North Saskatchewan River to a point "some miles south of the city of Helena" in the Montana Territory. "Being a wild, uncivilized set," he contended, "they of course do not take into consideration any treaties we have with Great Britain in regard to our boundary line, but look upon the whole of the country both north and south of the line as theirs."[12]

Sully's comments were echoed a year later by the American agent to the Blackfoot, who noted that his charges crossed and recrossed the boundary between Canada and the United States yet stopped short of encroaching on the lands of other aboriginal peoples. "They seem . . . to be governed by imaginary boundary-lines," he wrote, blissfully ignorant of the irony of his words, but "express themselves as perfectly willing to remain in what they consider their own country."[13] Many Blackfoot who had retreated north of the border after experiencing trouble with various American fur traders returned to American territory during the winter of 1855–56 after hearing news of the Blackfeet Treaty negotiated that year. They were "greatly pleased when informed that they were to receive a portion of the benefits resulting from the late treaty."[14] Afterward they returned to British territory. When they and many of the Bloods missed the treaty payments in 1858, their agent explained that this was because they were "so far north"—undoubtedly in British territory—that they were unable to attend.[15] The agent set out to pay annuities in June 1862 but found few Native people at Fort Benton as "nearly all were off to the north on their hunting grounds."[16]

American officials grew increasingly concerned about the presence of "foreigners" at American treaty payments. In September 1864 the Blackfeet agent recorded that the people attached to the agency had arrived for the annual payments and remarked that the Bloods "live mostly on the other side of the line in the British possessions . . . and it is questionable whether they can properly be called subjects of the United States."[17] The Blackfoot, he continued, "live entirely in the British possessions and never come this way except to trade, get their annuities, or commit some depredation. . . . [W]ere it not that the [Blackfeet] treaty expires next year, [I] would recommend that their next annuity be paid them in powder and ball from the mouth of a six-pounder, but as it is, I recommend that when the present treaty expires they be turned over to the tender mercies of the British crown, whose subjects they undoubtedly are."[18] When the United States proposed a new treaty with the Blackfoot peoples in 1865 and most of the Blackfoot and many of the Bloods were absent from the negotiations, T. F. Meagher, the acting governor of the Montana Territory and superintendent of Indian affairs, questioned whether the United States was obligated to treat with "Indian tribes who voluntarily abandon their lands, seeking shelter and protection in a foreign country."[19]

The American and Canadian treaties were significant to many Blackfoot people. Both treaties were commemorated in a Blackfoot winter count made, probably, by Teddy Yellow Fly for James Willard Schultz in February 1929.[20] More than a few Blackfoot people, in fact, took treaty in both countries. Of the forty-three Blackfoot, Blood, Peigan, and Sarcee leaders who signed Treaty Seven in Canada in 1877, seven had taken treaty with the Americans in 1855. Other individuals who attended the Blackfeet Treaty in the United States later ended up in British territory but did not attend the negotiations for the Canadian treaty. One signatory of the American treaty, Three Bulls, entered Treaty Seven by adhesion three months after negotiations ended.[21] Another, Calf Shirt, fled the United States after involvement in the murder of twelve Americans in 1865 and lived the last eight years of his life in British territory. He was shot and killed by an American trader at the confluence of the Oldman and Belly Rivers during the winter of 1873–74, only three years before Treaty Seven was concluded.[22]

Another individual, Broken Arm, signed the Blackfeet Treaty as a witness and was a perfect example of a borderlands person. Although Cree, he was the influential leader of an Assiniboine band. His group wintered at Wood Mountain in British territory but traded regularly at Fort Union in the United States, and he traveled to Washington as part of a Native delegation in 1831. He was well-known to the missionaries of the north, being baptized by the Wesleyan Methodist Thomas Woolsey, and befriending the missionary John McDougall. Broken Arm died in 1869 trying to promote peace between the Crees and the Blackfoot, the victim of a Blackfoot bullet.[23]

The Blood leader Medicine Calf, who was present at the negotiations for the Blackfeet Treaty in 1855, used provisions of this American treaty as the basis for negotiations at Treaty Seven. "I hope and expect to get plenty," he began:

> [W]e think we will not get so much as the Indians receive from the Americans on the other side; they get large presents of flour, sugar, tea, and

blankets. The Americans gave at first large bags of flour, sugar, and many blankets; the next year it was only half the quantity, and the following years it grew less and less, and now they give only a handful of flour. We want to get fifty dollars for the Chiefs and thirty dollars each for all the others, men, women, and children, and we want the same every year for the future.[24]

Clearly, he wanted the Canadian treaty to have long-term benefits that the American one lacked.

Like the Blackfoot peoples, Assiniboines who resided for most of the year in British territory took advantage of treaties in the United States. In 1862, Upper Missouri Agent Samuel Latta noted that the Assiniboines were "a good and well-disposed people, and try to keep their treaty obligations." However, owing to their general fear of Lakota attacks, they had abandoned lands to the south of the Missouri River and spent "a portion of their time in the British country."[25] Two years later Agent M. Wilkinson arrived at Fort Union with goods for the Assiniboines. He met a band of Assiniboines who had been absent from the post for several years and who told him that they owned "immense tracts of land" and that Europeans "must not walk through it." After receiving gifts from Wilkinson this group of "American" Indians left for their hunting grounds in Rupert's Land.[26]

When Canadian treaties were signed, "American" Indians, not unexpectedly, presented themselves at treaty payments in Canada. This was simply the reverse of the trend that began when only American treaties existed. John Young, the Blackfeet agent in the United States, noted that prior to the signing of the Canadian Treaty Seven "the Indians from north of the line made use of their family relationship to gravitate towards the agency that issued food and rations, thus swelling the number on the agency roll and drawing from its supplies."[27] Once Treaty Seven had been signed in Canada, the movement of Native peoples was reversed. Young reported that between fifteen hundred and two thousand people had moved north to receive annuities in Canada.[28]

Likewise, Assiniboines from American territory moved north to receive the benefits of Canadian treaties. Alexander Culbertson, an interpreter at Fort Belknap, complained to Special Indian Agent William H. Fanton that Pheasant Belly, a headman who was "for years known as a beneficiary of Milk River Agency at Forts Browning and Belknap M.T.," had gone north in the summer of 1875 and had been "induced to become a beneficiary of the Canadian Government and sign some articles of allegiance." Long Lodge, a headman from another band, had also gone north that summer but had refused to make an adhesion to a Canadian treaty. Culbertson noted that American officials responded by refusing assistance to the members of both bands at the Fort Belknap Agency during the winter of 1875–76. [29] Agent W. L. Lincoln of Fort Belknap in the United States summed up that some Assiniboines "go north and take their money, thus becoming British Indians," and noted: "[T]here are always some of my Indians at Wolf Point and Cypress [Hills, in Canada], and probably as many from those places here."[30]

The Canadian government responded to cross-border movement just as the American government had. Both were unwilling to spend more on annuities than was absolutely necessary and rejected the claims of "foreign" Indians. When a group of Ojibwas told Commissioner Alexander Morris at the negotiations for Treaty Three in 1873 that they expected their American relatives to be included in the Canadian treaty, he replied that it was only for "*bona fide British Indians.*" But, recognizing the transboundary nature of this community, he allowed that any "who should *within two* years be found *resident* on British soil would be recognized."[31] In 1876 the policeman James Morrow Walsh told a group of Assiniboines, including Long Lodge, who had assembled in the Cypress Hills that to receive their annuities they would have to prove to his satisfaction that they were "British Indians." The leaders advised Walsh that the nontreaty Assiniboines who were arriving were "really British Indians" who had been obliged to cross into American territory because of declining buffalo herds in Canada. They assured him that these people "had been living as much on this side of the line as the other, and were surely as much entitled to all the provisions of the treaty as the Indians who are living further North."[32] Walsh refused to pay the followers of Little Chief and Shell and struck from the pay sheets anyone who he discovered received annuities in both countries. Long Lodge, whom Walsh considered a "good man and very friendly to the Whites," found his band weakened on account of objections that many of his followers were American Indians. [33]

Canadian Indian Agent Allan MacDonald refused to take the adhesion of a number of Assiniboines at Fort Qu'Appelle in the fall of 1877 because Piapot, Ocean Man, and Pheasant Rump could not assure him that they "belonged to our country." "Unless great caution is exercised," he concluded, "we will find Indians in a few years drawing annuities from both Governments." [34] In the end, however, the Canadian government recognized all three as Canadian Indians.

Sitting Bull understood the fluidity of the border as well as anyone. He recognized that leaders like Piapot, Ocean Man, and Pheasant Rump could easily be Canadian one day and American the next. In fact he viewed Pheasant Rump as essentially an American but one who nonetheless made the successful transition to the Canadian side. Sitting Bull hoped to do as well for himself. "The Santee Sioux and 'Pheasant Rump' the Assiniboine," he said in the spring of 1881, "have received Reservations in this Country and I am going to try for one also."[35]

By the early 1880s both the American and the Canadian governments were taking steps to stop aboriginal peoples from crossing the boundary. Over the course of a single generation the boundary was closed and the borderlands destroyed.[36] In Canada the North-West Mounted Police (NWMP) used the tactic of arresting Indians who brought stolen horses into Canada to control Indian movement.[37] In addition the Canadian government withheld rations from Native people who refused to go to their assigned reserves farther north in an effort to "starve them out" of border areas, especially near Fort Walsh.[38] Native people were "not [to] be permitted to think that they can go to any Post and receive a similar Ration to those Indians who belong there."[39] The policy had disastrous effects on Native health. Agent Allan MacDonald reported from Fort Walsh in 1882: "The Indians look very bad, I know they are not getting enough flour but I like to punish them a little, I will have to increase their rations, but not much."[40] Yet Native peoples responded to the curtailment of rations, not by giving up and going to the reserves, but by crossing "the line in strong armed parties" to get what food they could in the United States.[41]

As far as the American government was concerned, the presence of so many "British" Indians served only to deprive "American" Indians of their food supply. The government gave instructions to the army to drive "Canadian" Indians back into Canada. The U.S. Army began encountering hunting parties of aboriginal peoples from Canada in 1878 and just as soon began sending them back north. Soldiers from Fort Belknap warned them that they would be sent to prison for two years and have their horses and carts confiscated if they returned to American soil.[42] But such threats often had little effect as the Americans were reluctant to carry them out.

At first American policy was lenient toward "British" Indians, who were the subjects of a foreign power, Great Britain. Not wanting to jeopardize its fragile but improving relations with the British, the American government reined in the army and prevented it from using the force necessary to keep "Canadian"

Indians out of the United States. Native peoples from Canada took advantage of this diplomatic decision.

Frederick White, the comptroller of the NWMP, reported: "Dominion Indians have raided across the Border, and meeting with no effective punishment or loss when confronted or turned back by American troops, have had apparently, in their own view, no risk to run in their incursions beyond temporary delays when discovered, as, when arrested and put across the boundary, they often return soon after the backs of the troops are turned."[43] Agent Lincoln noted that Native people from Canada "pay but little attention to my representations thinking that we, the American Soldiers, are afraid of them."[44]

By 1881 the Americans had become increasingly aware of the depredations allegedly committed by Native people from Canada and were "determined to deal with them severely."[45] Yet American policy had no teeth and remained unsuccessful. Cecil Denny, an ex-policeman turned Canadian Indian agent, noted that a large party of troops from Fort Assinniboine had come across 250 lodges of Crees and tried to intimidate them into leaving: "The soldiers placed their guns in position and ordered the camp to leave, but the Indians paid no attention to them, and the troops had to return to Assinniboine without having made the Indians move."[46] At the same time as Denny was relating this incident to his superiors it was rumored that two Native people caught horse stealing had been hanged by Montana ranchers. Stockmen had been petitioning the departmental military commander since May to remove Canadian Indians from the United States. Denied satisfaction through this channel, they took the law into their own hands in November.[47] This action, more forceful than any the army was prepared to take, had the desired effect. Denny noted that Native peoples, fearing similar actions on the part of other American settlers, "seem afraid to go across the lines."[48]

By the middle of 1882 the American government had decided to pursue a more vigorous policy. That summer four companies of troops from Fort Assinniboine, established in 1879 in part to control movement over the border, were detailed to patrol the boundary along Milk River.[49] A party of Métis and Natives was captured that summer, and their horses, rifles, ammunition—"nearly all they possessed"—were taken from them.[50] Although bison were reported to be plentiful on the American side of the line as late as October 1882, the Indians were afraid to cross over as "the American Troops are watching them closely to try and catch them."[51] The possibility of capture now had greater meaning. No longer were Native peoples simply to be taken to the Canadian border and set free. Now their possessions were confiscated, and they were deposited at the border with only four or five days' rations. [52]

Nearly thirty years ago Irene Spry outlined the process whereby aboriginal peoples on the Canadian plains were dispossessed of their lands and, eventually, confined to reserves. The "Great Transformation," she argued, involved the replacement of the "commons"—lands exploited by Indians, mixed-bloods, and Europeans alike—by private property where access to resources was strictly controlled. [53] Spry may well have substituted *borderlands* for *commons* and *bordered land* for *private property*. Over the course of a generation the Canadian-American borderlands on the Northern Plains were divided first by an international boundary and then into a patchwork of individual landholdings. The borderland in which competing polities, both Native and newcomer, pursued their own objectives had become bordered lands.

Most of the Lakotas who fled to Canada following the Great Sioux War had surrendered to American authorities by 1881, thus bringing to a dramatic close the story of their exodus across the boundary. They were removed from the region to reservations lower down the Missouri River, while Dakotas, Yanktons, and Yanktonais were settling on reserves and reservations on both sides of the border. The relationships among the various Sioux living in the borderlands were disrupted, as were Sioux relationships with others. The Métis were also becoming rooted, settling in communities such as Willow Bunch in Saskatchewan and Zortman in Montana or on individual landholdings.

In December 1883 nineteen Sisseton families from the Poplar River Agency—members of the elder Standing Buffalo's band who had not followed his son to Canada—arrived in Canada to visit relatives on the Standing Buffalo and Birdtail Creek reserves. [54] In September 1886 another twenty-two Sisseton and Yanktonai families from Poplar River arrived in Canada in the company of some "Canadian" Dakotas to visit relatives. [55] They were the last Sioux to cross the boundary in appreciable numbers. These recent arrivals had lived in the borderlands for years, often at the Poplar River Agency in the United States, but also—unnoticed by Canadian officials—with the Sioux on Canadian territory. Many had relatives among White Cap's followers on the Moose Woods Reserve, while others had close family ties to the Dakotas on the Oak River Reserve. Among the arrivals of 1886 was Two Dogs, the man who had met Pascal Breland at Wood Mountain in 1873 and had spent so much time with Valentine Rowe during the latter's convalescence at Wood Mountain in 1874, still carrying the "credentials" that Donald Cameron of the North American Boundary Commission had given him in 1874.

What is significant about contact between Sioux communities at the end of the century is that it occurred within bordered lands, not in the borderlands. Native peoples had lost their independence, and their leaders could no longer use the boundary as a tool. Settling on reserves and reservations, made necessary when the buffalo herds failed, was also having consequences. Children went to European-run schools; former hunters became enmeshed in and dependent on European-style agriculture; government administrators collected data on aboriginal people and where they "belonged." The collapse of the buffalo economy tied aboriginal people to government agencies where they could obtain rations.

The historiography of aboriginal peoples and the Canada–United States boundary is still in its infancy. The historian Paul F. Sharp advocated in the early 1950s that scholars employ regional rather than national approaches to the history of the Northern Plains. His *Whoop-Up Country* was a first attempt to draw the people of southern Alberta, Saskatchewan, and Montana into a single historical frame. [56] Nearly fifty years later Beth LaDow examined much of the same geography as Sharp, retracing some lines and drawing many new ones. [57] Yet very few book-length transboundary studies were undertaken in the years between these two books. Like the Spanish Borderlands in the days of their pioneering historian, Herbert Eugene Bolton, the Canadian-American borderlands have been seen as a fringe area in the history of the Canadian and American Wests and consequently have been largely ignored. [58] As late as 1992 Donald Worster pointed out the scant attention paid to this region. "We have no real school of northern borderlands history," he wrote. There was "no Herbert Bolton or John Francis Bannon for these parts." [59]

The absence of a borderlands paradigm in Sioux historiography means that significant aspects of Sioux history receive little attention. The nineteenth-century Sioux are, in fact, best conceptualized as a borderlands people. This characterization tells something about where they lived but something also about who they were. They made tremendous tactical use of their proximity to different groups of Europeans. They were pragmatic, switching their support from one group to another, always with Sioux needs uppermost in their minds. Sioux in the upper Mississippi Valley supported French traders during the early eighteenth century but quickly accepted British ones after the British conquest of New France in 1763. While they fought alongside British troops during the American Revolution and the War of 1812, they then reversed themselves and made peace with the Americans. By 1800 the Sioux had developed a trade network that gave them access to British, American, and Spanish goods. Dakotas from Minnesota and Lakotas from Montana used the boundary as a shield against the U.S. Army during times of conflict, while Dakotas, Yanktonais, and Lakotas profited from their trade in buffalo products and contraband arms and ammunition with the Métis from the north. As members of the borderlands community Dakota and Yanktonai leaders petitioned Indian agents and other government officials in both Canada and the United States for goods and land. Throughout the history of their interaction with incoming national powers, the Sioux used their position in the borderlands as a tool to improve their lives.

The Sioux have had a complicated relationship with the Canada–United States boundary. Long expert in promoting their own goals by taking advantage of opportunities offered by different groups of Europeans, the Sioux added the boundary itself to the list of tools useful in achieving these ends. Canadian and American government policy regarding the common border evolved over the course of the nineteenth century. Neither government patrolled or monitored the boundary for much of the century; by century's end, however, they had all but closed it. Yet the Sioux, by virtue of the opportunities offered by the boundary, ended up residing on both sides of it and maintained transboundary ties throughout the century. Their diplomacy had significance for the relationships among aboriginal peoples along the entire length of the western Canada–United States boundary and invites comparisons with boundary situations involving indigenous peoples throughout the world. A borderlands perspective shifts the historical lens away from Canadian and American history and, in so doing, offers clearer insights into Sioux history.

NOTES

The following abbreviations have been used in the notes:

AAG   Assistant Adjutant General;
AASB   Archives de l'archevêché, Saint-Boniface;
ARCIA   *Annual Report of the Commissioner of Indian Affairs*;
ARSW   *Annual Report of the Secretary of War*;
BCARS   British Columbia Archives and Records Service;
CIA   Commissioner of Indian Affairs;
CO   Commanding Officer;
GA   Glenbow Archives;
HBCA   Hudson's Bay Company Archives;
LR   Letters Received;
LRCIA   Letters Received by the Commissioner of Indian Affairs;
LS   Letters Sent;
MHSA   Montana Historical Society Archives;
NAC   National Archives of Canada;
NARA   National Archives and Records Administration;
PAA   Provincial Archives of Alberta;
PAM   Provincial Archives of Manitoba;
SAB   Saskatchewan Archives Board;
SGIA   Superintendent General of Indian Affairs;
SW   Secretary of War

Preface

1. Axtell, *The Invasion Within*, xi.

Note on Sioux Groups and Leaders

1. See DeMallie, "The Sioux in Dakota and Montana Territories," 20–21; Parks and DeMallie, "Sioux, Assiniboine, and Stoney Dialects"; and the Sioux essays in DeMallie, ed., *Plains*.

2. In some Canadian sources, Big Road is referred to as Broad Tail. This appears to be a simple typographic error. *Big Road* and *Broad Trail* are alternate translations of the same name. At some point, a Canadian recordkeeper accidentally dropped the *r* from *Trail*, and the incorrect appellation has been perpetuated ever since.

Partitioning Sioux History

1. An extensive body of work on cultural borderlands could be cited. For a selection of useful

studies providing vistas into "peoples in-between," see Brown, *Strangers in Blood*; Van Kirk, *Many Tender Ties*; White, *The Roots of Dependency*, and *The Middle Ground*; Anderson, *Kinsmen of Another Kind*; Axtell, *The Invasion Within*; Calloway, *Crown and Calumet*; Jennings, *Empire of Fortune*; Dowd, *A Spirited Resistance*; Seed, *Ceremonies of Possession*; Adelman and Aron, "From Borderlands to Borders"; and Brooks, *Captives and Cousins*.

2. Even so, aboriginal peoples understood that there was a geographic component of these borderlands. Those Santees who moved into the Milk River country in the 1860s appear to have believed that the Missouri River was the boundary. See Diedrich, *The Odyssey of Chief Standing Buffalo*, 82, 110 n. 20.

3. Literature that deals directly with Plains Indians and the Canada–United States boundary is very sparse: in addition to works cited below, see Peterson, "Imasees and His Band"; Dempsey, "Little Bear's Band"; Hubner, "Horse Stealing and the Borderline"; Hogue, "Disputing the Medicine Line"; McLeod, "Plains Cree Identity"; and Sasges, "Divided Loyalties."

4. For examples of contraband trade across colonial territorial boundaries, see Collins, "Clandestine Movement"; Asiwaju, ed., *Partitioned Africans*; and Asiwaju, "Problem Solving along African Borders," 173–74.

5. DeMallie, "The Sioux in Dakota and Montana Territories."

6. The expression *bordered lands* is from Adelman and Aron, "From Borderlands to Borders."

7. Excellent recent works include Gray, *Custer's Last Campaign*; Greene, *Yellowstone Command*; Hedren, ed., *The Great Sioux War*; Hutton, ed., *The Custer Reader*; Fox, *Custer's Last Battle*; and Greene, ed., *Lakota and Cheyenne*.

8. See, e.g., DeMallie's editions of the Black Elk and Walker materials: DeMallie, ed., *The Sixth Grandfather*; and Walker, *Lakota Belief and Ritual*, *Lakota Society*, and *Lakota Myth*. Parks and DeMallie discuss the forthcoming fourth volume of Walker material, manuscripts written by George Sword, in "Plains Indian Native Literatures." DeMallie discusses the place of Lakota texts in ethnohistory in " 'These Have No Ears.' "

9. DeMallie, ed., *Plains*.

10. For Standing Buffalo's actions south of the border, see DeMallie, "The Sioux in Dakota and Montana Territories." For his actions north of the border, see Elias, *The Dakota of the Canadian Northwest*; and Diedrich, *The Odyssey of Chief Standing Buffalo*.

11. Anderson, *Little Crow*, chap. 9.

12. Anderson, *Kinsmen of Another Kind*, 278.

13. Elias, *The Dakota of the Canadian Northwest*, chap. 2.

14. Utley, *The Lance and the Shield*.

15. Kehoe, *The Ghost Dance*.

From Contested Ground to Borderlands

1. A useful account of Sioux-French relations during the final years of the French regime is Baily, ed. and trans., *Journal of Joseph Marin*. Marin's journal is owned by the Henry E. Huntington Library and was first published (in French) in Champagne, ed., "Journal de Marin, Fils."

2. Parker, ed., *The Journals of Jonathan Carver*, 117–18 (see also Parker's introduction). See also Carver, *Travels*.

3. Abel, "Trudeau's Description," 176–77, and *Tabeau's Narrative*, 121–23; Thwaites, ed., *Journals of the Lewis and Clark Expedition*, 6:45, 89; and Pike, *Exploratory Travels*, 127–31, 134–37. For numerous references to British traders, see Jackson, ed., *The Journals of Zebulon Montgomery Pike*, vol. 1, passim.

4. Carondelet to Alcudia, New Orleans, 8 January 1796, Nasatir, ed., *Before Lewis and Clark*, 2:385–95.

5. Sioux involvement in the American Revolution is discussed in Thwaites, ed., "Papers from the Canadian Archives," 144–47; and Perrault, "Narrative," 544–45. Their involvement in the War of 1812 can be gleaned from a number of collections of primary documents: see Wood, ed., *Select British Documents*; Gruesel, ed., "Copies of Papers . . . Pertaining to the Relations of the British Government with the United States during the Period of the War of 1812," and "Copies of Papers . . . Pertaining to the Relations of the British Government with the United States during and subsequent to the Period of the War of 1812"; Thwaites, ed., "Dickson and Grignon Papers," and "Bulger Papers"; Draper, ed., "Lawe and Grignon Papers"; and Carter, ed., *The Territory of Louisiana-Missouri*.

6. Wood, ed., *Select British Documents*, 1:425 (speech of Wabasha).

7. Robert McDouall to Sir, Drummond Island, 19 June 1816, Gruesel, ed., "Copies of Papers . . . Pertaining to the Relations of the British Government with the United States during and subsequent to the Period of the War of 1812," 468–69.

8. "Indian Council," 29 June 1816, Gruesel, ed., "Copies of Papers . . . Pertaining to the Relations of the British Government with the United States during and subsequent to the Period of the War of 1812," 479–87. See also Keating, *Narrative*, 400. Keating's account of Little Crow's speech is significantly more hostile in tone than the one reprinted in Gruesel.

9. Information about Dickson can be found in Cruikshank, "Robert Dickson"; and Tohill, "Robert Dickson."

10. James, *Narrative*, 223–26.

11. Peers, *The Ojibwa of Western Canada*, 94, 124; Ross, *The Red River Settlement*, 55–56; West, *The Substance of a Journal*, 70–71.

12. Anonymous to Sir, Ft. Douglas, 10 September 1822, National Archives of Canada (hereafter NAC), Andrew Bulger Papers, MG19 E5, vol. 2, pp. 322–23.

13. West, *The Substance of a Journal*, 82–84.

14. Ross, *The Red River Settlement*, 162–65.

15. Ross, *The Red River Settlement*, 158–62, 162–65; and Thomas Simpson to James Hargrave, Red River, 28 November 1836, Glazebrook, ed., *The Hargrave Correspondence*, 249–50.

16. Ross, *The Red River Settlement*, 324.

17. Wallace, *John McLean's Notes*, 377.

18. Ross, *The Red River Settlement*, 258–59, 264–72.

19. Ross, *The Red River Settlement*, 330–32. See also Kane, *Wanderings of an Artist*, 49. For a commentary on the event, see Peers, *The Ojibwa of Western Canada*, 157–58.

20. Kane, *Wanderings of an Artist*, 54–55.

21. Morton, "The Battle at the Grand Coteau"; and Woodcock, *Gabriel Dumont*, 55–62.

22. Denig, *Five Indian Tribes*, 30–31.

23. Morton, "The Battle at the Grand Coteau," 47–49.

24. Denig, *Five Indian Tribes*, 31.

25. Morton, "The Battle at the Grand Coteau," 49.

26. Wheeler-Voegelin and Hickerson, *The Red Lake and Pembina Chippewa*, 165.

27. Prud'Homme, "Georges-Antoine Belcourt," 63. Prud'Homme did not identify the "trois nations siousses." For an English translation of Prud'Homme's essay, see Aldrich, "George Antoine Belcourt."

28. Hind, *Narrative*, 1:143–44, 2:153–54. Both the Canadian Red River Exploring Expedition and the

Assinniboine and Saskatchewan Exploring Expedition were funded by the Canadian government to learn about the Northwest.

29. H. L. Hime, Diary Entry, 1 July 1858, Provincial Archives of Manitoba (hereafter PAM), Records of the Assinniboine and Saskatchewan Exploring Expedition, P5404, file 9, Diary of H. L. Hime, 29 April 1858 to 30 November 1858. (This is a copy; the original diary is in the York Pioneer and Historical Society, Toronto.)

30. Taché, *Vingt Années de missions*, 117.

31. Ross, *The Red River Settlement*, 324–32.

32. "The Fall Hunt," *The Nor'-Wester*, 15 November 1861, p. 2, col. 5.

33. White, *The Middle Ground*, x, xiv.

The Dakota Conflict and Migration

1. Anderson (*Little Crow*, 171) states, without providing a source, that this delegation was made up of Standing Buffalo's people.

2. The "Canadian Party" was made up of Canadian settlers at Red River who advocated the annexation of Rupert's Land by Canada.

3. Schultz to Colonel Peteler (commanding officer [CO] Ft. Abercrombie), Red River Settlement, 2 January 1862 [1863], Libby, "Fort Abercrombie," 25–26; Pfaller, "The Peace Mission of 1863–1864," 297–99.

4. Libby, "Fort Abercrombie," 25–26. See also Anderson, *Little Crow*, 171; Hargrave, *Red River*, 266; "Sioux at Fort Garry," *The Nor'-Wester*, 24 January 1863, p. 3, col. 3. Less authoritative accounts can be found in Cheadle, *Cheadle's Journal*, 121; and Milton and Cheadle, *The North-West Passage by Land*, 163–64.

5. "News from St. Joseph," *The Nor'-Wester*, 9 February 1863, p. 3, col. 3.

6. "Visit from the Sioux," *The Nor'-Wester*, 2 June 1863, p. 2, col. 4.

7. Hargrave, *Red River*, 291. "The red flag of the north" was the British red ensign with "HBC" printed in white on the fly that the Hudson's Bay Company was authorized to use.

8. Dallas to General Sibley, Ft. Garry, 3 June 1863, U.S. Commissioner of Indian Affairs, *Annual Report of the Commissioner of Indian Affairs* (hereafter CIA, ARCIA), 1863, 336. See also Anderson, *Little Crow*, 174–75.

9. "Another Sioux Visit," *The Nor'-Wester*, 1 September 1864, p. 3, cols. 1–2.

10. "Arrival of the Sioux," *The Nor'-Wester*, 3 December 1864, p. 2, cols. 4–5.

11. Dumont, *Gabriel Dumont Speaks*, 34–35. See also Woodcock, *Gabriel Dumont*, 75–76.

12. Kerr, "Gabriel Dumont," 53.

13. Weekes, *The Last Buffalo Hunter*, 273–74.

14. Elias, *The Dakota of the Canadian Northwest*, 20–21.

15. *St. Cloud Democrat*, 20 May 1863, reprinted in Libby, "Fort Abercrombie," 29–30.

16. Pfaller, "The Peace Mission of 1863–1864," 299. See also Anderson, *Little Crow*, 174.

17. Pfaller, "The Peace Mission of 1863–1864," 302–4. See also H. H. Sibley to John Pope, St. Paul, 16 September 1863, Board of Commissioners, *Minnesota in the Civil and Indian Wars*, 2:309–10. Sibley had engaged the Sioux at Big Mound on 24 July, at Dead Buffalo Lake on 26 July, and at Stony Lake on 28 July.

18. Angus McKay, biographical sketch of William McKay I, 30 November 1948, Glenbow Archives (hereafter GA), Robert H. Hougham Fonds; McKay, *Fighting Parson*, 13–39.

19. Fort Ellice Journal of Daily Occurrences, Entry, 1 June 1864, PAM, MG1 C6, folder E; Angus McKay, biographical sketch of William McKay I, 30 November 1948, GA, Robert H. Hougham Fonds.

20. W. E. Traill to Mother [Catherine Parr Traill], Ft. Ellice, 22 July 1865, and W. E. Traill to Kate [sister], Ft. Ellice, 17 August 1865, GA, Traill Family Fonds, M1241, box 1, file 2. A brief account of this meeting is found in Zachary M. Hamilton, "Indians of Saskatchewan," n.d., 38–39, PAM, Zachary M. Hamilton Papers, MG9 A50, box 2, file 113, microfilm reel M107.

21. Fort Ellice Journals, PAM, Hudson's Bay Company Archives (hereafter HBCA), 1 July 1868–19 September 1869, B.63/a/10, microfilm reel 1M52; 1 June 1871–24 May 1872, B.63/a/11, microfilm reel 1M1003; and 1 November 1875–30 June 1876, 11 November 1876–9 December 1876, B.63/a/12, microfilm reel 1M1003.

22. W. E. Traill, "Lo the Poor Indian," n.d., GA, Traill Family Fonds, M1241, box 3, file 20. Traill was married to McKay's daughter Harriet.

23. Angus McKay, biographical sketch of William McKay I, 30 November 1948, GA, Robert H. Hougham Fonds.

24. Valentine McKay, "The McKays in Saskatchewan," *Grand Rapids Star*, 3 May 1961, GA, Charles D. Denny Fonds, newspaper clipping.

25. Steele, *Forty Years in Canada*, 161.

26. Gad. E. Upson to Dole, Ft. Benton, 19 February 1864, CIA, *ARCIA, 1864*, 446–47.

27. Throne, ed., "Iowa Troops in Dakota Territory," 137, 139–41.

28. Bartlett to Pell, Ft. Sully, 2 December 1863, National Archives and Records Administration (hereafter NARA), Records of the United States Army Continental Commands, RG393, Ft. Sully, Letters Sent (hereafter LS), vol. 19, pp. 24–25, no. 8.

29. Pfaller, "The Peace Mission of 1863–1864," 306–9. Norbert Welsh wintered on the south side of the Souris River the following winter, intending to trade with the Dakotas, but found that they were away on the Missouri. He traded only with a small Dakota camp of two lodges. Weekes, *The Last Buffalo Hunter*, 66–69.

30. De Smet to Dole, on board the *Yellow Stone*, 15 July 1864, CIA, *ARCIA, 1864*, 423–24 (quotation from 423).

31. F. F. Girard to De Smet, enclosed in De Smet to Dole, 23 August 1864, CIA, *ARCIA, 1864*, 425.

32. De Smet to W. P. Dole, Washington DC, 23 September 1864, CIA, *ARCIA, 1864*, 427.

33. Sully to Assistant Adjutant General (AAG), Ft. Berthold, 29 August 1864, U.S. War Department, *The War of the Rebellion*, ser. 1, vol. 1, pt. 1, pp. 150–51.

34. Dimon to TenBroeck, Ft. Rice, 24 January 1865, U.S. War Department, *The War of the Rebellion*, ser. 1, vol. 48, pt. 1, pp. 636–38.

35. Kane, ed. and trans., *Military Life in Dakota*, 122 (see also 138–39, 148).

36. Otis to Crossman, 17 July 1867, NARA, RG393, Ft. Abercrombie, Letters Received (hereafter LR) 1867; Stanley to Campbell, 1 June 1867, Ft. Sully, LS, vol. 20, pp. 99–100, no. 1867-101.

37. Kane, ed. and trans., *Military Life in Dakota*, 122 n. 71, 224–25.

38. "Report of Major General Hancock," St. Paul, 20 October 1869, U.S. Secretary of War, *Annual Report of the Secretary of War* (hereafter SW, *ARSW*), *1869*, H. Ex. Doc. 1, pt. 2, 41st Cong., 2d sess., vol. 2, pt. 1, serial 1412, pp. 56–67.

39. Pfaller, "The Peace Mission of 1863–1864," 299–300; *Expedition of Captain Fisk to the Rocky Mountains*, 7–8; Clandening, "Across the Plains in 1863–1865," 256.

40. Hall to AAG, Department of Dakota, Ft. Abercrombie, 18 May 1867, NARA, RG393, Ft. Abercrombie, LS, vol. 3 (1866–67), pp. 65–66, no. 63 [*sic*; no. 64]; Hall to Hayman, Ft. Abercrombie, 17 June 1867, NARA, RG393, Ft. Wadsworth (Sisseton), LR, unnumbered; Hayman to CO Ft. Thompson, Ft. Wadsworth, 29 June 1867, NARA, RG393, Ft. Abercrombie LR 1867, no. 115 H and W.

41. Kane, ed. and trans., *Military Life in Dakota*, 138–39. The mail carriers were given this warning by a party of mixed-blood traders who, in turn, had been told this by Medicine Bear's Yanktonais.

42. Kane, ed. and trans., *Military Life in Dakota*, 171; Wright, "The Fort Totten–Fort Stevenson Trail," 73.

43. Kane, ed. and trans., *Military Life in Dakota*, 192–93.

44. Kane, ed. and trans., *Military Life in Dakota*, 287–90.

45. Sully to Meline, camp at mouth of Little Cheyenne River, 11 September 1863, U.S. War Department, *The War of the Rebellion*, ser. 1, vol. 22, pt. 1, pp. 555–61; Sibley to Meline, St. Paul, 12 September 1863, Board of Commissioners, *Minnesota in the Civil and Indian Wars*, 2:308–9.

46. Sibley to Pope, St. Paul, 25 January 1864, U.S. War Department, *The War of the Rebellion*, ser. 1, vol. 34, pt. 2, pp. 152–56.

47. Pfaller, "The Peace Mission of 1863–1864," 307–8.

48. Sully to AAG, Ft. Berthold, 29 August 1864, U.S. War Department, *The War of the Rebellion*, ser. 1, vol. 41, pt. 1, pp. 150–51.

49. Sully to Pope, Ft. Rice, 17 July 1865, and Sully to AAG Department of the Northwest, Camp No. 22, 20 July 1865, U.S. War Department, *The War of the Rebellion*, ser. 1, vol. 48, pt. 2, pp. 1090–91, 1109–10.

50. Sully to AAG Department of the Northwest, Camp No. 30, Devil's Lake, 31 July 1865, and Sully to AAG Department of the Northwest, Camp No. 37, Ft. Berthold, 8 August 1865, U.S. War Department, *The War of the Rebellion*, ser. 1, vol. 48, pt. 2, pp. 1145–47, 1172–74.

51. Pope to [Halleck], Milwaukee, 6 October 1864, and Pope to Halleck, Milwaukee, 3 November 1864, U.S. Department of War, *The War of the Rebellion*, ser. 1, vol. 41, pt. 1, pp. 131–33, 133–40; Pope to Grant, St. Louis, 23 May 1865, U.S. War Department, *The War of the Rebellion*, ser. 1, vol. 48, pt. 2, pp. 565–68.

52. Edmunds to Dole, Executive Office, Yankton, Dakota Territory, 15 May 1865, CIA, *ARCIA*, *1865*, 195.

53. Anderson, *Little Crow*, 174.

54. Aahdamane [H'damani] to Cameron, Turtle Mountain, 26 January 1874, enclosed in George Arthur Hill to Cameron, Turtle Mountain, 26 January 1874, NAC, Archives of the North-West Boundary Commission, 1872–76, MG16 F.O.302, vol. 8, Letterbook, microfilm reel B-5324, pp. 79–80. (An inexact copy of this document is in NAC, Records Relating to Indian Affairs, RG10, vol. 3607, file 2988, microfilm reel C-10105.)

55. Adams to Olin, Ft. Abercrombie, 12 August 1864, NARA, RG393, Ft. Abercrombie, LS, vol. 2 (1863–66), pp. 92–93, no. 90. See also the account of Sioux-Cree conflict in Messiter, *Sport and Adventures among the North-American Indians*, 12–14, 32–36. Messiter's work has a certain ring of unreliability. Cheadle makes no reference to the incidents described by Messiter, although Messiter was still with Cheadle's party at the time (see Cheadle, *Cheadle's Journal*; and Milton and Cheadle, *The North-West Passage by Land*).

56. Corse to Sherburn, St. Paul, 11 January 1866, CIA, *ARCIA*, *1866*, 162.

57. Copies of White Cap's statement, dated Wood Mountain, 14 March 1870, can be found in three places: PAM, Adams George Archibald Papers, MG12 A1, no. 3, microfilm reel M1; PAM, Lieutenant-Governor Collection, MG12 B1, no. 266; and PAM, Louis Riel Correspondence and Papers (hereafter Riel Papers), MG3 D1, no. 26.

58. Atwood, ed., *In Rupert's Land*, 120–21. William Edward Traill, the son-in-law of William McKay, was Walter's brother. The rather complacent post journal does not mention any altercation, stating only: "Great excitement was caused by Some of the men fancying they saw Sioux about"

(Fort Ellice Journals, 1 July 1868–19 September 1869, Entry, 20 July 1868, PAM, HBCA, B.63/a/10, microfilm reel 1M52.)

59. "The Sioux Invasion," *The Nor'-Wester*, 18 January 1864, p. 2, cols. 3–4; and "The Sioux," *The Nor'-Wester*, 5 February 1864, p. 2, col. 3.

60. For a discussion that, in contrast, attributes almost all Ojibwa-Dakota conflict to the Red River Ojibwas, see Neufeld, "Picheito."

61. "Fighting between the Sioux and Chippewas," *The Nor'-Wester*, 10 May 1864, p. 2, col. 3. The Dakotas subsequently fortified this camp and two others. The remains of these fortifications are still visible. See Manitoba, Historic Resources Branch, *The Dakota Fortified Camps of the Portage Plain*.

62. Atwood, ed., *In Rupert's Land*, 44–45. Elias identifies these as Ojibwas from Red Lake (*The Dakota of the Canadian Northwest*, 27–29).

Sioux Migration to the Milk River Country

1. Potter, "The Missouri River Journal of Leonard W. Gilchrist," 267–300, entry for 23 June 1866.

2. NARA, RG393, Ft. Buford Document File, Lt. Col. Henry A. Morrow, Ft. Buford, 14 June 1870.

3. DeMallie ("The Sioux in Dakota and Montana Territories," 28) identifies these Sioux as the Cuthead band of Upper Yanktonais under Medicine Bear, Thunder Bull, and His Road to Travel; the C'an'óna band of Upper Yanktonais under Shoots the Tiger, Afraid of Bear, Catches the Enemy, and Heart; the Takíni band of Upper Yanktonais under Calumet Man, Afraid of Bull, Long Fox, Eagle Dog, and Standing Bellow; and a band of Sissetons under Brave Bear and Your Relation to the Earth.

4. Pease to Viall, Ft. Parker, n.d., enclosed in Viall to Parker, Helena, 24 December 1870, NARA, Records of the Bureau of Indian Affairs, RG75, Letters Received by the Commissioner of Indian Affairs (hereafter LRCIA), Montana Superintendency, no. 1871-V2, microcopy M234, roll 491, frames 408–11.

5. Elias, *The Dakota of the Canadian Northwest*, 26–27.

6. Isaac Cowie to Donald A. Smith, Draft Memorandum, Elbow of the South Branch, South Saskatchewan River, 16 December 1873, PAM, HBCA, Isaac Cowie Papers, E.86/59; S. J. Clarke, Diary Entry, 18 March 1879, GA, Edward Barnett Fonds, M3875, S. J. Clarke Diary.

7. DeMallie, "The Sioux in Dakota and Montana Territories."

8. Petition, Ft. Buford, 7 September 1869, enclosed in Morrow to Greene, Ft. Buford, 8 September 1869, NARA, RG393, Ft. Buford, LS 1869, no. 144.

9. Morrow to Greene, Ft. Buford, 8 September 1869, NARA, RG393, Ft. Buford, LS 1869, no. 144. A. J. Simmons, the Milk River Indian agent, shared this position. See Simmons to Viall, Milk River Agency, 20 September 1871, NARA, RG75, LRCIA, Montana Superintendency, no. 1871-V165, microcopy M234, roll 491, frames 938–40.

10. DeMallie, "The Sioux in Dakota and Montana Territories," 28.

11. Simmons to Parker, Ft. Browning, 12 May 1871, NARA, RG75, LRCIA, Montana Superintendency, no. 1871-V78, microcopy M234, roll 491, frames 635–52. Another account of these events in found in Quinton to Sanborne, Ft. Shaw, 19 May 1871, NARA, RG75, LRCIA, Montana Superintendency, no. 1871-W533, microcopy M234, roll 491, frames 1106–19. See also Viall to Parker, Helena, 20 May 1871, NARA, Records of the Adjutant General's Office, RG94, LR, file 2019 AGO 1871, microcopy M666, roll 16, frames 510–11.

12. Viall to Parker, Telegram, Helena, 18 May 1871, NARA, RG75, LRCIA, Montana Superintendency,

file 1871-V52-V97, microcopy M234, roll 491, frame 603; Viall to Parker, Helena, 21 May 1871, NARA, RG75, LRCIA, file 1871-V80, microcopy M234, roll 491, frames 657–59.

13. Viall to CIA, Helena, 21 August 1871, NARA, RG75, LRCIA, file 1871-V139-V197, microcopy M234, roll 491, frames 871–75.

14. See Friesen, "Magnificent Gifts." Friesen advances the position that aboriginal peoples expected the Canadian government to provide them with a new economic livelihood in exchange for their lands in Canada.

15. Simmons to Viall, Ft. Browning, 5 December 1871, enclosed in Viall to F. A. Walker (CIA), Helena, 23 December 1871, NARA, RG75, LRCIA, Montana Superintendency, no. 1872-V222, microcopy M234, roll 492, frames 636–63. Simmons's report was subsequently republished in *Appropriations for Sioux Indians*; and *Teton-Sioux Indians*. Black Moon's remarks were substantially the same as those he had made in June 1868 to Father Pierre-Jean De Smet during the latter's peace envoy to the Lakotas. See Chittenden and Richardson, eds., *Father Pierre-Jean De Smet*, 916–17.

16. "Report of Hon. B. R. Cowen, Assistant Secretary of the Interior, Hon. N. J. Turney, and Mr. J. W. Wham, commissioners to visit the Teton-Sioux at or near Fort Peck, Montana," Washington DC, 15 October 1872, *Teton-Sioux Indians*, 4–8. This report was also published in CIA, *ARCIA, 1872*, 456–60.

17. Finerty, *War-Path and Bivouac*, 275.

18. Cowie, *The Company of Adventurers*, 445–48.

19. Breland to Morris, White Horse Plains, 18 May 1873, PAM, Lieutenant-Governor Collection, MG12 B1, no. 164, microfilm reel M134.

20. Cowie, *The Company of Adventurers*, 448.

21. Grant, *Ocean to Ocean*, 87–88; and George M. Grant, Diary Entry, 4 August 1872, NAC, George M. Grant Papers, MG29 D38, vol. 8, Diary 1872. John Macoun, the expedition's botanist, recorded the event in his memoirs but lifted the passage from Grant's *Ocean to Ocean*. See Macoun, *Autobiography*, 58–59.

22. *Report of Colonel Robertson-Ross, Adjt.-General of Militia, on the Northwest Provinces and Territories of the Dominion* (Ottawa, 1872), 25–26, NAC, Patrick Robertson-Ross Papers, MG29 E39, file 3.

23. McKay to Archibald, Ft. Ellice, 25 May 1872, NAC, RG10, vol. 3596, file 1275, microfilm reel C-10103.

24. Henri Bouthillier to William McKay, Ft. Garry, 6 June 1872, NAC, RG10, vol. 3596, file 1275, microfilm reel C-10103; [Bouthillier] to Simpson, Ft. Garry, 8 June 1872 (draft), PAM, MG12 A1, no. 679, microfilm reel M3.

25. William McKay to Archibald, Ft. Ellice, 24 June 1872, PAM, MG12 A1, no. 681, microfilm reel M3.

26. Archibald to McKay, Ft. Garry, 8 June 1872, NAC, RG10, vol. 3596, file 1275, microfilm reel C-10103; and Archibald to Secretary of State for the Provinces, Ft. Garry, 8 June 1872, PAM, A. G. Archibald Papers, MG12 A1, Dispatch Book No. 3, no. 73, microfilm reel M3. Lord Dufferin, the Canadian governor-general, offered a different explanation for Archibald's refusal to meet the Lakotas and Yanktonais. Writing the British secretary of state for the colonies, Lord Kimberley, Dufferin explained that, when the delegation had arrived and Indian Commissioner Simpson was absent, Adams Archibald "considered it was not proper for him to receive them, and consequently said 'not at home.'" See Dufferin to Kimberley, Ottawa, 2 May 1873, NAC, John Wodehouse Papers, MG27 I A4, microfilm reel A-315.

27. Goossen, "'A Wearer of Moccasins.'" James was not related to Chief Trader William McKay of Ft. Ellice.

28. [James McKay] to Nap-cho-kah, Mah-too-yankee, Me-nah-che-kan, and Their Braves, Deer

Lodge, 26 August 1872, PAM, MG12 B1, no. 266, microfilm reel M134. McKay mistakenly believed that Archibald had thought these Sioux were from Portage la Prairie, when Archibald had actually thought they were from Ft. Ellice.

29. Affidavit of George Racette, Lac Qu'Appelle, 5 May 1873, PAM, MG12 B1, no. 266, microfilm reel M134.

30. For an account of Standing Buffalo's death during a raid against the Gros Ventres and Assiniboines in the Bear Paw Mountains, see Diedrich, *The Odyssey of Chief Standing Buffalo*, 86–87.

31. Morris to Secretary of State for the Provinces, Ft. Garry, 16 December 1872, PAM, MG12 A1, Dispatch Book No. 3, no. 123, microfilm reel M3. The Canadian government quickly informed Morris that it would grant eighty acres of land to each Dakota family (see Howe to Morris, Ottawa, 8 January 1873, PAM, MG12 B1, no. 50, microfilm reel M134). For an extended treatment of this topic, see Elias, *The Dakota of the Canadian Northwest*.

32. Morris to Minister of the Interior, Ft. Garry, 13 July 1874, NAC, RG10, vol. 3611, file 3679, microfilm reel C-10106.

33. Extracts, Isaac Cowie to Archibald McDonald, Ft. Qu'Appelle, 29 January 1873, PAM, HBCA, Isaac Cowie Papers, E.86/59.

34. Petition, Martin L. West, Rev. John McNabb, and 52 Others to Morris, Palestine, 4 March 1873, NAC, RG10, vol. 3600, file 1567, microfilm reel C-10104.

35. "Extract of a letter from Arch^d McDonald, Esquire, Chief Trader, addressed to D. A. Smith, C.C. dated 11 Febry 1873, from Fort Ellice," enclosed in Smith to Morris, Ft. Garry, 6 March 1873, PAM, MG12 B1, no. 128, microfilm reel M134.

36. Morris to Secretary of State for the Provinces, Ft. Garry, 11 March 1873, PAM, Ketcheson Collection, MG12 B2, no. 24, microfilm reel M140; Morris to Macdonald, Cipher Telegram, [Ft. Garry], 10 March 1873, PAM, Ketcheson Collection, MG12 B1, Letterbook "G," no. 1, microfilm reel M138.

37. Norquay to Morris, Winnipeg, 17 March 1873, PAM, MG12 B1, no. 139, microfilm reel M134. (A copy can be found in NAC, RG10, vol. 3600, file 1567, microfilm reel C-10104.)

38. Norquay to Macdonald, Ft. Garry, 28 March 1873, NAC, Records of the Department of the Secretary of State, RG6, ser. C1, vol. 31.

39. Cowie, *The Company of Adventurers*, 456.

40. Breland to Judge McKeagney, Lac Qu'Appelle, 9 April 1873, PAM, MG12 B1, no. 161, microfilm reel M134. (A copy is found in NAC, RG10, vol. 3602, file 1831½, microfilm reel C-10104.)

41. Information about American traders operating in the North-West Territories can be found in Dempsey, *Firewater*.

42. McDonald to McKeagney, Ft. Ellice, 16 April 1873, PAM, MG12 B1, no. 189, microfilm reel M134. (A copy is found in NAC, RG10, vol. 3602, file 1848½.) "*Memorandum* of a *Conversation* with Mr Edmund [Edward] McKay, formerly of the Hudson Bay Company's service, and a man said, on good authority, to be thoroughly reliable and respectable—*Fort Garry May 19th 1873*," enclosed in Urquhart to McKeagney, Ft. Garry, 19 May 1873, PAM, MG12 B1, no. 165, microfilm reel M134.

43. For Breland's official report (in French), see "Montagne de Bois," [10 May 1873], PAM, MG12 B1, no. 162, microfilm reel M134. For an English translation, see "Copy of Honb^le Mr Breland's Report," 12 May 1873, PAM, MG12 B2, no. 27, microfilm reel M140. I have quoted from the English translation.

44. "Lo's Oration," *Daily British Colonist*, 31 July 1873, p. 3, col. 3. It is unclear who "Lo" is.

45. Interview between Morris, the Minister of the Interior, and a party of Sioux from Wood Mountain, 16 September 1874, enclosed in Morris to Secretary of State, Ft. Garry, 3 October 1874, NAC,

RG10, vol. 3613, file 4049½. (A copy of Morris's letter is in PAM, MG12 B1, Letterbook "J," no. 199; a copy of the minutes of the interview is found in PAM, MG12 B1, no. 847.)

46. Christie and Dickieson to Minister of the Interior, Winnipeg, 7 October 1875, PAM, MG12 B1, no. 1102, microfilm reel M136.

47. "Notes of an Interview with the Sioux Indians Chief 'White Cap' and others, delegates from 53 Tents of Sioux Camped near the Hudson's Bay Company's Post at Lakes Q'appelle [sic], 10th September 1875," enclosed in Christie to Morris, Winnipeg, 7 October 1875, PAM, MG12 B1, no. 1101, microfilm reel M136.

48. Morris to White Cap and Standing Buffalo, Ft. Garry, 9 October 1875, PAM, MG12 B1, Letterbook "J," no. 295, microfilm reel M138. (A copy of this letter, dated 11 October, is found in NAC, RG10, vol. 3625, file 5494.)

49. Dickieson to Minister of the Interior, Winnipeg, 7 October 1876, Canadian House of Commons, Annual Report of the Department of the Interior, 1876, Sessional Papers (1877), vol. 7, p. xxxvi; Laird to Morris, Livingstone, Swan River, 25 November 1876, Saskatchewan Archives Board (hereafter SAB), David Laird Papers, R-1170, file 2, Letterbook, fols. 8–11d.

50. For a fuller discussion of this topic, see Elias, The Dakotas of the Canadian Northwest, 147–85.

51. Howard, "Dakota Winter Counts," 393 (the Jaw and Jaw Variant counts); Vestal, New Sources of Indian History, 350 (an unidentified Hunkpapa count).

52. Lestanc to Taché, Montagne de Bois, 21 March 1871, Archives de l'archevêché, Saint-Boniface (hereafter AASB), Fonds Taché, T8570-T8573. Information about Ouellette's trading operations can be found in Cowie, The Company of Adventurers, 433; and Wood Mountain Historic Park (pamphlet), 2, SAB, S-F453.2.

53. Cowie, The Company of Adventurers, 422.

54. Lestanc to Taché, Montagne de Bois, 21 March 1871, AASB, Fonds Taché, T8570-T8573; and "Souvenirs 1860–1880," 1910, Provincial Archives of Alberta (hereafter PAA), Joseph-Jean-Marie Lestanc papiers personnel, 71.220, box 170, item 6873.

55. For a discussion of American attempts to enforce the Intercourse Act of 1834, see Dempsey, Firewater, chap. 2.

56. Simmons to Parker, Ft. Browning, 12 May 1871, NARA, RG75, LRCIA, Montana Superintendency, no. 1871-V78, microcopy M234, roll 491, frames 635–52. (A copy is located in NARA, RG94, LR, file 2019 AGO 1871, microcopy M666, roll 16, frames 513–25.) See also Simmons to Viall, Ft. Browning, 5 December 1871, in Viall to Walker, Helena, 23 December 1871, NARA, RG75, LRCIA, Montana Superintendency, no. 1872-V222, microcopy M234, roll 492, frames 636–63.

57. Quinton to Sanborne, Ft. Shaw, 19 May 1871, NARA, RG75, LRCIA, Montana Superintendency, no. 1871-W533, microcopy M234, roll 491, frames 1106–19.

58. DeMallie, "The Sioux in Dakota and Montana Territories," 30.

59. White Bull Interviews, University of Oklahoma, Campbell Collection, box 105, notebook 8, pp. 29–31 and notebook 28, pp. 7–8. Possibly owing to translation and transcription problems, the location of Sitting Bull's camp is not clear in the text; it may have been on the Missouri River, at the mouth of Frenchman River (also known as White Mud River).

60. DeBarthe, Life and Adventures of Frank Grouard, 48–49.

61. DeBarthe, Life and Adventures of Frank Grouard, 49–54.

62. Cowie to Donald A. Smith, Draft Memorandum, Elbow of the South Branch, South Saskatchewan River, 16 December 1873, PAM, HBCA, Isaac Cowie Papers, E.86/59. Cowie incorporated this note into his published memoirs (see The Company of Adventurers, 483).

63. Simmons to Viall, Ft. Benton, 15 October 1871, NARA, RG75, LRCIA, Montana Superintendency,

file v139-v197, microcopy M234, roll 491, frames 995–99; Viall to Walker, Helena, 25 September 1872, CIA, ARCIA, 1872, 658–59; Simmons to Viall, Milk River Agency, 1 September 1872, CIA, ARCIA, 1872, 660–62; Hildebrandt and Hubner, *The Cypress Hills*, 60.

64. Viall to Gibbon, Ft. Shaw, 18 October 1871, NARA, RG75, LRCIA, Montana Superintendency, file v139-v197, microcopy M234, roll 491, frames 993–94. (An incomplete copy of this letter is in PAM, MG12 A1, no. 697.) Sams to Freeman, Ft. Shaw, 19 October 1871, NARA, RG75, LRCIA, Montana Superintendency, file v200-w1045, microcopy M234, roll 491, frames 1165–68. (A copy is in PAM, MG12 A1, no. 697.)

65. Freeman to Gibbon, Ft. Browning, 6 November 1871, NARA, RG75, LRCIA, Montana Superintendency, file 1871-v200-w1045, microcopy M234, roll 491, frames 1031–35; Simmons to Viall, Ft. Browning, 6 November 1871, NARA, RG75, LRCIA, Montana Superintendency, file 1871-v200-w1045, microcopy M234, roll 491, frames 1036–38; Gibbon to Viall, Ft. Shaw, 12 November 1871, NARA, RG75, LRCIA, Montana Superintendency, file 1871-v200-w1045, microcopy M234, roll 491, frame 1039; and Viall to Clum, Helena, 16 November 1871, NARA, RG75, LRCIA, Montana Superintendency, file 1871-v200-w1045, microcopy M234, roll 491, frames 1027–30.

66. Freeman to AAG, Ft. Shaw, 27 November 1871, PAM, MG12 A1, no. 697, microfilm reel M3; Freeman to Bonson, Ft. Shaw, 22 April 1872, "Enclosures to 5th Endorsement," PAM, MG12 A1, no. 697, microfilm reel M3; Archibald to Secretary of State for the Provinces, Ft. Garry, 12 January 1872, PAM, MG12 A1, Dispatch Book No. 3, no. 6, microfilm reel M3.

67. Affidavit of Jean Louis Légaré, 16 June 1874, PAM, MG12 B1, no. 772, microfilm reel M135; PAM, MG12 B1, no. 824 and three enclosures, microfilm reel M135 (the follow-up correspondence with American authorities); Hard to Alderson, Ft. Peck, 16 May 1874, in Alderson to Smith, Ft. Peck, 1 June 1874, NARA, RG75, LRCIA, Montana Superintendency, no. 1874-A554, microcopy M234, roll 498, frames 145–52.

68. Rondeau, *La Montagne de Bois*, 46; Lestanc to Taché, Montagne de Bois, 21 March 1871, AASB, Fonds Taché, T8570-T8573.

69. Légaré and François Ouellette, Memorandum, 6 June 1874, PAM, MG12 B1, no. 760, microfilm reel M135.

70. Cameron to Morris, Dufferin, 30 May 1874, PAM, MG12 B1, no. 751, microfilm reel M135.

71. Viall to Parker, Helena, 14 April 1871, NARA, RG75, LRCIA, Montana Superintendency, file 1871-v52-v97, microcopy M234, roll 491, frames 561–65. On the migration of traders north of the border, see Dempsey, *Firewater*, chaps. 4–5.

The Sioux, Surveyors, and Mounted Police

1. "Messages from The Cree Chiefs of The Plains Saskatchewan, To His Excellency Governor Archibald, our Great Mother's Representative at Fort Garry Red River Settlement, 13 April 1871," enclosed in W. J. Christie to George W. Hill, Edmonton, 26 April 1871, PAM, MG12 A1, no. 272, microfilm reel M2. This letter was reprinted in Morris, *The Treaties of Canada with the Indians*, 169–171.

2. Cree of Whitefish Lake to Archibald, Wesleyan Mission, Whitefish Lake, 9 January 1871, PAM, MG12 A1, no. 169, microfilm reel M1.

3. Morris to Campbell, Ft. Garry, 4 August 1873, PAM, MG12 B2, no. 36, microfilm reel M140. These settlements were on the "South Branch"—the lower portion of the river roughly from Saskatoon to Prince Albert.

4. Morris to Minister of the Interior, Ft. Garry, 20 September 1873, NAC, RG10, vol. 3604, file 2543, microfilm reel C-10104; Breland, "Rapport de ma mission au milieu des Cris, des Sauteux et des

Assiniboines," enclosed in Breland to Morris, S[ain]t Fr[ançoi]s Xavier, 17 November 1873, PAM, MG12 B1, no. 170, microfilm reel M134.

5. Robert Bell to Morris, Ft. Garry, 14 October 1873, PAM, MG12 B1, no. 524, microfilm reel M134. See also Morris to Minister of the Interior, Ft. Garry, 23 October 1873, PAM, MG12 B2, no. 69, microfilm reel 140.

6. Charles N. Bell, Memorandum, "Our Indians," 23 March 1874, PAM, MG12 B1, no. 677, microfilm reel M135.

7. See Utley, *The Lance and the Shield*, 106–11.

8. Morris to Secretary of State, Ft. Garry, 13 December 1872, PAM, MG12 B1, no. 1983, microfilm reel M138. (A nearly identical copy of this document is located in PAM, MG12 A1, Dispatch Book No. 3, no. 122, microfilm reel M3. Morris's letter was published in Canadian House of Commons, Annual Report of the Department of Indian Affairs, 1872, *Sessional Papers* [1873], vol. 5, pp. 12–13.)

9. Cameron to Secretary of State for Foreign Affairs, Dufferin, 27 February 1873, NAC, MG16 F.O.302, vol. 9, Letterbook, microfilm reel B-5324, pp. 242–45. This view was accepted by the Colonial Office. See Kimberley (Secretary of State for the Colonies) to Dufferin, 22 May 1873, NAC, MG27 I A4, microfilm reel A-315.

10. D. R. Cameron to Morris, Dufferin, 23 April 1874, PAM, MG12 B1, no. 715, microfilm reel M135. (A copy of Cameron's letter [without its enclosures] is in NAC, MG16 F.O.302, vol. 12, Letterbook, microfilm reel B-5325, pp. 176–79.) George Arthur Hill to Cameron, Turtle Mountain, 18 May 1874, PAM, MG12 B1, no. 751, microfilm reel M135.

11. Cameron to Governor-General, Ottawa, 29 November 1873, NAC, MG16 F.O.302, vol. 8, Letterbook, microfilm reel B-5324, pp. 165–67.

12. Anderson to My Dearest Mamma, camp on the plains, 270 miles west of Pembina, 10 August 1873, Yale University, Beinecke Rare Book and Manuscript Library, Western Americana Collection, Samuel Anderson Papers, WA MSS S-1292; and see Parsons, *West on the 49th Parallel*, 73–74.

13. L. F. Hewgill, *In the Days of Pioneering: Crossing the Plains in the Early 70's. The Prairie Black with Buffalo* (n.p., 1894), 3, PAM, Records of the North American Boundary Commission, MG1 B23-5.

14. Samuel Anderson, "Report of Operations during the Summer Season of 1874 and Winter 1874–75," 30 April 1875, fols. 90–99d, PAM, MG1 B23-1, Report of Capt. D. R. Cameron, vol. 29.

15. Anderson, "The North-American Boundary," 244. See also Featherstonhaugh, "Narrative," 40.

16. Morris to Minister of the Interior, Ft. Garry, 27 May 1874, NAC, RG10, vol. 3610, file 3499, microfilm reel C-10106. (A copy of this document is in PAM, MG12 B2, no. 114, microfilm reel M141.) See also [Morris], Memorandum, 26 May 1874, PAM, MG12 B1, no. 745, microfilm reel M135.

17. Morris to Dorion, Ft. Garry, 29 May 1874, PAM, MG12 B2, no. 116, microfilm reel M141.

18. "Memorandum of Statement Made to the Lieut. Governor of the North-West Territories, by Joseph Tanner, otherwise known as 'Kissoway' a Saulteaux trader from the South Branch of the Saskatchewan—May 30th 1874," NAC, RG10, vol. 3610, file 3528, microfilm reel C-10106. (A copy is in PAM, MG12 B1, no. 750.) Details of Tanner's trading operations are found in Morris to Minister of the Interior, Ft. Garry, 6 June 1874, NAC, RG10, vol. 3610, file 3528, microfilm reel C-10106. (A copy is in PAM, Ketcheson Collection, MG12 B2, no. 119.)

19. Jean-Louis Légaré and François Ouillette, Memorandum, 6 June 1874, PAM, MG12 B1, no. 760, microfilm reel M135. The relationship between Antoine Ouellette and François Ouellette is unclear.

20. "Substance of the information given by Michael Klyne Junr to the Lieut. Governor, June 6th

1874," enclosed in Morris to Minister of the Interior, Ft. Garry, 6 June 1874, NAC, RG10, vol. 3610, file 3529-2, microfilm reel C-10106.

21. Cameron to Morris, Dufferin, 22 June 1874, PAM, MG12 B2, Telegram Book No. 2, no. 32, microfilm reel M141.

22. Cameron to Morris, Dufferin, 30 May 1874, PAM, MG12 B1, no. 751, microfilm reel M135.

23. Cameron to Alexander McKenzie, Dufferin, 24 June 1874, NAC, MG16 F.O.302, vol. 8, Letterbook, microfilm reel B-5324, pp. 179–82.

24. Capt. J. S. McNaught to Post Adjutant Ft. Totten, Ft. Pembina, 8 July 1874, NARA, RG393, Ft. Totten, LR, box 3.

25. Morris to McKenzie, Ft. Garry, [16] July 1874, PAM, MG12 B2, no. 122, microfilm reel M141.

26. U.S. Department of State, *Reports upon the Survey of the Boundary*, 280–83, 339.

27. Valentine McGillycuddy, Diary Entry, 25 July 1874, Yale University, Beinecke Rare Book and Manuscript Library, Western Americana Collection, Valentine McGillycuddy Northwest Boundary Survey Diary, WA MSS S-242. See also Parsons, *West on the 49th Parallel*, 109.

28. "Six Months in the Wilds of the North-west," 8, PAA, Henri Julien Papers, 69.98.

29. D'Artigue, *Six Years in the Canadian North-West*, 49–50.

30. James Finlayson, Diary Entry, 31 August 1874, NAC, James Finlayson Papers, MG29 E58, Diary, June–November 1874; "Six Months in the Wilds of the North-west," 13, PAA, Henri Julien Papers, 69.98.

31. Francis V. Greene, "Down the Missouri by Mackinaw Boat: Journal of Lieut. Francis Vinton Greene, September, 1874," reprinted in Parsons, *West on the 49th Parallel*, 169–70.

32. Anderson to My Dearest Mother, camp at eastern base of Rocky Mountains, 23 August 1874, Yale University, Beinecke Rare Book and Manuscript Library, Western Americana Collection, Samuel Anderson Papers, WA MSS S-1292.

33. Maj. J. E. Yard to AAG, Department of Dakota, Telegram, Ft. Pembina, 24 July 1874, NARA, RG75, LRCIA, Dakota Superintendency, no. 1874-W1216, microcopy M234, roll 253, frames 628–29.

34. Featherstonhaugh, "Narrative," 43.

35. Burgess to Cameron, Dufferin, 13 October 1874, enclosed in Cameron to Deputy Adjutant General, Royal Engineers, Dufferin, 18 October 1874, NAC, MG16 F.O.302, vol. 13, Letterbook, microfilm reel B-5325, pp. 214–16; Featherstonhaugh, "Narrative," 42.

36. The circumstances surrounding this fight are found in George Arthur French, Diary Entry, 12 August 1874, PAM, George Arthur French Papers, MG6 A3, Diary, North West Mounted Police Expedition, 8 July–7 November 1874.

37. "Extracts from Notebook of John E. Edwards, R.E. (with the British North America Boundary Commission surveying the 49th parallel from the Lake of the Woods to the Rocky Mountains, 1874)," entry for 17 July 1874, PAM, MG1 B23-4.

38. Valentine Francis Rowe, Memoir, pp. 5–8, NAC, Valentine Francis Rowe Papers, MG29 C24.

39. J. A. Markle to Indian Commissioner, Birtle, 4 May 1891, NAC, RG10, vol. 3596, file 1319, microfilm reel C-10103. Two Dogs showed Markle this piece of paper at this time.

40. Frederick Augustus Bagley, Diary Entry, 12 August 1874, GA, Frederick Augustus Bagley Fonds, Diary, M44; Denny, *The Riders of the Plains*, 35. Denny's posthumously published *The Law Marches West*, 28, identifies these people as Assiniboines; this mistake was made by Denny's editor, W. B. Cameron.

41. Frederick Augustus Bagley, Diary Entry, 12 August 1874, GA, Frederick Augustus Bagley Fonds, Diary, M44; George Arthur French, Diary Entry, 12 August 1874, PAM, MG6 A3, Diary, North West Mounted Police Expedition, 8 July–7 November 1874. French's diary was published in Canadian

House of Commons, Annual Report of the North-West Mounted Police, 1874, *Sessional Papers* (1875), app. A.

42. John H. McIllrie, Diary Entry, 13 August 1874, British Columbia Archives and Records Service (hereafter BCARS), John H. McIllrie Diaries and Notebooks, Add.Mss 1434, microfilm reel A-530, vol. 1, Diary 1874, 1876–1877.

43. George Arthur French, Diary Entry, 13 August 1874, PAM, MG6 A3, Diary, North West Mounted Police Expedition, 8 July–7 November 1874.

44. John H. McIllrie, Diary Entry, 13 August 1874, BCARS, John H. McIllrie Diaries and Notebooks, Add.Mss 1434, microfilm reel A-530, vol. 1, Diary 1874, 1876–1877.

45. Frederick Augustus Bagley, Diary Entry, 13 August 1874, GA, Frederick Augustus Bagley Fonds, Diary, M44; John H. McIllrie, Diary Entry, 13 August 1874, BCARS, John H. McIllrie Diaries and Notebooks, Add.Mss 1434, microfilm reel A-530, vol. 1, Diary 1874, 1876–1877; James Finlayson, Diary Entry, 13 August 1874, NAC, James Finlayson Papers, MG29 E58, Diary, June–November 1874; Joseph J. Carscadden, Diary Entry, 12 August 1874, GA, Joseph J. Carscadden Fonds, M6608, Diary, 1874 (this entry is misdated and should read 13 August).

46. Frederick Augustus Bagley, Diary Entry, 14 August 1874, GA, Frederick Augustus Bagley Fonds, Diary, M44.

47. John H. McIllrie, Diary Entry, 15 August 1874, BCARS, John H. McIllrie Diaries and Notebooks, Add.Mss 1434, microfilm reel A-530, vol. 1, Diary 1874, 1876–1877.

48. George Arthur French, Diary Entry, 14 August 1874, PAM, MG6 A3, Diary, North West Mounted Police Expedition, 8 July–7 November 1874.

49. North-West Mounted Police, *North-West Mounted Police Report for 1875*, 22–23. This annual report was not published, as was usual in other years, in the Canadian House of Commons' *Sessional Papers*.

50. John H. McIllrie, Diary Entry, 17 August 1874, BCARS, John H. McIllrie Diaries and Notebooks, Add.Mss 1434, microfilm reel A-530, vol. 1, Diary 1874, 1876–1877; James Finlayson, Diary Entry, 17 August 1874, NAC, James Finlayson Papers, MG29 E58, Diary, June–November 1874; "Six Months in the Wilds of the North-west," 13, PAA, Henri Julien Papers, 69.98.

51. George Arthur French, Diary Entry, 4 September 1874, PAM, MG6 A3, Diary, North West Mounted Police Expedition, 8 July–7 November 1874.

52. Joseph J. Carscadden, Diary Entry, 4 September 1874, GA, Joseph J. Carscadden Fonds, M6608, Diary, 1874.

The Great Sioux War

1. Morris to Secretary of State, Ft. Garry, 6 June 1876, PAM, MG12 B2, no. 178, microfilm reel M141.

2. Irvine to Richardson, Ft. Walsh, 21 June 1876, NAC, RG18, A1, vol. 11, file 209-76.

3. Crozier to Irvine, Ft. Walsh, 19 June 1876, NAC, RG18, A1, vol. 11, file 209-76.

4. Mitchell to Smith, Bismarck, 19 July 1876, NARA, RG94, LR, file 4163 AGO 1876, microcopy M666, roll 277, frame 338; Mitchell to Smith, Ft. Peck, 29 July 1876, NARA, RG94, LR, file 4163 AGO 1876, microcopy M666, roll 278, frames 515–18.

5. Crozier to Irvine, Ft. Walsh, 19 June 1876, NAC, RG18, A1, vol. 11, file 209-76.

6. "Life in the Nor'-West," *The Globe*, 24 July 1876, p. 4, col. 3. This report was telegraphed on 27 June.

7. Wood to CIA, Blackfeet Agency, 25 August 1876, CIA, *ARCIA, 1876*, 86.

8. Wood to CIA, Blackfeet Agency, 25 August 1876, CIA, *ARCIA, 1876*, 86. An account of the council written by Robert Vaughn was based on Wood's report. See Vaughn, *Then and Now*, 300.

9. Morris to Minister of the Interior, Ft. Garry, 27 March 1877, PAM, MG12 B2, no. 251, microfilm reel M141. This is Morris's draft; the sent copy would have spoken only of "American Indians."

10. "Life in the Nor'-West," *The Globe*, 24 July 1876, p. 4, col. 3.

11. Barrie to Lizzie, Ft. Macleod, 21 June 1876, GA, Richard Barrington Nevitt Fonds, M893, box 2, file 9. This letter was written over several days, but 21 June appears on the first page.

12. Morris to Secretary of State for the Provinces, Ft. Garry, 11 July 1876, PAM, MG12 B2. These events are also reported in "The Indian War," *The Globe*, 29 July 1876, p. 1, col. 7.

13. White to Scott, 30 December 1876 (including an extract of Report of Sub-Inspector C. E. Denny, July 1876), in Canadian House of Commons, Annual Report of the Secretary of State of Canada, 1876, *Sessional Papers* (1877), pp. 21–25. Copies of Denny's report were also sent to American authorities: see Irvine to Secretary of State, Ft. Benton, 5 August 1876, NARA, RG94, LR, file 4163 AGO 1876, microcopy M666, roll 278, frames 611–20; and W. Hunter (Acting Secretary of State) to James D. Cameron (Secretary of War), Washington DC, 2 September 1876, NARA, RG393, Department of Dakota, LR 1876, box 18, no. 1876-2641. Denny's report was reprinted, with small editorial changes, in his *The Riders of the Plains*, 98–100, and in his posthumous *The Law Marches West*, 98–100.

14. Ruhlen to AAG, Department of Dakota, Cheyenne River Agency, 19 April 1876, NARA, RG393, Department of Dakota, LR 1872–76, box 16, no. 1876-1142.

15. "Interview with He Dog, July 13, 1910; William Berger, Interpreter," in Hammer, ed., *Custer in '76*, 205–8.

16. One Bull Interview, Standing Rock, 1912, p. 346, Indiana University, Lilly Library, Walter Mason Camp Papers, box 5, folder 1, field notes, envelope 41.

17. For a discussion of firearms and ammunition commonly found at Métis sites in Canada, see Doll, Kidd, and Day, *The Buffalo Lake Metis Site*, 215–23.

18. Scott, Fox, Connor, and Harmon, *Archaeological Perspectives on the Battle of the Little Bighorn*, 181. A photograph of this item appears on p. 157, fig. 51, j.

19. Solomon, Affidavit, Ft. Walsh, 18 August 1876, and Crozier to Irvine, Ft. Walsh, 18 August 1876, Canadian House of Commons, Annual Report of the Secretary of State of Canada, 1877, *Sessional Papers* (1878), pp. 25–26, 26–27.

20. Mitchell to Smith, Wolf Point, 14 September 1876, NARA, RG393, "Special Files" of Headquarters, Division of the Missouri, Relating to Military Operations and Administration, 1863–1885, microcopy M1495, roll 4, frames 373–75. (Another copy is in NARA, RG94, LR, file 4163 AGO 1876, microcopy M666, roll 279, frames 139–41.)

21. Boyd to Jordan, Ft. Peck, 8 October 1876, in Hazen to AAG, Department of Dakota, Telegram, Ft. Buford, 11 October 1876, NARA, RG94, LR, file 4163 AGO 1876, microcopy M666, roll 279, frames 209–11. See also Little to Jourdan [Jordan], Ft. Buford, 8 October 1876, NARA, RG393, Ft. Buford Document File (1873–1877).

22. Gibbon to Walsh, Ft. Shaw, 2 November 1876, NARA, RG393, Department of Dakota, LR 1876, box 19, no. 1876-3370.

23. Dickieson to Minister of the Interior, Winnipeg, 7 October 1876, Canadian House of Commons, Annual Report of the Department of the Interior, 1876, *Sessional Papers* (1877), vol. 7, p. xxxvi. William J. McLean was the trader in charge of Ft. Qu'Appelle. His papers (PAM, HBCA, E.218) do not mention the incident.

24. Mitchell to CIA, Ft. Peck, 18 September 1876, NARA, RG75, Montana Superintendency, no. 1876-M1015, microcopy M234, roll 505, frames 532–34. (A copy is located in NARA, RG94, LR, file 4163 AGO 1876, microcopy M666, roll 279, frames 243–44.)

25. Mitchell to Smith, Ft. Peck, 11 November 1876, NARA, RG94, LR, file 4163 AGO 1876, microcopy M666, roll 279, frames 521–23; Mitchell to Smith, Ft. Peck, 13 November 1876, NARA, RG94, LR, file 4163 AGO 1876, microcopy M666, roll 279, frames 525–26; Mitchell to Smith, Ft. Peck, 11 November 1876, NARA, RG94, LR, file 4163 AGO 1876, microcopy M666, roll 279, frames 551–52; Hazen to Miles, Ft. Peck, 2 November 1876, NARA, RG393, District of the Yellowstone, LS 1876–77, box 1, unregistered.

26. Mitchell to Gibbon, Ft. Peck, 25 October 1876, NARA, RG393, Department of Dakota, LR 1876, box 19, no. 1876-3370; Gibbon to AAG, Department of Dakota, Telegram, Ft. Shaw, 2 November 1876, NARA, RG393, District of Montana, LS 1870–79, p. 107, no. 1876-49.

27. Ilges to Gibbon, Ft. Benton, 22 October 1876, NARA, RG393, Department of Dakota, LR 1876, box 19, no. 1876-3952.

28. Day to Hazen, Ft. Peck, 9 November 1876, and Day to Hazen, Ft. Peck, 23 November 1876, NARA RG393, Ft. Buford Document File 1873–1877.

29. Légaré to Camp, Willow Bunch, 22 October 1910, Brigham Young University, Harold B. Lee Library, Walter M. Camp Papers, MS 57, box 1, folder 14.

30. Day to Hazen, Ft. Peck, 25 November 1876, NARA, RG393, "Special Files" of Headquarters, Division of the Missouri, microcopy M1495, roll 4, frames 517–20.

31. Mitchell to Hazen, Wolf Point, 6 December 1876, NARA, RG393, Department of Dakota, LR 1876, box 19, no. 1876-3868.

32. Wood to AAG, Department of Dakota, Cheyenne River Agency, 28 December 1876, NARA, RG393, "Special Files" of Headquarters, Division of the Missouri, microcopy M1495, roll 4, frames 568–71. (A copy is located in NARA, RG94, LR, file 4163 AGO 1876, microcopy M666, roll 279, frames 730–34.)

33. Mitchell to Smith, Wolf Point, 9 December 1876, NARA, RG94, LR, file 4163 AGO 1876, microcopy M666, roll 279, frames 622–25; Miles to Terry, Telegram, Tongue River Cantonment, 20 December 1876, NARA, RG94, LR, file 4163 AGO 1876, microcopy M666, roll 279, frames 766–68.

34. Frank D. Baldwin, Diary Entry, 11 December 1876, Henry E. Huntington Library, Frank D. Baldwin Papers, Diary. (A copy of this diary is located in the Montana Historical Society Archives as Small Collection 382.)

35. Transcript, Baldwin to Miles, camp on Cedar Creek, 19 December 1876, University of Colorado Archives, Historical Collections, William Carey Brown Papers, box 21, folder 27.

36. White Eagle (Wambdiska), originally from Mazomani's Wahpeton village in Minnesota, entered Rupert's Land in the winter of 1862–63. His people settled first on the Souris River and at Oak Lake but had moved to the Assiniboine River by 1865–66. He and his band had occupied the region around Wood Mountain for several years before 1876 but eventually returned to Manitoba. Their descendants live today on the Oak River reserve. See Elias, *The Dakota of the Canadian Northwest*, 20–21 and passim.

37. Walsh to Macleod, Ft. Walsh, 31 December 1876, NAC, RG10, vol. 3646, file 8044, microfilm reel C-10113; and Anonymous to Cora, Brockville, 21 May 1890, NAC, Cora Mowat Walsh Papers, MG29 C45. The NAC has attributed the latter letter to A. R. Macdonnell, a junior officer of the NWMP, while Pakes (in *Sitting Bull in Canada*, 23) attributes it to Macleod and Utley (in *The Lance and the Shield*, 359) to Walsh.

38. Day to Post Adjutant Ft. Buford, Ft. Peck, 10 February 1877, NARA, RG393, "Special Files" of Headquarters, Division of the Missouri, microcopy M1495, roll 4, frames 704–6. Langer also told Day of a discussion between Walsh and Inkpaduta, which Walsh also did not note in his official report.

39. Walsh to Irvine, Ft. Walsh, 15 March 1877, NAC, RG10, vol. 3646, file 8044, microfilm reel C-10113. The British father was George III.

40. Day to Post Adjutant Ft. Buford, Ft. Peck, 10 February 1877, NARA, RG393, "Special Files" of Headquarters, Division of the Missouri, microcopy M1495, roll 4, frames 704–6; Boyd to Baldwin, Ft. Peck, 7 February 1877, NARA, RG393, District of the Yellowstone, LS 1876–77, box 1, unregistered.

41. Boyd to Miles, Ft. Peck, 19 February 1877, NARA, RG393, District of the Yellowstone, LS 1876–77, box 1, unregistered.

42. Wood to AAG, Department of Dakota, Cheyenne River Agency, 16 February 1877, NARA, RG393, "Special Files" of Headquarters, Division of the Missouri, microcopy M1495, roll 4, frames 667–71. (Another copy, with related documents, is in NARA, RG94, LR, file 4163 AGO 1876, microcopy M666, roll 280, frames 164–71.)

43. Wood to AAG, Department of Dakota, Cheyenne River Agency, 21 February 1877, NARA, RG393, "Special Files" of Headquarters, Division of the Missouri, microcopy M1495, roll 4, frames 673–81. (Another copy, with related documents, is in NARA, RG94, LR, file 4163 AGO 1876, microcopy M666, roll 280, frames 130–37.) See also Clark to Bourke, Camp Robinson, 3 March 1877, NARA, RG393, "Special Files" of Headquarters, Division of the Missouri, microcopy M1495, roll 4, frames 727–30. (Another copy is in NARA, RG94, LR, file 4163 AGO 1876, microcopy M666, roll 280, frames 218–22).

44. Day to Post Adjutant Ft. Buford, Ft. Peck, 14 April 1877, NARA, RG393, "Special Files" of Headquarters, Division of the Missouri, microcopy M1495, roll 4, frames 964–67.

45. Day to Post Adjutant Ft. Buford, Ft. Peck, 2 May 1877, NARA, RG393, "Special Files" of Headquarters, Division of the Missouri, microcopy M1495, roll 4, frames 1016–17.

46. Day to the Post Adjutant Ft. Buford, Ft. Buford, 7 June 1877, NARA, RG75, Dakota Superintendency, no. 1877-W647, microcopy M234, roll 262, frames 631–35. (Another copy is in NARA, RG94, LR, file 4163 AGO 1876, microcopy M666, roll 282, frames 154–58.)

47. Irvine to Scott, Ft. Benton, 23 May 1877, Canadian House of Commons, Annual Report of the Secretary of the State of Canada, 1877, *Sessional Papers* (1878), p. 33. In addition to Irvine's official report other accounts of Walsh's meeting with Sitting Bull can be found in Day to the Post Adjutant Ft. Buford, Ft. Buford, 7 June 1877, NARA, RG75, Dakota Superintendency, no. 1877-W647, microcopy M234, roll 262, frames 631–35; Anonymous to Cora, Brockville, 21 May 1890, NAC, Cora Mowat Walsh Papers, MG29 C45; "Transcript of Tape Recording made by Gabriel (Gabe) Leveillie at Maple Creek Detachment, February 14, 1957. Interview by Inspector T. E. Mudiman, o/c Swift Current Sub-Division," GA, Southern Alberta Research Project Fonds, M4561, box 2, file 10; and General Archibald Macdonell, "How Sitting Bull Came to Canada: Recollections of an Old Royal Mounted Police Officer," n.d., SAB, Saskatchewan Historical Society Papers, file 205, Siouan Indians.

48. John H. McIllrie, Diary Entries, 30 April, 8, 10, 15 May 1877,, BCARS, John H. McIllrie Diaries and Notebooks, Add.Mss 1434, microfilm reel A-530, vol. 1, Diary 1874, 1876–1877.

49. Dufferin to Carnarvon, Ottawa, 1 June 1877, and Dufferin to Carnarvon, Ottawa, 27 July 1877, De Kiewiet and Underhill, eds., *Dufferin-Carnarvon Correspondence*, 353, 361.

50. Taylor to Seward, Winnipeg, 24 July 1877, NARA, General Records of the Department of State, RG59, Consular Dispatches, Winnipeg, file T-24 10-9-5, microcopy T24, roll 5, vol. 5. (A copy is in NAC, Records of the Office of the Governor General, RG7, G21, vol. 319, file 2001, pt. 3d, *Papers relating to the Sioux Indians of the United States who have taken refuge in Canadian Territory*, p. 38, microfilm reel T-1386, frame 39.)

51. Walsh to Macleod, Ft. Walsh, 31 December 1876, NAC, RG10, vol. 3646, file 8044, microfilm reel

C-10113; Walsh to Irvine, Ft. Walsh, 15 March 1877, NAC, RG10, vol. 3646, file 8044, microfilm reel C-10113; Irvine to Scott, Ft. Benton, 23 May 1877, Canadian House of Commons, Annual Report of the Secretary of State of Canada, 1877, *Sessional Papers* (1878), app. "E," p. 33; Howard to Miles, Ft. Keogh, 10 January 1878, NARA, RG393, District of the Yellowstone, LR, box 3.

52. Brotherton to AAG, Department of Dakota, Ft. Buford, 26 May 1881, NARA, RG94, LR, file 4163 AGO 1876, microcopy M666, roll 290, frames 123–24; Ilges to Breck, Telegram, Ft. Keogh, 12 June 1881, NARA, RG94, LR, file 4163 AGO 1876, microcopy M666, roll 290, frame 241; Ilges to Breck, Telegram, Ft. Keogh, 15 June 1881, NARA, RG94, LR, file 4163 AGO 1876, microcopy M666, roll 290, frames 237–38; and Gilbert to the AAG, Department of Dakota, Ft. Yates, 2 August 1881, NARA, RG94, LR, file 4163 AGO 1876, microcopy M666, roll 290, frame 418.

53. "Interview between Lieut.-Col. J. F. Macleod, C.M.G. Commissioner of N.W.M.P., and Sitting Bull and other Chiefs of the Sioux Nation," Ft. Walsh, 17 October 1877, enclosed in Macleod to Mills, 27 October 1877, NAC, Records of the Office of the Governor General, RG7, G21, vol. 319, file 2001, pt. 3d, microfilm reel T-1386.

54. Steele, *Forty Years in Canada*, 159.

The Lakotas and Métis at Wood Mountain

1. *Report of the Commission . . . to Meet the Sioux Indian Chief, Sitting Bull*, 8. A record of this council was also made by the North-West Mounted Police. See Sitting Bull Commission, Proceedings, Ft. Walsh, 17 October 1877, enclosed in Macleod to Scott, Ft. Macleod, 31 October 1877, NAC, RG7, G21, vol. 319, file 2001, pt. 3d, microfilm reel T-1386, frames 76–84, which was published as Canadian House of Commons, Annual Report of the Secretary of State of Canada, 1877, *Sessional Papers* (1878), pp. 47–48.

2. This point is made emphatically in Rivard and Littlejohn, *The Metis of Willow Bunch*, chap. 7.

3. Raymond J. DeMallie, personal communication, 18 May 1996.

4. Marty to Very Rev. Dear Father, Ft. Peck, Montana, 9 June 1877, Marquette University Archives, Bureau of Catholic Indian Mission Records, Abbot Martin Marty Correspondence.

5. Marty, "Abbot Martin Visits Sitting Bull."

6. Barrie to Lizzie, Ft. Macleod, 11 June 1877, GA, Richard Barrington Nevitt Fonds, M893, box 2, file 12.

7. "Council held June 2nd 1877, at the Teton or Sitting Bull's Camp," Canadian House of Commons, Annual Report of the Secretary of State of Canada, 1877, *Sessional Papers* (1878), app. "E," pp. 37–41.

8. Slaughter, "Leaves from Northwestern History," 277–81; Miles to AAG, Department of Dakota, Ft. Buford, 19 June 1877, NARA, RG393, Department of Dakota, LR 1877, box 22, no. 1877-2590.

9. Ouellette spent the summer of 1877 working as a guide for an English couple who were in the North-West Territories on a hunting trip; troublesome news about Sitting Bull's Sioux hastened his return to the Cypress Hills, where his family lived. See Percy, *Journal of Two Excursions*, 8. Information on Larivée is found in Rondeau, *La Montagne de Bois*, 90.

10. Slaughter, "Leaves from Northwestern History," 280–81. Information on Morin is found in Allen to Vankoughnet, Ft. Walsh, 12 December 1880, NAC, RG10, vol. 3652, file 8589, pt. 1, microfilm reel C-10114; and Irvine to Minister of the Interior, Ft. Walsh, 8 December 1880, NAC, RG18, B3, vol. 2185, no pagination, microfilm reel T-6269. Information on Leveillé is found in Gabriel Leveillé, Statement, Maple Creek, 27 October 1956; and "Transcript of Tape Recording made by Gabriel (Gabe) Leveillie at Maple Creek Detachment, February 14, 1957. Interview by Inspector

T. E. Mudiman, o/c Swift Current Sub-Division," GA, Southern Alberta Research Project Fonds, M4561, box 2, file 10,

11. Walsh to Macleod, Ft. Walsh, 12 October 1877, and Walsh to Macleod, Ft. Walsh, 16 October 1877, reprinted in "Sitting Bull: The United States Commission Arrive at Fort Walsh," *New York Herald*, 22 October 1877, p. 5, cols. 1–4, and p. 10, cols. 1–3. Macleod to Mary [Macleod], Ft. Walsh, 12 October 1877, GA, James Farquharson Macleod Family Fonds, M776, box 1, file 12. (A photocopy of this letter is the sole item in GA, James Farquharson Macleod Family Fonds, M781. Another copy is found in PAM, James Farquharson Macleod Papers, MG6 A5.)

12. Extract, Irvine to Sister, Ft. Macleod, 18 June 1877, SAB, Saskatchewan Historical Society Papers, file 204, Siouan Indians. See also Letter from E. Dalrymple Clark, *Regina Leader*, 17 March 1885, 416–17, Indiana University, Lilly Library, Walter Mason Camp Papers, box 5, folder 13, field notes, envelope 67. Sub-Inspector Edmund Dalrymple Clark, one of the policemen present, also wrote of the Marty council in "In the North West with Sitting Bull."

13. Charette, *L'Espace de Louis Goulet*, 103, 105–7 (quotation from 106). Goulet (or Charette) incorrectly dated this event to 1879.

14. Old Bull Interview, University of Oklahoma, Campbell Collection, box 105, notebook 11, p. 2.

15. Morris Bob-Tailed Bull Interview, University of Oklahoma, Campbell Collection, box 105, notebook 11, pp. 24–27.

16. Charette, *L'Espace de Louis Goulet*, 107–10. A summary of this incident, based on Charette's original manuscript but varying from it, is found in Turner, *The North-West Mounted Police: 1873–1893*, 1:459–61.

17. Miles to Terry, camp near mouth of Squaw Creek, on the Missouri River, 24 September 1877, NARA, RG393, Department of Dakota, LR 1877, box 23, no. 1877-4043.

18. Slaughter, "Leaves from Northwestern History," 274.

19. Miles, *Personal Recollections*, 310.

20. Miles to Ruggles, camp on Rock Creek, 31 July 1879, NARA, RG94, LR, file 4163 AGO 1876, microcopy M666, roll 286, frames 317–19.

21. Sheridan to Townsend, Telegram, Chicago, 2 February 1879, NARA, RG94, LR, file 4163 AGO 1876, microcopy M666, roll 285, frames 441–50; Lincoln to CIA, Ft. Belknap Agency, 1 August 1879, CIA, ARCIA, 1879, pp. 98–100.

22. Finerty, *War-Path and Bivouac*, 280, 290–91. The interpreter during the council was André Larivée.

23. Louis Riel to Julie Riel [his mother], [Montana], 15 September, 1879, PAM, Riel Papers, MG3 D2, box 2, file 13.

24. Walsh, Handwritten Notes on Riel, n.d., PAM, James Morrow Walsh Papers, MG6 A1, microfilm reel M705, pp. 552–90.

25. Woodcock, *Gabriel Dumont*, 84.

26. Riel to Julie Riel, Ft. Belknap, 13 October 1879, PAM, Riel Papers, MG3 D2, box 2, file 13; O'Hanlon to Riel, Milk River Crossing, 19 October 1879, PAM, Riel Papers, MG3 D1, no. 376, microfilm reel M162; Hamelin to Riel, Wood Mountain, 31 October 1879, PAM, Riel Papers, MG3 D1, no. 377, microfilm reel M162.

27. L'Heureux to Dewdney, Ft. Walsh, 29 September 1880, NAC, RG10, vol. 3771, file 34527, microfilm reel C-10135.

28. L'Heureux to Macdonald, Ft. Macleod, 1 November 1886, NAC, John A. Macdonald Papers, MG26 A, vol. 110, pp. 44894–99, reel C-1525. A similar account, supposedly in Crowfoot's words, appears in Maclean, *Canadian Savage Folk*, 380–81. Maclean did not provide a source. An even more terse

reference to Crowfoot's involvement in this affair appeared in "Points for Mr. Amyot," *Toronto Mail*, 2 March 1886, p. 4, col. 2.

29. Hugonnard to Taché, Montagne de Bois, 6 March 1880, AASB, Fonds Taché, T23446–T23449.

30. L'Heureux to Riel, n.p., n.d., PAM, Riel Papers, MG3 D1, no. 436, microfilm reel M162.

31. Black to Acting AAG, District of Montana, Ft. Assinniboine, 26 November 1879, NARA, RG94, LR, file 4163 AGO 1876, microcopy M666, roll 287, frames 190–91.

32. Macleod to Dennis, Ft. Walsh, 1 December 1879, NAC, RG10, vol. 3652, file 8589, pt. 1, microfilm reel C-10114. (A copy is located in NAC, RG7, G21, vol. 320, file 2001, pt. 4b, microfilm reel T-1386, frames 5–7.) Macleod says that the mail carrier's name was Levallier. This may have been Louis Leveillé.

33. Walsh, Draft Account of Sitting Bull, 1879–81 [1881], PAM, MG6 A1, microfilm reel M705, pp. 333–42.

34. Crozier to Dennis, Ft. Walsh, 22 February 1880, NAC, RG10, vol. 3652, file 8589, pt. 1, microfilm reel C-10114. (A copy is located in NAC, RG7, G21, vol. 319, file 2001, pt. 3c, microfilm reel T-1386, frames 93–94.) See also Crozier to Commissioner, Ft. Walsh, 24 March 1880, NAC, RG18, B3, vol. 2233, fols. 52d–54d, microfilm reel T-6573, frames 512–14; and Crozier to Lt. Governor, Ft. Walsh, 29 March 1880, NAC, RG18, B3, vol. 2233, fols. 61–64, microfilm reel T-6573, frames 520–23. Edward Lambert worked as an interpreter at Ft. Walsh until the end of July 1879. At that time, the trader Frederick Cadd wrote that the Sioux had great confidence in him. Not surprisingly, Lambert became a trader after leaving police employ. See Cadd to [Miles], Poplar River, 20 July 1879, NARA, RG393, District of the Yellowstone, L&TR, box 5.

35. Black to AAG, Department of Dakota, Ft. Assinniboine, 10 February 1880, NARA, RG393, Department of Dakota, LR 1880, box 33, no. 1880-612; Riel, "About the Titons," [Montana, February 1880], PAM, Riel Papers, MG3 D1, no. 565, microfilm reel M163. Black does not identify Riel's memorandum in his letter. However, I am certain that "About the Titons" was the memorandum that Riel gave to Black as the first endorsement attached to Black's letter (written by the CO of the district, Col. Thomas T. Ruger) parrots what Riel wrote in that piece.

36. Ochoupe to Riel, Montagne de Bois, 16 April 1880, PAM, Riel Papers, MG3 D1, no. 384, microfilm reel M162. The author's name is unclear in the original; it is given as Odroupe in the archive's finding aid.

37. Walsh to Commissioner, Wood Mountain, 19 May 1880, NAC, RG10, vol. 3691, file 13893, microfilm reel C-10121; and Walsh to Minister of the Interior, Brockville, 11 September 1880, NAC, RG10, vol. 3691, file 13893, microfilm reel C-10121.

38. Black to AAG, Department of Dakota, Ft. Assinniboine, 19 March 1880, and enclosures, NARA, RG94, file 4163 AGO 1876, microcopy M666, roll 287, frames 350–52; Riel to Colonel [Black], Ft. Assinniboine, 16 March 1880, NARA, RG94, file 4163 AGO 1876, microcopy M666, roll 287, frames 355–58; Riel to Black, Ft. Assinniboine, 18 March 1880, NARA, RG94, file 4163 AGO 1876, microcopy M666, roll 287, frames 360–63; and Riel to Black, Ft. Assinniboine, 18 March 1880, NARA, RG94, file 4163 AGO 1876, microcopy M666, roll 287, frames 360–63. The quotation is from Riel's second letter of 18 March. (A copy of Riel's letter of 16 March is located in PAM, Riel Papers, MG3 D1, no. 383, microfilm reel M162.) See also Black to AAG, Department of Dakota, Ft. Assinniboine, 6 September 1880, NARA, RG393, Department of Dakota, LR 1880, box 36, no. 1880-3300.

39. Flanagan, *Louis "David" Riel*, 101–11.

40. Stanley, *The Birth of Western Canada*, 297.

1. Manzione, "*I Am Looking to the North for My Life*," 5, credits the Canadian government's "rather barbaric policy of starving the Sioux" with forcing the Lakotas to surrender.

2. Vestal, *New Sources of Indian History*, 236, 269–70, 334. See also Kennedy, *Recollections of an Assiniboine Chief*, 76–78, which discusses another early encounter between Hunkpapas and Assiniboines—this one in the winter of 1876–77.

3. Dempsey, *Crowfoot*, 91–92; John Peter Turner to Hamilton, Ottawa, 12 August 1944, SAB, Saskatchewan Historical Society Papers, file 204, Siouan Indians; Turner, *The North-West Mounted Police: 1873–1893*, 1:400.

4. "Statement by Henry Oscar One Bull in Sioux and in English Regarding Sitting Bull's Life from the Custer Fight until His Surrender, 1876–1881," University of Oklahoma, Campbell Collection, box 104; and Old Bull and One Bull Interview, University of Oklahoma, Campbell Collection, box 5, notebook 4, no. 3, pp. 26–28.

5. North-West Mounted Police, Extract from Commissioner's Report, 1877, Canadian House of Commons, Annual Report of the Secretary of State of Canada, 1878, *Sessional Papers* (1879), app. "D," pp. 21–22.

6. Dempsey, *Crowfoot*, 108–9, and *Red Crow*, 120–21.

7. Brooke to AAG, Department of Dakota, Ft. Shaw, 22 November 1878, NARA, RG393, Department of Dakota, LR 1878, box 29, no. 1878-5688.

8. John Young to CIA, Blackfeet Agency, 28 July 1879, CIA, ARCIA, 1879, 89.

9. S. J. Clarke, Diary Entry, 4 March 1879, GA, Edward Barnett Fonds, M3875, S. J. Clarke Diary.

10. Morris Bob-Tailed Bull Interview, University of Oklahoma, Campbell Collection, box 105, notebook 11, pp. 30–31. Bob-Tailed Bull did not say that the naming took place at this meeting. Children were often given names during the sun dance (see Walker, *Lakota Belief and Ritual*, 180, 192).

11. Gooderham to Campbell, Norman, 6 September 1930, quoted in Vestal, *New Sources of Indian History*, 236–38.

12. Dempsey, *Crowfoot*, 123.

13. "Sitting Bull and His Comrades," *New-York Times*, 4 August 1878, p. 2, col. 3. This article was reprinted from the *Ottawa Free Press*, 1 August 1878.

14. Macleod to Scott, Ft. Macleod, 9 July 1878, NAC, RG18, B3, vol. 2230, microfilm reel T-6572, frames 76–79.

15. Crozier to Macleod, Ft. Walsh, 18 July 1879, NAC, RG18, B3, vol. 2232, pp. 547–49, microfilm reel T-6573, frames 124–26; and Crozier to Walsh, Ft. Walsh, 20 July 1879, NAC, RG18, B3, vol. 2232, pp. 554–56, microfilm reel T-6573, frames 131–33.

16. Crozier to Macleod, Ft. Walsh, 29 December 1879, Canadian House of Commons, Annual Report of the Department of the Interior, 1879, *Sessional Papers* (1880), pt. 3, North-West Mounted Police Force, p. 18.

17. Cadd to [Miles], Poplar River, 20 July 1879, NARA, RG393, District of the Yellowstone, L&TR, box 5.

18. Dewdney to Superintendent General of Indian Affairs (SGIA), Ottawa, 31 December 1880, Canadian House of Commons, Annual Report of the Department of Indian Affairs, 1880, *Sessional Papers* (1881), p. 81.

19. Macleod to Dewdney, Ft. Macleod, 29 December 1880, Canadian House of Commons, Annual Report of the Department of Indian Affairs, 1880, *Sessional Papers* (1881), p. 97.

20. Lincoln to Hayt, Ft. Belknap, 6 October 1879, NARA, RG94, LR, file 4163 AGO 1876, microcopy M666, roll 287, frames 81–84. (A copy is in NAC, RG10, vol. 3691, file 13893.)

21. L'Heureux to Dewdney, Ft. Walsh, 24 September 1880, NAC, RG10, vol. 3771, file 34527, microfilm reel C-10135.

22. L'Heureux to Dewdney, Ft. Walsh, 29 September 1880, NAC, RG10, vol. 3771, file 34527, microfilm reel C-10135.

23. Dewdney to Dennis, Ft. Macleod, 22 July 1879, NAC, RG10, vol. 3696, file 15266, microfilm reel C-10122. This information was also included in Dewdney's year-end report (see Dewdney to SGIA, Ottawa, 2 January 1880, Canadian House of Commons, Annual Report of the Department of the Interior, 1879, *Sessional Papers* [1880], pp. 78–79).

24. Young to CIA, Blackfeet Agency, 6 August 1880, CIA, *ARCIA*, 1880, p. 106.

25. S. J. Clarke, Diary Entry, 31 January 1880, GA, Edward Barnett Fonds, M3875, S. J. Clarke Diary.

26. DeMallie, ed., *The Sixth Grandfather*, 210–11.

27. Parker to AAG, District of Montana, Ft. Maginnis, 26 September 1880, NARA, RG393, Ft. Maginnis, LS, vol. 7, p. 9, no. 1880-31; and Parker to AAG, District of Montana, 6 October 1880, NARA, RG393, Ft. Maginnis, LS, vol. 7, p. 13, no. 1880-44.

28. Dempsey, *The Amazing Death of Calf Shirt*, 210–33.

29. Allison, "Surrender of Sitting Bull," 242–47. (Allison's original manuscript is located in the Smithsonian Institution, National Anthropological Archives, MS 1755. It was published as Allison, *The Surrender of Sitting Bull*, of which Allison, "Surrender of Sitting Bull" is an edited reprinting.) See also Brotherton to AAG, Department of Dakota, Telegram, Ft. Buford, 7 November 1880, NARA, RG94, file 4163 AGO 1876, microcopy M666, roll 288, frames 472–82; and Morris Bob-Tailed Bull Interview, University of Oklahoma, Campbell Collection, box 105, notebook 11, pp. 28–29.

30. Lang to Davidson, Telegram, Ft. Keogh, 12 November 1880, NARA, RG393, District of the Yellowstone, LR, box 6.

31. Whistler to AAG, Department of Dakota, Ft. Keogh, 16 December 1880, NARA, RG94, LR, file 4163 AGO 1876, microcopy M666, roll 289, frames 104–9.

32. Dempsey, *Crowfoot*, 124–25.

33. Allen to Vankoughnet, Ft. Walsh, 12 December 1880, NAC, RG10, vol. 3652, file 8589, pt. 1, microfilm reel C-10114.

34. Everette to Miles, Wolf Point, 15 October 1880, NARA, RG393, District of the Yellowstone, LR, box 6.

35. Crozier to Irvine, Wood Mountain, 19 April 1881, NAC, RG10, vol. 3652, file 8589, pt. 1, microfilm reel C-10114. A fanciful account of this incident is in General Archibald Macdonell, "How Sitting Bull Came to Canada: Recollections of an Old Royal Mounted Police Officer," n.d., SAB, Saskatchewan Historical Society Papers, file 205, Siouan Indians. Both the policeman Cecil Denny (*The Riders of the Plains*, 125; and *The Law Marches West*, 148–49) and the historian John Peter Turner (*The North-West Mounted Police: 1873–1893*, 1:568–70) mention the event and state that the man was a Blood, but the contemporary account identifies him clearly as Cree.

36. Read to AAG, Department of Dakota, 13 June 1881, University of Vermont, Ogden B. Read, Camp Poplar River Letterbooks, LS, pp. 59–61.

37. Snyder to Williams, Ft. Peck, 16 February 1878, NARA, RG393, Department of Dakota, LR 1878, box 27, no. 1878-1486; Gibbon to Terry, Telegram, Ft. Shaw, 22 February 1878, NARA, RG393, District of Montana, LS 1870–79, pp. 160–61, no. 1878-138; and Williams to Acting AAG, District of Montana,

Ft. Belknap, 23 February 1878, NARA, RG393, Department of Dakota, LR 1878, box 27, no. 1878-1486.

38. [Walsh to co Ft. Walsh], Wood Mountain Post, 27 October 1878, PAM, MG6 A1, pp. 293–94. This material is repeated in Irvine to White, Ft. Walsh, 10 November 1878, NAC, RG18, B3, vol. 2232, pp. 77–81, microfilm reel T-6572, frames 668–72.

39. Walsh to Assistant Commissioner, Wood Mountain, 25 March 1879, NAC, RG7, G21, vol. 318, file 2001, pt. 3b, microfilm reel T-1386, frames 124–36. This information was later sent to the British Colonial Office: Deputy Minister of the Interior to the Governor-General's Secretary, Ottawa, 8 May 1879, Public Record Office, Colonial Office, Original Correspondence, Canada, C.O.42/757, no. 133.

40. Ilges to Acting AAG, District of Montana, Ft. Benton, 19 July 1877, NARA, RG75, LRCIA, Montana Superintendency, no. 1877-W771, microcopy M234, roll 508, frames 870–80; Ilges to Acting AAG, District of Montana, Ft. Benton, 24 July 1877, NARA, RG75, LRCIA, Montana Superintendency, no. 1877-W770, microcopy M234, roll 508, frames 861–69; Gibbon to Drum, Telegram, Ft. Shaw, 26 July 1877, NARA, RG393, District of Montana, LS 1870–79, p. 125, no. 1877-47.

41. Howard to Miles, Ft. Benton, 27 September 1877, NARA, RG393, District of the Yellowstone, LR, box 3; and Gibbon to Terry, Telegram, Ft. Shaw, 22 February 1878, NARA, RG393, District of Montana, LS 1870–79, pp. 160–61, no. 1878-138.

42. Ilges to Brooke, Ft. Benton, 13 April 1878, NARA, RG393, Department of Dakota, LR 1878, box 27, no. 1878-2272. (Copies are in NARA, RG75, LRCIA, Montana Superintendency, no. 1878-W34, microcopy M234, reel 515, frames 478–79; and NARA, RG94, LR, file 4163 AGO 1876, microcopy M666, reel 285, frames 129–33.)

43. Ilges to Acting AAG, District of Montana, Ft. Benton, 8 May 1878, NARA, RG94, LR, file 4163 AGO 1876, microcopy M666, roll 285, frames 125–28.

44. Lincoln to Commissioner of Indian Affairs, Ft. Belknap, 26 December 1878, NARA, RG94, LR, file 4163 AGO 1876, microcopy M666, roll 285, frames 423–25.

45. Lincoln to Brooke, Ft. Belknap, 4 January 1879, NARA, RG94, LR, file 4163 AGO 1876, microcopy M666, roll 285, frames 433–35. These visits were, in fact, routine: Assiniboines from Canadian territory often visited those at Ft. Belknap, "with whom they intermarry and are nearly all related." See Irvine to Dennis, Ft. Walsh, 15 March 1879, NAC, RG18, B3, vol. 2232, p. 313, microfilm reel T-6572, frame 890.

46. "News from the Plains," Saskatchewan Herald, 18 November 1878.

47. Irvine to Minister of the Interior, Ft. Walsh, 11 January 1879, NAC, RG18, B3, vol. 2232, pp. 200–201, microfilm reel T-6572, frames 786–87.

48. Lincoln to Sir [CIA], Ft. Belknap, 6 March 1879, NARA, RG94, LR, file 4163 AGO 1876, microcopy M666, roll 286, frames 16–18; and Lincoln to CIA, Ft. Belknap, 19 May 1879, NARA, RG94, LR, file 4163 AGO 1876, microcopy M666, roll 286, frames 68–69.

49. Lincoln to Hayt, Ft. Belknap, 16 June 1879, NARA, RG94, LR, file 4163 AGO 1876, microcopy M666, roll 286, frames 104–6; Thomas J. Bogy, Diary Entries, 10, 21 June 1879, Montana Historical Society Archives (hereafter MHSA), Thomas J. Bogy Diary, microfilm reel 292; Lincoln to CIA, Ft. Belknap Agency, Montana, 11 August 1880, CIA, ARCIA, 1880, 114.

50. Crozier to Commissioner, Wood Mountain, 28 March 1881, NAC, RG10, vol. 3691, file 13893, microfilm reel C-10121. This appears to be the same attack related to Indian Agent William Graham by a Moose Mountain Assiniboine years later. See Graham, Treaty Days, 23.

51. Beal, "I Will Fight No More Forever," 27–38.

52. Chalmers, The Last Stand of the Nez Perce, 176.

53. Turner, *Across the Medicine Line*, 112. Nez Percé accounts of the flight north are presented in McWhorther, *Hear Me, My Chiefs!* 508–24.

54. Walsh to CO Ft. Walsh, Wood Mountain Post, 8 October 1878, PAM, MG6 A1, microfilm reel M705, pp. 288–90.

55. Irvine to White, Ft. Walsh, 10 November 1878, NAC, RG18, B3, vol. 2232, pp. 77–81, microfilm reel T-6572, frames 668–72. (A copy is in NAC, RG7, G21, vol. 319, file 2001, pt. 3d, *Papers relating to the Sioux Indians*, pp. 125–26, microfilm reel T-1386, frames 125–26.)

56. Walsh to CO Ft. Walsh, Wood Mountain, 30 December 1878, NAC, RG7, G21, vol. 319, file 2001, pt. 3d, *Papers relating to the Sioux Indians*, pp. 127–28, microfilm reel T-1386, frames 127–28. (A copy is in PAM, MG6 A1, pp. 309–12.)

57. Walsh to Assistant Commissioner, Wood Mountain, 25 January 1879, NAC, RG7, G21, vol. 319, file 2001, pt. 3d, *Papers relating to the Sioux Indians*, pp. 129–130, microfilm reel T-1386, frames 129–130.

58. Irvine to Dennis, Ft. Walsh, 25 May 1879, NAC, RG18, B3, vol. 2232, pp. 413–14, microfilm reel T-6572, frames 984–85.

59. DeMallie, ed., *The Sixth Grandfather*, 205–7. The original text reads "Muddy Creek," which probably refers to White Mud River—an alternate name for Frenchman River.

60. Moses Old Bull to Campbell, Bull Head, 21 January 1932, and Moses Old Bull Pictorial Autobiography, drawings 10 and 12, University of Oklahoma, Campbell Collection. The autobiography has been published (see Miles and Lovett, "The Pictorial Autobiography of Moses Old Bull," 48–57).

61. Gordon Rolph, Memorandum, "Ouelette's Coulee," Cypress Hills, 14 February 1879, NAC, RG7, G21, vol. 319, file 2001, pt. 3d, *Papers relating to the Sioux Indians*, p. 132, microfilm reel T-1386, frame 132. This appears to be the same attack mentioned by American Indian Agent W. L. Lincoln in his monthly report for February 1879. See Lincoln to Sir [CIA], Ft. Belknap, 6 March 1879, NARA, RG94, LR, file 4163 AGO 1876, microcopy M666, roll 286, frames 16–18.

62. Antrobus to Irvine, Ft. Walsh, 24 February 1879, NAC, RG7, G21, vol. 319, file 2001, pt. 3d, *Papers relating to the Sioux Indians*, p. 135, microfilm reel T-1386, frame 135.

63. Cadd to [Miles], Poplar River, 20 July 1879, NARA, RG393, District of the Yellowstone, L&TR, box 5.

64. Lincoln to Hayt, Ft. Belknap, 16 June 1879, NARA, RG94, LR, file 4163 AGO 1876, microcopy M666, roll 286, frames 104–6.

65. Walsh to CO Ft. Walsh, Wood Mountain, 25 July 1879, NAC, RG10, vol. 3652, file 8589, pt. 1, microfilm reel C-10114.

66. See the High Dog count for the years 1877–78 and 1878–79 and the Jaw and Jaw Variant count for 1878–79 published in Howard, "Dakota Winter Counts, 397; the unattributed Hunkpapa count for 1879 published in Vestal, *New Sources of Indian History*, 351; and the Swift Dog count for the years 1877, 1878, and 1879 published in Praus, *The Sioux*. Ascribing Julian dates to events depicted in winter counts is difficult because Lakota years do not correspond exactly to Julian years and because different counts sometimes place the same events in different years. My reading of these counts is that One Star (or Lone Star) was killed in 1878, Bear Lice (or Little Bear) in 1879, and Brings Arrow in 1880.

67. Statement of Spotted Eagle, Ft. Walsh, May 1879, NAC, RG18, B3, vol. 2232, pp. 385–86, microfilm reel T-6572, frames 958–59.

68. Woolworth, "A Disgraceful Proceeding."

69. Finerty, *War-Path and Bivouac*, 269. McKenzie refers to General Ranald S. Mackenzie, the officer

who led the Americans' first illegal raid into Mexico in 1873. Canada's governor-general, John Douglas Sutherland Campbell, the Marquess of Lorne, was, as we have seen, married to Queen Victoria's daughter, Princess Louise.

70. Walsh to Assistant Commissioner, Wood Mountain, 25 January 1879, NAC, RG7, G21, vol. 319, file 2001, pt. 3d, *Papers relating to the Sioux Indians*, pp. 129–30, microfilm reel T-1386, frames 129–30.

71. Walsh to Assistant Commissioner, Wood Mountain, 25 March 1879, NAC, RG7, G21, vol. 318, file 2001, pt. 3b, microfilm reel T-1386, frames 124–36.

72. "[Sitting Bull] Interviewed," *Chicago Daily Tribune*, 5 July 1879, p. 1, cols. 2–7, and p. 2, cols. 1–2.

73. "Report of Brigadier-General Terry," 4 October 1880, and "Report of Col. N. A. Miles," 21 September 1880, SW, ARSW, *1880*, H. Ex. Doc. 1, pt. 2, 46th Cong., 3d sess., vol. 2, serial 1952, pp. 58–67, 74–76; CO Ft. Custer to AAG, Department of Dakota, Telegram, Ft. Custer, 24 March 1880, NARA, RG94, LR, file 4163 AGO 1876, microcopy M666, roll 287, frames 290–91; Davidson to AAG, Department of Dakota, Telegram, Ft. Custer, 2 April 1880, NARA, RG94, LR, file 4163 AGO 1876, microcopy M666, roll 287, frames 305–8; Miles to AAG, Department of Dakota, Telegram, O'Fallon Creek Station, 2 April 1880, NARA, RG94, LR, file 4163 AGO 1876, microcopy M666, roll 287, frames 314–15; Haines, ed., "Letters of an Army Captain."

74. *Report of the Commission . . . to Meet the Sioux Indian Chief, Sitting Bull*, 8–9. Nine was identified as a member of Struck by the Ree's band by Pascal Breland and Valentine Rowe (see "Montagne de Bois," 10 May 1873, PAM, MG12 B1, no. 162, reel M134; and Valentine Francis Rowe, Memoir, p. 10, NAC, Valentine Francis Rowe Papers, MG29 C24).

75. "Report of Brigadier-General Terry," 12 November 1877, SW, ARSW, *1877*, H. Ex. Doc. 1, pt. 2, 45th Cong., 2d sess., vol. 2, serial 1794, pp. 481–520.

76. Buell to Acting AAG, District of the Yellowstone, Ft. Custer, 2 February 1878, NARA, RG94, LR, file 4163 AGO 1876, microcopy M666, roll 284, frames 241–43.

77. Irvine to Scott, Ft. Macleod [actually Ft. Walsh], 14 July 1878, NAC, RG7, G21, vol. 319, file 2001, pt. 3d, *Papers relating to the Sioux Indians*, pp. 119–20, microfilm reel T-1386, frames 119–20; and Irvine to Scott, Ft. Macleod, 11 August 1878, NAC, RG7, G21, vol. 319, file 2001, pt. 3d, *Papers relating to the Sioux Indians*, p. 121, microfilm reel T-1386, frame 121.

78. [Walsh to CO Ft. Walsh], Wood Mountain Post, 27 October 1878, PAM, MG6 A1, microfilm reel M705, pp. 293–94. This information is repeated in Irvine to White, Ft. Walsh, 10 November 1878, NAC, RG18, B3, vol. 2232, pp. 77–81, microfilm reel T-6572, frames 668–72.

79. Buell to AAG, Department of Dakota, Telegram, Ft. Custer, 16 February 1879, NARA, RG94, LR, file 4163 AGO 1876, microcopy M666, roll 285, frames 509–12; and Henry to Acting AAG, District of Montana, Ft. Benton, 12 March 1879, NARA, RG94, LR, file 4163 AGO 1876, microcopy M666, roll 285, frames 573–76.

80. Lincoln to Hayt, Ft. Belknap, 21 January 1879, NARA, RG75, LRCIA, Montana Superintendency, no. 1879-L37, microcopy M234, roll 514, frames 374–82.

81. Thomas J. Bogy, Diary Entry, 17 March 1878, MHSA, Thomas J Bogy Diary, microfilm reel 292.

82. Williams to Acting AAG, District of Montana, Ft. Belknap, 23 February 1878, NARA, RG393, Department of Dakota, LR 1878, box 27, no. 1878-1486.

83. Lincoln to CIA, Ft. Belknap, 26 June 1878, NARA, RG75, LRCIA, Montana Superintendency, no. 1878-L491, microcopy M234, roll 511, frames 130–39; Bird to CIA, Poplar River, 6 August 1878, NARA, RG75, LRCIA, Montana Superintendency, no. 1878-B1152, microcopy M234, roll 509, frames 395–402. Two Assiniboines involved in the fight traveled to Ft. Walsh and informed the NWMP of the incident. See "Substance of a Report of Two Milk River Assiniboines, in Re. A Fight

Between the Assiniboines, Gros Ventres and Yanktons, Given to Lieut.-Colonel Irvine, 14th July, 1878," NAC, RG7, G21, vol. 319, file 2001, pt. 3d, *Papers relating to the Sioux Indians*, pp. 120–21, microfilm reel T-1386, frames 120–21.

84. Lincoln to Hayt, Ft. Belknap, 21 January 1879, NARA, RG75, LRCIA, Montana Superintendency, no. 1879-L37, microcopy M234, roll 514, frames 374–82.

85. Thomas J. Bogy, Diary Entry, 24 April 1879, MHSA, Thomas J. Bogy Diary, microfilm reel 292; Gilson to Hathaway, Ft. Belknap, 30 April 1879, NARA, RG393, Ft. Keogh Document File 1878–79.

86. Fort Belknap, Fort Peck, and Poplar River Agency Journal, Entries, 20, 21 February 1880, MHSA, Small Collection 251.

87. Kislingbury to Terry, Bismarck, 6 May 1879, NARA, RG94, LR, file 4163 AGO 1876, microcopy M666, roll 286, frames 29–34; and Bird to Miles, Poplar River, 6 June 1879, NARA, RG94, LR, file 4163 AGO 1876, microcopy M666, roll 286, frames 117–21.

88. Ewers to Post Adjutant Ft. Keogh, Ft. Keogh, 2 July 1880, NARA, RG393, Department of Dakota, LR 1880, box 35, no. 1880-2477.

89. "Arrival of Major Walsh," *Manitoba Daily Free Press*, 30 July 1880, GA, James Morrow Walsh Papers, M8065, box 2, file 11, Scrapbook.

90. Culbertson to Miles, Poplar River, 30 October 1880, NARA, RG393, District of the Yellowstone, LR, box 6.

91. Read to AAG, Department of Dakota, 13 June 1881, and Telegrams, University of Vermont, Ogden B. Read, Camp Poplar River Letterbooks, LS, pp. 59–61; Read to Breck, 16 June 1881, University of Vermont, Ogden B. Read, Camp Poplar River Letterbooks, LS, p. 44.

92. Recent examples are Manzione, *"I Am Looking to the North for My Life,"* 140–49; and Utley, *The Lance and the Shield*, chaps. 17 and 18. Both Manzione and Utley carefully document the surrender of various individuals and groups to American authorities without making any detailed mention of their ties to the Poplar River Yanktonais.

93. Porter to Brotherton, Poplar Creek, 1 April 1881, NARA, RG94, LR, file 4163 AGO 1876, microcopy M666, roll 290, frames 37–38; Porter to Brotherton, Poplar Creek, 5 April 1881, NARA, RG94, LR, file 4163 AGO 1876, microcopy M666, roll 290, frames 39–40; Brotherton to Porter, Ft. Buford, 5 April 1881, NARA, RG94, LR, file 4163 AGO 1876, microcopy M666, roll 290, frames 41–42; Porter to Trowbridge, Poplar Creek, 6 April 1881, NARA, RG94, LR, file 4163 AGO 1876, microcopy M666, roll 290, frames 43–46. Porter's position was supported Captain Read, who was in command of the troops stationed at the agency. See Read to CO Ft. Buford, 5 April 1881, University of Vermont, Ogden B. Read, Camp Poplar River Letterbooks, LS, pp. 48–50. Porter had discussed the marital relations between the hostiles and the Yanktonais in his annual report for 1880. See Porter to CIA, Ft. Peck Agency, Poplar River, Montana, 12 August 1880, CIA, *ARCIA, 1880*, 113.

94. Brotherton to Terry, Telegram, Ft. Buford, 25 December 1880, NARA, RG94, LR, file 4163 AGO 1876, microcopy M666, roll 289, frames 150–53.

95. Statement of Joseph Culbertson, Ft. Peck Agency, 9 February 1881, NARA, RG94, LR, file 4163 AGO 1876, microcopy M666, roll 289, frame 521. It seems ironic that this information came from Culbertson, a scout at Camp Poplar River, as Black Horn was his father-in-law. For information on Black Horn, see Read to AAG, Department of Dakota, Poplar River, 8 November 1880, NARA, RG393, Camp Poplar River, LS 1880–86, pp. 11–12.

96. Statement of Phillip Alvarez, Ft. Peck Agency, 9 February 1881, NARA, RG94, LR, file 4163 AGO 1876, microcopy M666, roll 289, frames 517–18.

97. Eli L. Huggins, "Surrender of Rain in the Face, the Reported Slayer of Gen. Custer," Smithsonian Institution, National Anthropological Archives, MS 2107.

98. Read to AAG, Department of Dakota, Telegram, Camp Poplar River, 26 November 1880, NARA, RG94, LR, file 4163 AGO 1876, microcopy M666, roll 288, frames 574–76. See Whistler to CO District of the Yellowstone, Telegram, Ft. Keogh, 27 November 1880, RG393, District of the Yellowstone, LR, box 6, which provides Joseph Culbertson's account of Read's conversations with Gall.

99. Read to Acting AAG, District of the Yellowstone, Poplar River, 1 December 1880, University of Vermont, Ogden B. Read, Camp Poplar River Letterbooks, Telegrams, pp. 9–10.

100. Lt. Col. Whistler to AAG, Department of Dakota, Ft. Keogh, 26 April 1881, NARA, RG94, LR, file 4163 AGO 1876, microcopy M666, roll 290, frames 87–90.

101. Extract from Commissioner's Report, 1877, Canadian House of Commons, Annual Report of the Secretary of State of Canada, 1878, *Sessional Papers* (1879), app. "D," North-West Mounted Police, pp. 21–22.

102. Whistler to AAG, Department of Dakota, Ft. Keogh, 26 April 1881, NARA, RG94, LR, file 4163 AGO 1876, microcopy M666, roll 290, frames 87–90; and Shrimp, Rain in the Face, Spotted Eagle, Bull Dog, Big Road, Little Hawk, Two Eagles, Iron Thunder, Horn Cloud, and Buffalo Runner to the Great Father, Ft. Yates, 15 July 1881, NARA, RG94, LR, file 4163 AGO 1876, microcopy M666, roll 290, frames 389–90.

The Northern Borderlands

1. Turner, *History, Frontier, and Section*; and Innis, *The Fur Trade in Canada*.
2. Trigger, "Indian and White History."
3. See Clifton, *Being and Becoming Indian*.
4. For an alternate view, see Haefeli, "The Use of North American Borderlands." Haefeli argues that, by the time aboriginals and Europeans found themselves in a common borderland, the days of aboriginal autonomy were already numbered: "Borderlands restrict natives' options at least as much as they increase them. Within a borderland, the choice is not between their way and our way but between the alliance of one or another empire. Trying to play one colonial power off of another only ups the ante of potential destruction to local autonomy" (1223). While I take the point, this view tends to efface the very real give-and-take of some encounters, however temporally limited they may have been.
5. For an introduction to boundary studies in Africa, see Musambachime, "Protest Migrations in Mweru-Luapula"; Cordell and Gregory, "Labour Reservoirs and Population"; Killingray, "Military and Labour Recruitment in the Gold Coast"; Echenberg, "Les Migrations militaires en Afrique occidentale française"; and Asiwaju, "Migrations as Revolt."
6. Ryder, "The Demarcation of the Turco-Persian Boundary," 235.
7. Quoted in Asiwaju, ed., *Partitioned Africans*, 9.
8. Elizabeth Gravelle, quoted in Fraser, *Walking the Line*, 140.
9. Davison, ed., "The Bannock-Paiute War of 1878," 134.
10. Sherman to Hayt, Telegram, Washington DC, 6 August 1878, NARA, RG393, Department of Dakota, LR 1878, box 28, no. 1878-4165.
11. Evarts to Plunkett, Washington DC, 31 July 1877, NAC, RG7, G21, vol. 319, file 2001, pt. 3d, *Papers relating to the Sioux Indians*, pp. 30–31, microfilm reel T-1386, frames 31–32.
12. Sully to Parker, Helena, 20 September 1870, CIA, *ARCIA, 1870*, 190.
13. Armitage to CIA, Teton Valley, 1 September 1871, CIA, *ARCIA, 1871*, 428.
14. Hatch to Cumming, 12 July 1856, CIA, *ARCIA, 1856*, 76.
15. Vaughan to Robinson, Ft. Benton, 10 September 1858, CIA, *ARCIA, 1858*, 78.
16. Reed to Jayne, Blackfeet Agency, 1 October 1862, CIA, *ARCIA, 1862*, 179.

17. Upson to Dole, Ft. Benton, 28 September 1864, CIA, *ARCIA, 1864*, 300.

18. Upson to Dole, Ft. Benton, 28 September 1864, CIA, *ARCIA, 1864*, 300.

19. Meagher to CIA, Virginia City, 14 December 1865, CIA, *ARCIA, 1866*, 196.

20. See University of British Columbia, Special Collections and University Archives Division, Frederick W. Howay Fonds, AX10 14, box 26, folder 6, Blackfoot Calendar.

21. The seven were Low Horn, Bad Head, Bull Backfat, Heavy Shield, Medicine Calf, Running Rabbit, and White Eagle. See Morris, *The Treaties of Canada with the Indians*, 368–75; and Kappler, comp., *Indian Affairs*, 2:737–40.

22. Dempsey, "The Amazing Death of Calf Shirt," 65. Hudson's Bay Company traders noted that many Blackfoot left the United States in 1865 following this violent confrontation with the Americans: see Brazeau to Cheadle, Rocky Mountain House, 1 January 1866, McGill University, McLennan Library, Department of Rare Books and Special Collections, W. B. Cheadle Papers, MS 657, item 67.

23. Dempsey, "Maskepetoon"; Ewers, "Ethnological Report," 54–56, 70; Milloy, *The Plains Cree*, 111–16.

24. Morris, *The Treaties of Canada with the Indians*, 270.

25. Latta to Dole, Yancton, Dakota Territory, 27 August 1862, CIA, *ARCIA, 1862*, 195.

26. Wilkinson to Edmunds, 31 August 1864, CIA, *ARCIA, 1864*, 263.

27. Young to CIA, Blackfeet Agency, 6 August 1883, CIA, *ARCIA, 1883*, 96.

28. Young to CIA, Blackfeet Agency, 11 August 1882, CIA, *ARCIA, 1882*, 100.

29. Statement of Alex Culbertson, enclosed in Fanton to CIA, Ft. Belknap, 1 April 1876, NARA, RG75, LRCIA, Montana Superintendency, no. 1876-F108, microcopy M234, roll 504, frames 797–802.

30. Lincoln to CIA, Ft. Belknap, 20 August 1881, CIA, *ARCIA*, 1881, 117–18.

31. Morris to Secretary of State for the Provinces, Ft. Garry, 14 October 1873, Canadian House of Commons, Annual Report of the Department of the Interior, 1874, *Sessional Papers* (1875), p. 17. The discussion on which Morris based this letter is reported in "Indian Treaty: Closing Proceedings," *Manitoban*, 18 October 1873, p. 1, col. 6.

32. Walsh to Minister of the Interior, Ft. Walsh, 12 September 1876, NAC, RG10, vol. 3637, file 7088.

33. Canadian House of Commons, Annual Report of the Department of the Interior, 1877, *Sessional Papers* (1878), vol. 8, special app. B, Walsh, pp. xxxi–xxxii.

34. McDonald to Lieutenant Governor of the North-West Territories, Livingstone, North-West Territories, 20 October 1877, NAC, RG10, vol. 3656, file 9092.

35. Crozier to Irvine, Wood Mountain, 1 May 1881, NAC, RG10, vol. 3691, file 13893, microfilm reel C-10121.

36. The closing of the borderlands is told from the perspective of Cree history in Hogue, "Disputing the Medicine Line."

37. See Hubner, "Horse Stealing and the Borderline."

38. Irvine to White, Ft. Walsh, 20 May 1882, NAC, RG10, vol. 3744, file 29506-2.

39. Extract, Galt to Wadsworth, 13 July 1881, NAC, RG10, vol. 3744, file 29506-1.

40. McDonald to [Dewdney], Ft. Walsh, 11 November 1882, NAC, RG10, vol. 3744, file 29506-3.

41. McIllrie to Indian Commissioner, Ft. Calgary, 2 December 1882, NAC, RG10, vol. 3744, file 29506-3. See also McIllrie to Indian Commissioner, Ft. Walsh, [received DIA (Department of Indian Affairs)], 30 July 1882, NAC, RG10, vol. 3744, file 29506-2.

42. Patrice Breland to Chèr Docteur, Cypress Hills, 24 November 1878, NAC, RG10, vol. 3687, file 13607.

43. White to Minister of the Interior, Ottawa, 9 June 1883, NAC, RG10, vol. 3740, file 28748–1.

44. Lincoln to Hayt, Ft. Belknap, 6 October 1879, NAC, RG10, vol. 3691, file 13893.

45. Allen to Dewdney, Ft. Walsh, 4 May 1881, NAC, RG10, vol. 3744, file 29506-1.

46. Denny to Indian Commissioner, Ft. Walsh, 16 November 1881, NAC, RG10, vol. 3744, file 29506-1.

47. Allen to Dewdney, Ft. Walsh, 4 May 1881, and Denny to Dewdney, Ft. Walsh, 1 November 1881, NAC, RG10, vol. 3744, file 29506-1.

48. Denny to [Dewdney], Ft. Walsh, 9 November 1881, NAC, RG10, vol. 3744, file 29506-1.

49. McIllrie to Indian Commissioner, Ft. Walsh, 27 June 1882, NAC, RG10, vol. 3744, file 29506-1 file 29506-2.

50. McIllrie to Indian Commissioner, Ft. Calgary, 2 December 1882, NAC, RG10, vol. 3744, file 29506-3.

51. Peter Houri to McDonald, Ft. Walsh, 13 October 1882, NAC, RG10, vol. 3744, file 29506-3.

52. Paul to Bates, Ft. Assinniboine, 3 May 1883, and Adams to Bates, Ft. Assinniboine, 30 May 1883, NAC, RG10, vol. 3740, file 28748-1.

53. Spry, "The Great Transformation."

54. Macdonald to Indian Commissioner, Indian Head, 28 December 1883, NAC, RG10, vol. 3652, file 8589, pt. 2, microfilm reel C-10114.

55. Reed to SGIA, Regina, 9 September 1886, NAC, RG10, vol. 3766, file 32957, microfilm reel C-10135; Vankoughnet to Macdonald, Ottawa, 21 September 1886, NAC, RG10, vol. 3766, file 32957, microfilm reel C-10135; Vankoughnet to Reed, Ottawa, 28 September 1886, NAC, RG10, vol. 3599, file 1564, pt. A, microfilm reel C-10104.

56. Sharp, "The Northern Great Plains," and *Whoop-Up Country*.

57. LaDow, *The Medicine Line*.

58. Caughey, "Historians of the West," 79.

59. Worster, *Under Western Skies*.

BIBLIOGRAPHY

Archival Sources
Archives de l'archevêché (Saint-Boniface)

>   Fonds Alexandre-Antonin Taché.

Brigham Young University, Harold B. Lee Library (Provo UT)

>   Walter Mason Camp Papers.

British Columbia Archives and Records Service (Victoria)

>   John H. McIllrie Diaries and Notebooks.

Glenbow Archives (Calgary)

>   Frederick Augustus Bagley Fonds.
>   Edward Barnett Fonds.
>   Joseph J. Carscadden Fonds.
>   Charles D. Denny Fonds.
>   Robert H. Hougham Fonds.
>   James Farquharson Macleod Family Fonds.
>   Richard Barrington Nevitt Fonds.
>   Southern Alberta Research Project Fonds.
>   Traill Family Fonds.
>   James Morrow Walsh Fonds.

Henry E. Huntington Library (San Marino CA)

>   Frank Baldwin Papers.

Indiana University, Lilly Library (Bloomington)

>   Walter Mason Camp Papers.

Marquette University Archives (Milwaukee)

>   Bureau of Catholic Indian Mission Records. Abbot Martin Marty, O.S.B., Correspondence. 1877–1878.

McGill University, McLennan Library, Department of Rare Books and Special Collections (Montréal)

W. B. Cheadle Papers.

Montana Historical Society Archives (Helena)

Thomas J. Bogy Diary.
Fort Belknap, Fort Peck and Poplar River Agency Journal.

National Archives of Canada (Ottawa)

Government Archives Division. Records of the Department of the Secretary of State
————. Records of the Office of the Governor General.
————. Records Relating to Indian Affairs. Black (Western) Series.
————. Records of the Royal Canadian Mounted Police. Office of the Commissioner, Letter-
   books.
————. Records of the Royal Canadian Mounted Police. Office of the Comptroller, Official
   Correspondence.
Manuscript Division. Archives of the American North-West Boundary Commission.
————. Andrew Bulger Papers.
————. James Finlayson Papers.
————. Fort Ellice Journals.
————. George M. Grant Papers.
————. Jean-Louis Légaré Papers.
————. Marquis of Lorne Papers.
————. John A. Macdonald Papers.
————. Patrick Robertson-Ross Papers.
————. Valentine Francis Rowe Papers.
————. United States, Court of Claims, J.-L. Legaré.
————. Cora Mowat Walsh Papers.
————. John Wodehouse Papers.

National Archives and Records Administration (Washington DC)

General Records of the Department of State. Consular Dispatches, Winnipeg
Records of the Adjutant General's Office. Letters Received by the Office of the Adjutant General
   (Main Series).
Records of the Bureau of Indian Affairs. Letters Received by the Office of Indian Affairs
————. Records of the Inspection Division.
Records of the United States Army Continental Commands. Division of the Missouri, "Special
   Files."
————. Post Records.

Nebraska State Historical Society (Lincoln)

Eli S. Ricker Collection.

Provincial Archives of Alberta (Edmonton)

Henri Julien Papers.
Joseph-Jean-Marie Lestanc papiers personnel.

Provincial Archives of Manitoba (Winnipeg)

Adams George Archibald Papers.
Fort Ellice Journal of Daily Occurrences.
George Arthur French Papers.
Zachary M. Hamilton Papers.
James Farquharson Macleod Papers.
Alexander Morris Papers. Lieutenant-Governor Collection.
————. Ketcheson Collection.
Records of the Assiniboine and Saskatchewan Exploring Expedition. Diary of H. L. Hime. 1858.
Records of the North American Boundary Commission. Report of Capt. D. R. Cameron.
————. Extracts from Notebook of John E. Edwards.
————. L. F. Hewgill. *In the Days of Pioneering: Crossing the Plains in the Early 70's: The Prairie Black with Buffalo*. N.p.: n.p., 1894.
————. Notebook and Journal of Capt. A. C. Ward.
————. Riel Family Papers.
————. James Wickes Taylor Papers.
————. James Morrow Walsh Papers.

Provincial Archives of Manitoba, Hudson's Bay Company Archives (Winnipeg)

Section B: Post Records. Fort Ellice District Reports. B.63/e/1.
————. Fort Ellice Journals. B.63/a/11–12.
Section E: Private Manuscripts. W. J. Christie Papers. E.23.
————. Isaac Cowie Papers. E.86/1–65.
————. William J. McLean. E.218.

Public Record Office (London)

Colonial Office. Original Correspondence, Canada.

Saskatchewan Archives Board (Regina and Saskatoon)

Clippings File. Local Histories—Moose Jaw.
Arsène Godin Papers.
Indians of North America Collection. John O'Kute-sica File.
David Laird Papers.
Saskatchewan Historical Society Papers. Johnny Chartrand File.
————. Siouan Indians Files.
Wood Mountain Historic Park. Pamphlet.

Smithsonian Institution, National Anthropological Archives (Washington DC)

E. H. Allison. "Surrender of Sitting Bull." 1897. With notes by John Galen Carter. 1933.

Eli L. Huggins. "Surrender of Rain in the Face, the Reported Slayer of Gen. Custer."

University of British Columbia, Special Collections and University Archives Division (Vancouver)

Frederick W. Howay Fonds.

University of Colorado, Archives (Boulder)

William Carey Brown Papers.

University of Oklahoma Archives (Norman)

Western History Collections. Walter S. Campbell Collection.

University of Vermont (Burlington)

Ogden B. Read Papers. Camp Poplar River Letterbooks.

Yale University, Beinecke Rare Book and Manuscript Library (New Haven CT)

Western Americana Collection. Samuel Anderson Papers.
————. Valentine McGillycuddy Northwest Boundary Survey Diary.

Newspapers

Daily British Colonist (Victoria). 1873.
Chicago Daily Tribune. 1879.
The Globe (Toronto). 1876–85.
The Manitoban (Winnepeg). 1873.
New-York Herald. 1877.
New-York Times. 1867, 1878–79.
New York Tribune. 1876.
The Nor'-Wester (Red River Settlement). 1861–64.
Saskatchewan Herald (Battleford). 1878–82.
Toronto Mail. 1886.

Published Sources

Abel, Annie Heloise. *Tabeau's Narrative of Loisel's Expedition to the Upper Missouri.* Translated by Rose Abel Wright. Norman: University of Oklahoma Press, 1939.
————. "Trudeau's Description of the Upper Missouri." *Mississippi Valley Historical Review* 8, nos. 1–2 (June–September 1921): 149–79.
Adelman, Jeremy, and Stephen Aron. "From Borderlands to Borders: Empires, Nation-States, and the Peoples in Between in North American History." *American Historical Review* 104, no. 3 (June 1999): 814–41.
Aldrich, Vernice M. "Father George Antoine Belcourt, Red River Missionary." *North Dakota Historical Quarterly* 2, no. 1 (October 1927): 30–52.
Allison, Edwin H. "Surrender of Sitting Bull." Edited by Doane Robinson. *South Dakota Historical Collections* 6 (1912): 233–70.
————. *The Surrender of Sitting Bull, Being a Full and Complete History of the Negotiations Con-*

ducted by Scout Allison Which Resulted in the Surrender of Sitting Bull and His Entire Band of Hostile Sioux in 1881. . . . Dayton OH: Walker Lithograph & Printing, 1891.

Anderson, Gary Clayton. *Kinsmen of Another Kind: Dakota-White Relations in the Upper Mississippi Valley, 1650–1862*. Lincoln: University of Nebraska Press, 1984.

————. *Little Crow: Spokesman for the Sioux*. St. Paul: Minnesota Historical Society Press, 1986.

Anderson, S. "The North-American Boundary from the Lake of the Woods to the Rocky Mountains." *Journal of the Royal Geographical Society* 46 (1876): 228–62.

Appropriations for Sioux Indians. 42d Cong., 2d sess., H. Ex. Doc. 102, vol. 8, serial 1511. Washington DC: U.S. Government Printing Office, 1872.

Asiwaju, A. I. "Migrations as Revolt: The Example of the Ivory Coast and Upper Volta before 1945." *Journal of African History* 17, no. 4 (1976): 577–94.

————, ed. *Partitioned Africans: Ethnic Relations across Africa's International Boundaries, 1884–1984*. London: C. Hurst; Lagos: University of Lagos Press, 1985.

————. "Problem Solving along African Borders: The Nigeria-Benin Case since 1889." In *Across Boundaries: Transborder Interaction in Comparative Perspective*, ed. Oscar J. Martínez. El Paso: Texas Western Press, 1986.

Atwood, Mae, ed. *In Rupert's Land: Memoirs of Walter Traill*. Toronto: McClelland & Stewart, 1970.

Axtell, James. *The Invasion Within: The Contest of Cultures in Colonial North America*. New York: Oxford University Press, 1985.

Baily, Kenneth P., ed. and trans. *Journal of Joseph Marin: French Colonial Explorer and Military Commander in the Wisconsin Country, August 7, 1753–June 20, 1754*. Los Angeles: privately printed, 1975.

Beal, Merrill D. *"I Will Fight No More Forever": Chief Joseph and the Nez Perce War*. Seattle: University of Washington Press, 1963.

Board of Commissioners. *Minnesota in the Civil and Indian Wars, 1861–1865*. 2 vols. St. Paul MN: Pioneer, 1890–93.

Brooks, James F. *Captives and Cousins: Slavery, Kinship, and Community in the Southwest Borderlands*. Chapel Hill: University of North Carolina Press, 2002.

Brown, Jennifer S. H. *Strangers in Blood: Fur Trade Company Families in Indian Country*. Vancouver: University of British Columbia Press, 1980.

Calloway, Colin G. *Crown and Calumet: British-Indian Relations, 1783–1815*. Norman: University of Oklahoma Press, 1987.

Canadian House of Commons. Annual Reports of the Department of Indian Affairs. *Sessional Papers*. Ottawa: Queen's Printer, 1881–85.

————. Annual Reports of the Department of the Interior. *Sessional Papers*. Ottawa: Queen's Printer, 1877–80.

————. Annual Reports of the North-West Mounted Police. *Sessional Papers*. Ottawa: Queen's Printer, 1877–86.

————. Annual Reports of the Secretary of State of Canada. *Sessional Papers*. Ottawa: Queen's Printer, 1877–79.

Carter, Clarence Edwin, ed. *The Territory of Louisiana-Missouri, 1806–1814*. Vol. 14 of *The Territorial Papers of the United States*. Washington DC: U.S. Government Printing Office, 1949.

Carver, Jonathan. *Travels through the Interior Parts of North-America, in the Years 1766, 1767, and 1768*. London: privately printed, 1778.

Caughey, John W. "Historians of the West." *American West* 1, no. 1 (1964): 31–43, 78–79.

Chalmers, Harvey, II. *The Last Stand of the Nez Perce: Destruction of a People*. New York: Twayne, 1962.

Champagne, R. P. Ant., ed. "Journal de Marin, Fils, 1753–1754." *Rapport des Archives du Québec* 41 (1963): 235–308.

Charette, Guillaume. *L'Espace de Louis Goulet*. Winnipeg: Editions Bois-Brûlés, 1976. Translated by Ray Ellenwood as *Vanishing Spaces: Memoirs of a Prairie Métis* (Winnipeg: Editions Bois-Brûlés, 1980).

Cheadle, Walter Butler. *Cheadle's Journal of Trip across Canada, 1862–1863*. Ottawa: Graphic, 1931.

Chittenden, Hiram Martin, and Alfred Talbot Richardson, eds. *Life, Letters and Travels of Father Pierre-Jean De Smet, S.J., 1801–1873*. 4 vols. New York: Francis P. Harper, 1905. Reprint, New York: Kraus, 1969.

Clandening, William H. "Across the Plains in 1863–1865: Being the Journal Kept by William H. Clandening of Walkertin, Upper Canada, now Ontario, Canada." *North Dakota Historical Quarterly* 2, no. 4 (July 1928): 247–72.

Clarke, E. D. "In the North West with Sitting Bull." *Rose-Belford's Canadian Monthly and National Review* 5 (July–December 1880): 66–73.

Clifton, James. *Being and Becoming Indian: Biographical Studies on North American Frontiers*. Chicago: Dorsey, 1989.

Collins, John Davison. "The Clandestine Movement of Groundnuts across the Niger-Nigeria Boundary." *Canadian Journal of African Studies* 10, no. 2 (1976): 259–78.

Cordell, Dennis D., and Joel W. Gregory. "Labour Reservoirs and Population: French Colonial Strategies in Kougoudou, Upper Volta, 1914 to 1939." *Journal of African History* 23, no. 2 (1982): 205–24.

Cowie, Isaac. *The Company of Adventurers: A Narrative of Seven Years in the Service of the Hudson's Bay Company during 1867–1874 on the Great Buffalo Plains with Historical and Biographical Notes and Comments*. Toronto: William Briggs, 1913.

Cruikshank, Ernest Alexander. "Robert Dickson, the Indian Trader." *Collections of the State Historical Society of Wisconsin* 12 (1892): 133–53.

D'Artigue, Jean. *Six Years in the Canadian North-West*. Translated by L. C. Corbett and Rev. S. Smith. Toronto: Hunter, Rose, 1882.

Davison, Stanley R., ed. "The Bannock-Paiute War of 1878: Letters of Major Edwin C. Mason." *Journal of the West* 11, no. 1 (January 1972): 128–42.

DeBarthe, Joe. *Life and Adventures of Frank Grouard*. Edited by Edgar I. Stewart. Norman: University of Oklahoma Press, 1958.

De Kiewiet, C. W., and F. H. Underhill, eds. *Dufferin-Carnarvon Correspondence, 1874–1878*. Toronto: Champlain Society, 1955.

DeMallie, Raymond J. "The Sioux in Dakota and Montana Territories: Cultural and Historical Background of the Ogden B. Read Collection." In *Vestiges of a Proud Nation*, ed. Glenn E. Markoe. Burlington VT: Robert Hull Fleming Museum, 1986.

————, ed. *The Sixth Grandfather: Black Elk's Teachings Given to John G. Neihardt*. Lincoln: University of Nebraska Press, 1984.

————. "'These Have No Ears': Narrative and the Ethnohistorical Method." *Ethnohistory* 40, no. 4 (fall 1993): 515–38.

————, ed. *Plains*. Vol. 13 of *The Handbook of North American Indians*. Washington DC: Smithsonian Institution, 2001.

Dempsey, Hugh A. "The Amazing Death of Calf Shirt." *Montana: The Magazine of Western History* 3, no. 1 (January 1953): 65–70.

————. *The Amazing Death of Calf Shirt and Other Blackfoot Stories: Three Hundred Years of Blackfoot History*. Saskatoon: Fifth House, 1994.

————. *Crowfoot: Chief of the Blackfeet*. Halifax: Goodread Biographies, 1988.

————. *Firewater: The Impact of the Whisky Trade on the Blackfoot Nation*. Calgary: Fifth House, 2002.

————. "Maskepetoon." In *Dictionary of Canadian Biography*, 9:537–38. Toronto: University of Toronto Press, 1976.

————. *Red Crow: Warrior Chief*. Saskatoon: Fifth House, 1995.

Dempsey, James. "Little Bear's Band: Canadian or American Indians?" *Alberta History* 41, no. 4 (autumn 1993): 2–9.

Denig, Edwin Thompson. *Five Indian Tribes of the Upper Missouri: Sioux, Arikaras, Assiniboines, Crees, Crows*. Edited by John C. Ewers. Norman: University of Oklahoma Press, 1961.

Denny, Cecil E. *The Law Marches West*. Edited by W. B. Cameron. London: J. M. Dent, 1939.

————. *The Riders of the Plains: A Reminiscence of the Early and Exciting Days in the North West*. Calgary: Herald, 1905.

Diedrich, Mark. *The Odyssey of Chief Standing Buffalo and the Northern Sisseton Sioux*. Minneapolis: Coyote, 1988.

Doll, Maurice F. V., Robert S. Kidd, and John P. Day. *The Buffalo Lake Metis Site: A Late Nineteenth Century Settlement in the Parkland of Central Alberta*. Provincial Museum of Alberta Human History Occasional Paper No. 4. Edmonton: Alberta Culture and Multiculturalism, Historical Resources Division, 1988.

Dowd, Gregory Evans. *A Spirited Resistance: The North American Indian Struggle for Unity, 1745–1815*. Baltimore: Johns Hopkins University Press, 1992.

Draper, Lyman C., ed. "Lawe and Grignon Papers, 1794–1821." *Collections of the State Historical Society of Wisconsin* 10 (1888): 90–141.

Dumont, Gabriel. *Gabriel Dumont Speaks*. Translated by Michael Barnholden. Vancouver: Talonbooks, 1993.

Echenberg, Myron J. "Les Migrations militaires en Afrique occidentale française, 1900–1945." *Canadian Journal of African Studies* 14, no. 3 (1980): 429–50.

Elias, Peter Douglas. *The Dakota of the Canadian Northwest: Lessons for Survival*. Winnipeg: University of Manitoba Press, 1988.

Ewers, John C. "Ethnological Report on the Chippewa Cree Tribe of the Rocky Boy Reservation, Montana, and the Little Shell Band of Indians." In *Chippewa Indians*, ed. David Agee Horr, vol. 6. New York: Garland, 1974.

Expedition of Captain Fisk to the Rocky Mountains: Letter from the Secretary of War, a Resolution of the House of February 26, Transmitting Report of Captain Fisk of His Late Expedition to the Rocky Mountains and Idaho. 38th Cong., 1st sess., H. Ex. Doc. 45, vol. 9, serial 1189. Washington DC: U.S. Government Printing Office, 1864.

Featherstonhaugh, Albany. "Narrative of the Operations of the British North American Boundary Commission, 1872–76." *Professional Papers of the Corps of Royal Engineers*, n.s., 23 (1876): 24–49.

Finerty, John F. *War-Path and Bivouac; or, The Conquest of the Sioux*. 1890. Norman: University of Oklahoma Press, 1961.

Flanagan, Thomas. *Louis "David" Riel: Prophet of the New World*. Halifax: Goodread Biographies, 1983.

Fox, Richard Allan, Jr. *Archaeology, History, and Custer's Last Battle: The Little Big Horn Reexamined*. Norman: University of Oklahoma Press, 1993.

Fraser, Marion Botsford. *Walking the Line: Travels along the Canadian/American Border*. Vancouver: Douglas & McIntyre, 1989.

Friesen, Jean. "Magnificent Gifts: The Treaties of Canada with the Indians of the Northwest, 1869–76." *Transactions of the Royal Society of Canada*, 5th ser., 1 (1986): 41–51.

Glazebrook, G. P. de T., ed. *The Hargrave Correspondence, 1821–1843*. Toronto: Champlain Society, 1938.

Goossen, N. Jaye. "'A Wearer of Moccasins': The Honourable James McKay of Deer Lodge." *Beaver* 309, no. 2 (autumn 1978): 44–53.

Graham, William M. *Treaty Days: Reflections of an Indian Commissioner*. Calgary: Glenbow Museum, 1991.

Grant, George M. *Ocean to Ocean: Sandford Fleming's Expedition through Canada in 1872*. Toronto: James Campbell & Son, 1873.

Gray, John S. *Custer's Last Campaign: Mitch Boyer and the Little Bighorn Reconstructed*. Lincoln: University of Nebraska Press, 1991.

Greene, Jerome A., ed. *Lakota and Cheyenne: Indian Views of the Great Sioux War, 1876–1877*. Norman: University of Oklahoma Press, 1994.

————. *Yellowstone Command: Colonel Nelson A. Miles and the Great Sioux War, 1876–1877*. Lincoln: University of Nebraska Press, 1991.

Gruesel, Joseph, ed. "Copies of Papers on File in the Dominion Archives at Ottawa, Canada, Pertaining to the Relations of the British Government with the United States during the Period of the War of 1812." *Michigan Pioneer and Historical Society Collections* 15 (1890; reprint, 1909): 1–744.

————, ed. "Copies of Papers on File in the Dominion Archives at Ottawa, Canada, Pertaining to the Relations of the British Government with the United States during and subsequent to the Period of the War of 1812." *Michigan Pioneer and Historical Society Collections* 16 (1890; reprint, 1910): 1–775.

Haefeli, Evan. "A Note on the Use of North American Borderlands." *American Historical Review* 104, no. 4 (October 1999): 1222–25.

Haines, Francis, ed. "Letters of an Army Captain on the Sioux Campaign of 1879–1880." *Pacific Northwest Quarterly* 39, no. 1 (January 1948): 39–64.

Hammer, Kenneth, ed. *Custer in '76: Walter Camp's Notes on the Custer Fight*. Provo UT: Brigham Young University Press, 1976.

Hargrave, Joseph James. *Red River*. Montréal: John Lovell, 1871.

Hedren, Paul L., ed. *The Great Sioux War, 1876–77*. Helena: Montana Historical Society Press, 1991.

Hewitt, J. N. B., ed. *Journal of Rudolph Friederich Kurz: An Account of His Experiences among Fur Traders and American Indians on the Mississippi and the Upper Missouri Rivers during the Years 1846 to 1852*. Translated by Myrtis Jarrell. Smithsonian Institution, Bureau of American Ethnology, Bulletin no. 115. Washington DC: U.S. Government Printing Office, 1937.

Hildebrandt, Walter, and Brian Hubner. *The Cypress Hills: The Land and Its People*. Saskatoon: Purich, 1994.

Hind, Henry Youle. *Narrative of the Canadian Red River Exploring Expedition of 1857 and of the*

Assinniboine and Saskatchewan Exploring Expedition of 1858. 2 vols. 1860. Reprint, New York: Greenwood, 1969.

Hogue, Michel. "Disputing the Medicine Line: The Plains Crees and the Canadian-American Border, 1876–1885." *Montana: The Magazine of Western History* 52, no. 4 (winter 2002): 2–17.

Howard, James H. "Dakota Winter Counts as a Source of Plains History." Smithsonian Institution, Bulletin no. 173, Anthropological Papers no. 61, pp. 335–416. Washington DC: U.S. Government Printing Office, 1960.

Hubner, Brian. "Horse Stealing and the Borderline: The NWMP and the Control of Indian Movement, 1874–1900." *Prairie Forum* 20, no. 2 (fall 1995): 281–300.

Hutton, Paul Andrew, ed. *The Custer Reader.* Lincoln: University of Nebraska Press, 1992.

Innis, Harold A. *The Fur Trade in Canada: An Introduction to Canadian Economic History.* Toronto: University of Toronto Press, 1956.

Jackson, Donald, ed. *The Journals of Zebulon Montgomery Pike with Letters and Related Documents.* 2 vols. Norman: University of Oklahoma Press, 1966.

James, Edwin, ed. *A Narrative of Captivity and Adventures of John Tanner (U.S. Interpreter at the Saut de Ste. Marie) during Thirty Years Residence among the Indians in the Interior of North America.* New York: G. & C. & H. Carvill, 1830.

Jennings, Francis. *Empire of Fortune: Crowns, Colonies and Tribes in the Seven Years War in America.* New York: Norton, 1988.

Kane, Lucile M., ed. and trans. *Military Life in Dakota: The Journal of Philippe Régis de Trobriand.* St. Paul MN: Alvord Memorial Commission, 1951.

Kane, Paul. *Wanderings of an Artist among the Indians of North America from Canada to Vancouver's Island and Oregon through the Hudson's Bay Company's Territory and Back Again.* Toronto: Radisson Society of Canada, 1925.

Kappler, Charles J., comp. *Indian Affairs: Laws and Treaties.* Vol. 2. New York: AMS, 1971.

Keating, William H. *Narrative of an Expedition to the Source of St. Peter's River, Lake Winnepeek, Lake of the Woods, &c., Performed in the Year 1823.* Minneapolis: Ross & Haines, 1959.

Kehoe, Alice B. *The Ghost Dance: Ethnohistory and Revitalization.* New York: Holt, Rinehart & Winston, 1989.

Kennedy, Dan. *Recollections of an Assiniboine Chief.* Edited by James R. Stevens. Toronto: McClelland & Stewart, 1972.

Kerr, John Andrew. "Gabriel Dumont: A Personal Memory." *Dalhousie Review* 15, no. 1 (April 1935): 53–59.

Killingray, David. "Military and Labour Recruitment in the Gold Coast during the Second World War." *Journal of African History* 23, no. 1 (1982): 83–95.

LaDow, Beth. *The Medicine Line: Life and Death on a North American Borderland.* New York: Routledge, 2001.

Libby, Orin G. "Fort Abercrombie, 1857–1877." *Collections of the State Historical Society of North Dakota* 2, pt. 2 (1908): 1–195.

Maclean, John. *Canadian Savage Folk: The Native Tribes of Canada.* Toronto: William Briggs, 1896.

Macoun, John. *Autobiography of John Macoun, M.A.: Canadian Explorer and Naturalist, Assistant Director and Naturalist to the Geological Survey of Canada, 1831–1920.* Ottawa: Ottawa Field-Naturalists' Club, 1922.

Manitoba. Historic Resources Branch. *The Dakota Fortified Camps of the Portage Plain.* Winnipeg: Historic Resources Branch, 1990.

Manzione, Joseph. *"I Am Looking to the North for My Life": Sitting Bull, 1876–1881*. Salt Lake City: University of Utah Press, 1991.

Marty, Martin. "Abbot Martin Visits Sitting Bull." *Annals of the Catholic Indian Missions of America* 2, no. 1 (January 1878): 7–10.

McKay, George. *Fighting Parson*. Kelowna BC: privately printed, 1968.

McLeod, Neil. "Plains Cree Identity: Borderlands, Ambiguous Genealogies and Narrative Irony." *Canadian Journal of Native Studies* 20, no. 2 (2000): 437–54.

McWhorter, L. V. *Hear Me My Chiefs! Nez Perce Legend and History*. Edited by Ruth Bordin. Caldwell ID: Caxton, 1992.

Messiter, Charles Alston. *Sport and Adventures among the North-American Indians*. London: R. H. Porter, 1890.

Miles, Nelson A. *Personal Recollections and Observations of General Nelson A. Miles*. Lincoln: University of Nebraska Press, 1992.

Miles, Ray, and John R. Lovett. "The Pictorial Autobiography of Moses Old Bull." *American Indian Art Magazine* 19, no. 3 (summer 1994): 48–57.

Milloy, John S. *The Plains Cree: Trade, Diplomacy and War, 1790 to 1870*. Winnipeg: University of Manitoba Press, 1988.

Milton, the Viscount, and W. B. Cheadle. *The North-West Passage by Land: Being the Narrative of an Expedition from the Atlantic to the Pacific, Undertaken with the View of Exploring a Route across the Continent to British Columbia through British Territory, by One of the Northern Passes in the Rocky Mountains*. Toronto: Coles, 1970.

Morris, Alexander. *The Treaties of Canada with the Indians of Manitoba and the North-West Territories*. Toronto: Coles, 1971.

Morton, W. L., ed. *Alexander Begg's Red River Journal and Other Papers Relative to the Red River Resistance of 1869–1870*. Toronto: Champlain Society, 1956.

————. "The Battle at the Grand Coteau, July 13 and 14, 1851." *Manitoba Scientific and Historical Society Papers*, 3d ser., no. 16 (1961): 37–49.

Musambachime, M. C. "Protest Migrations in Mweru-Luapula, 1900–1940." *African Studies* 47, no. 1 (1988): 19–34.

Nasatir, A. P., ed. *Before Lewis and Clark: Documents Illustrating the History of the Missouri, 1785–1804*. 2 vols. St. Louis: St. Louis Historical Documents Foundation, 1952.

Neufeld, Peter Lorenz. "Picheito, Manitoba's Last Saulteaux-Cree War Chief." *Indian Record* 48, no. 2 (April 1985): 19–20.

North-West Mounted Police. *A Chronicle of the Canadian West: North-West Mounted Police Report for 1875*. Calgary: Historical Society of Alberta, 1975.

Pakes, Fraser J. "Sitting Bull in Canada, 1877–81." *Brand Book* (English Westerners' Society), vol. 20, nos. 1–2 (October 1977–January 1978).

Parker, John, ed. *The Journals of Jonathan Carver and Related Documents, 1766–1770*. St. Paul: Minnesota Historical Society Press, 1976.

Parks, Douglas R., and Raymond J. DeMallie. "Plains Indian Native Literatures." *Boundary* 19, no. 3 (1992): 105–47.

————. "Sioux, Assiniboine, and Stoney Dialects: A Classification." *Anthropological Linguistics* 34, nos. 1–4 (1992): 233–55.

Parsons, John E. *West on the 49th Parallel: Red River to the Rockies, 1872–1876*. New York: William Morrow, 1963.

Peers, Laura. *The Ojibwa of Western Canada, 1780–1870.* Winnipeg: University of Manitoba Press, 1994.

Percy, Algernon Heber. *Journal of Two Excursions in the British North West Territory of North America by Algernon Heber Percy and Mrs. Heber Percy, 1877 and 1878.* Market Drayton: Bennion & Horne, 1879.

Perrault, Jean Baptiste. "Narrative of the Travels and Adventures of a Merchant Voyageur in the Savage Territories of Northern America Leaving Montreal the 28th of May 1783 (to 1820)." Edited by John Sharpless Fox. *Historical Collections and Researches Made by the Michigan Pioneer and Historical Society* 37 (1909–10): 508–619.

Peterson, Hans J. "Imasees and His Band: Canadian Refugees after the North-West Rebellion." *Western Canadian Journal of Anthropology* 8, no. 1 (1978): 21–37.

Pfaller, Rev. Louis. "The Peace Mission of 1863–1864." *North Dakota History* 37, no. 4 (fall 1970): 293–313.

Pike, Zebulon Montgomery. *Exploratory Travels through the Western Territories of North America: Comprising a Voyage from St. Louis, on the Mississippi, to the Source of That River, and a Journey through the Interior of Louisiana, and the North-Eastern Provinces of New Spain, Performed in the Years 1805, 1806, 1807, by Order of the Government of the United States.* Denver: W. H. Lawrence, 1889.

Potter, James E., ed. "The Missouri River Journal of Leonard W. Gilchrist, 1866." *Nebraska History* 58, no. 3 (fall 1977): 267–300.

Praus, Alexis A. *The Sioux, 1798–1922: A Dakota Winter Count.* Cranbrook Institute of Science, Bulletin no. 44. Bloomfield Hills MI: Cranbrook Institute of Science, 1962.

Prud'Homme, L.-A. "Monsieur Georges-Antoine Belcourt, missionnaire à la Rivière Rouge." *Proceedings and Transactions of the Royal Society of Canada,* 3d ser., 14 (1920): 23–64.

Report of the Commission Appointed by Direction of the President of the United States, Under Instructions of the Honorables the Secretary of War and the Secretary of the Interior, to Meet the Sioux Indian Chief, Sitting Bull, with a View to Avert Hostile Incursions into the Territory of the United States from the Dominion of Canada. Washington DC: U.S. Government Printing Office, 1877.

Rivard, Ron, and Catherine Littlejohn. *The History of the Metis of Willow Bunch.* Saskatoon: privately printed, 2003.

Rondeau, l'Abbé Clovis. *La Montagne de bois: Histoire de la Saskatchewan méridionale.* Edited by Rév. R. Alexis. Québec: L'Action sociale, 1923.

Ross, Alexander. *The Red River Settlement: Its Rise, Progress, and Present State with Some Account of the Native Races and Its General History, to the Present Day.* London: Smith, Elder, 1856.

Ryder, C. H. D. "The Demarcation of the Turco-Persian Boundary in 1913–14." *Geographical Journal* 66, no. 3 (September 1925): 227–42.

Sasges, Michael. "Divided Loyalties." *Beaver* 83, no. 3 (June/July 2003): 14–18.

Seed, Patricia. *Ceremonies of Possession in Europe's Conquest of the New World, 1492–1640.* Cambridge: Cambridge University Press, 1995.

Scott, Douglas D., Richard A. Fox Jr., Melissa A. Connor, and Dick Harmon. *Archaeological Perspectives on the Battle of the Little Bighorn.* Norman: University of Oklahoma Press, 1989.

Sharp, Paul F. "The Northern Great Plains: A Study in Canadian-American Regionalism." *Mississippi Valley Historical Review* 39, no. 1 (June 1952): 61–76.

———. *Whoop-Up Country: The Canadian-American West, 1865–1885.* Minneapolis: University of Minnesota Press, 1955.

Slaughter, Linda W. "Leaves from Northwestern History." *Collections of the State Historical Society of North Dakota* 1 (1906): 200–292.

Spry, Irene. "The Great Transformation: The Disappearance of the Commons in Western Canada." In *Man and Nature on the Prairies*, ed. Richard Allen. Regina: Canadian Plains Research Center, University of Regina, 1976.

Stanley, George F. G. *The Birth of Western Canada: A History of the Riel Rebellions*. Toronto: University of Toronto Press, 1960.

Steele, S. B. *Forty Years in Canada: Reminiscences of the Great North-West with Some Account of His Service in South Africa*. Winnipeg: Russell Lang; London: Herbert Jenkins, 1915.

Taché, Alexandre-Antonin. *Vingt Années de missions dans le Nord Ouest de l'Amérique*. Wakefield: S.R.; New York: Johnson Reprint, 1969.

Teton-Sioux Indians: Letter from the Secretary of the Interior, Relative to the Condition, Location, &c., of the Teton-Sioux. 42d Cong., 3d sess., H. Ex. Doc. 96, vol. 8, serial 1566. Washington DC: U.S. Government Printing Office, 1873.

Throne, Mildred, ed. "Iowa Troops in Dakota Territory, 1861–1864: Based on the Diaries and Letters of Henry J. Wieneke." *Iowa Journal of History* 57, no. 2 (April 1959): 97–190.

Thwaites, Reuben Gold, ed. "The Bulger Papers." *Collections of the State Historical Society of Wisconsin* 13 (1895): 10–153.

———, ed. "Dickson and Grignon Papers." *Collections of the State Historical Society of Wisconsin* 11 (1888): 271–315.

———, ed. *The Original Journals of the Lewis and Clark Expedition, 1804–1806*. 8 vols. New York: Antiquarian, 1959.

———, ed. "Papers from the Canadian Archives—1778–1783." *Collections of the State Historical Society of Wisconsin* 11 (1888): 97–212.

Tohill, Louis Arthur. "Robert Dickson, British Fur Trader on the Upper Missouri." *North Dakota Historical Quarterly* 3, no. 1 (October 1928): 5–49; 3, no. 2 (January 1929): 83–128; 3, no. 3 (April 1929): 182–203.

Trigger, Bruce. "Indian and White History: Two Worlds or One?" In *Extending the Rafters: Interdisciplinary Approaches to Iroquoian Studies*, ed. Michael K. Foster, Jack Campisi, and Marianne Mithun. Albany: State University of New York Press, 1984.

Turner, C. Frank. *Across the Medicine Line: The Epic Confrontation between Sitting Bull and the North-West Mounted Police*. Toronto: McClelland & Stewart, 1973.

Turner, Frederick Jackson. *History, Frontier, and Section: Three Essays*. Albuquerque: University of New Mexico Press, 1993.

Turner, John Peter. *The North-West Mounted Police, 1873–1893*. 2 vols. Ottawa: King's Printer, 1950.

U.S. Commissioner of Indian Affairs. *Annual Reports of the Commissioner of Indian Affairs*. Washington DC: U.S. Government Printing Office, 1856–83. All references to the *Annual Reports* are to the microfiche edition.

U.S. Department of State. *Reports upon the Survey of the Boundary between the Territory of the United States and the Possessions of Great Britain from the Lake of the Woods to the Summit of the Rocky Mountains*. Washington DC: U.S. Government Printing Office, 1878.

U.S. Secretary of War. *Annual Reports of the Secretary of War*. Washington DC: U.S. Government Printing Office, 1868–83.

U.S. War Department. *The War of the Rebellion: A Compilation of the Official Records of the Union and Confederate Armies*. 74 vols. Washington DC: U.S. Government Printing Office, 1885–1901.

Utley, Robert M. *The Lance and the Shield: The Life and Times of Sitting Bull*. New York: Henry Holt, 1993.

Van Kirk, Sylvia. *Many Tender Ties: Women in Fur-Trade Society, 1670–1870*. Winnipeg: Watson & Dwyer, 1980.

Vaughn, Robert. *Then and Now; or, Thirty-Six Years in the Rockies: Personal Reminiscences of Some of the First Pioneers of the State of Montana*. Minneapolis: Tribune, 1900.

Vestal, Stanley. *New Sources of Indian History, 1850–1891: The Ghost Dance—the Prairie Sioux, a Miscellany*. Norman: University of Oklahoma Press, 1934.

Walker, James R. *Lakota Belief and Ritual*. Edited by Raymond J. DeMallie and Elaine A. Jahner. Lincoln: University of Nebraska Press/Colorado Historical Society, 1980.

————. *Lakota Myth*. Edited by Elaine A. Jahner. Lincoln: University of Nebraska Press/Colorado Historical Society, 1983.

————. *Lakota Society*. Edited by Raymond J. DeMallie. Lincoln: University of Nebraska Press/Colorado Historical Society, 1982.

Wallace, W. S. *John McLean's Notes of a Twenty-five Year's Service in the Hudson's Bay Territory*. Toronto: Champlain Society, 1932.

Weekes, Mary. *The Last Buffalo Hunter*. Toronto: Macmillan, 1945.

West, John. *The Substance of a Journal during a Residence at the Red River Colony, British North America; and Frequent Excursions among the North-West American Indians, in the Years 1820, 1821, 1822, 1823*. Wakefield: S.R.; New York: Johnson Reprint, 1966.

Wheeler-Voegelin, Erminie, and Harold Hickerson. *The Red Lake and Pembina Chippewa*. New York: Garland, 1974.

White, Richard. *The Middle Ground: Indians, Empires, and Republics in the Great Lakes Region, 1650–1812*. New York: Cambridge University Press, 1991.

————. *The Roots of Dependency: Subsistence, Environment, and Social Change among the Choctaws, Pawnees, and Navajos*. Lincoln: University of Nebraska Press, 1983.

Wood, William, ed. *Select British Documents of the Canadian War of 1812*. 3 vols. Toronto: Champlain Society, 1920.

Woodcock, George. *Gabriel Dumont: The Métis Chief and His Lost World*. Edmonton: Hurtig, 1975.

Woolworth, Alan R. "A Disgraceful Proceeding: Intrigue in the Red River Country in 1864." *Beaver* 299 (spring 1969): 54–59.

Worster, Donald. *Under Western Skies: Nature and History in the American West*. New York: Oxford University Press, 1992.

Wright, Dana. "The Fort Totten–Fort Stevenson Trail, 1867–1872." *North Dakota History* 20, no. 2 (April 1953): 67–86.

INDEX

trade between Sioux, Métis, and mixed-bloods, 24

Dakotas, 4, 5, 9, 9–10, 23, 24, 26, 28, 30, 31, 43, 55, 57, 63, 112; and Cameron, Donald R., 51–52; and Carver, Jonathan, 8; and Dakota-Ojibwa hostilities, 29; delegation visits Alexander Morris, 39; and McKay, William, 21; and peace negotiations with Blackfeet and Assiniboines, 1865, 29; and trade with Métis and mixed-bloods during and after Dakota Conflict, 24, 45; Wahpetons, 6; War of 1812, 17–18

Dakota Territory, 28, 31, 32, 54

Dallas, Alexander Grant, 18–19, 19

Day, R. H., 68, 69, 72, 73

Deer Tail, 55

DeMallie, Raymond, 5, 32

Desmarais, François, 30

Desmerais, Joseph, 26

Denig, Edwin, 13

Denny, Cecil, 64, 111

De Smet, Pierre-Jean: facilitating peace between Sioux and American Government, 24–25

Des Moines River, 9

Dewdney, Edgar, 90, 91

Dickieson, M. G., 44, 67

Dickson, Robert, 10

Devil's Lake, 18, 20, 24, 28

Diedrich, Mark, 5

Dimon, Charles, 25

Dog Den Butte, 27

Double Runner, 91

Drag, The, 70

Drummond Island, 9

Dry Fork River, 46

Dufferin, 54

Dufferin, Earl of, 73

Dumont, Gabriel, 81; and Métis-Sioux peace negotiations, 20

Dumont, Isadore, 20

Dumont, Jean, 20

Durfee and Peck, 4

Eagle Dog, 33

Eagle Shield, 72

Eagle Sitting Down, The, 77

East End Post, 94

Edmunds, Newton, 28

Ehannaienke: and Breland, Pascal, 42–43

Elias, Peter Douglas, 5

Elk, The; and Valentine Francis Rowe, 56

Elk Horn, 67

Everette, William, 92

Fanton, William H., 108

Farwell, Abel, 46

Featherstonehaugh, Albany, 59; explaining purpose of boundary surveys to Sioux, 56

Finerty, John F., 36, 80; visiting Sitting Bull's camp, 97

Finlayson, James, 55

Fisher, Alick, 36

Fisk, James, 26

Flanagan, Thomas, 83

Fleming, Sandford, 37, 56

Fleury, 98

Forts; Abercrombie, 21, 26, 27; Assinniboine, 83, 111; Belknap, 81, 90, 93, 94, 99, 108, 109, 110; Benton, 20, 23, 45, 47, 91, 93, 98, 106; Berthold, 24, 25, 26; Browning, 33, 45, 47, 108; Buford, 26, 31, 33, 34, 46, 66, 74, 75, 100, 101; Custer, 98; Douglas, 10; Ellice, 21–22, 29, 32, 37, 38, 39, 40, 41, 42; Garry, 11, 12, 14, 17, 18, 19, 20, 72; Keogh, 74, 80, 98, 101, 102; Macleod, 64, 82, 88, 90; Maginnis, 91; N. J. Turney, 54; Peck, 4, 32, 34, 35, 46, 47, 50, 54, 61, 65, 66–68, 69, 71, 72, 75, 98; Pitt, 64; Qu'Appelle, 4, 23, 36, 40, 42, 44, 45, 61, 67, 68, 75, 109; Rice, 25, 28, 31; Shaw, 88; Stevenson, 25, 26; Sully, 24, 26; Totten, 26, 27; Union, 12, 13, 23, 108; Wadsworth, 29; Walsh, 63, 68, 69–70, 76, 77, 78, 82, 83, 89, 92, 96, 98, 110; Yates, 74, 102

Fort Belknap Agency, 80, 99, 109

Fort Belknap Reservation, 82

Fort Peck Agency, 72. See also Poplar River Agency

Forty-Ninth Parallel, 1, 2, 3, 89, 104

Four Horns, 4, 33, 34, 36, 59, 69, 70, 72, 73, 74, 75

France, 8

François, 47

Fréchette, Edmund, 69

Freeman, H. B., 47

French, George Arthur, 54, 58

Frenchman River, 40, 46, 47, 52, 53–55, 65, 70, 72, 73, 91, 92, 95, 96, 98

Frenier, Antoine, 23

Gall, 100, 101

Gardepie, 27

Garfield, James, 102

Genin, Jean Baptiste Marie, 77, 79

Laird, David: and Treaty 4 negotiations with Crees and Ojibwas, 43–44
Lake Manitoba, 29
Lake of the Woods, 2; Northwest Angle, 49
Lakotas, 1, 4, 9, 13, 24, 26, 27, 28, 33–36, 45, 46, 55, 59, 63, 64, 65, 67, 68, 70, 71, 73, 75, 90, 91, 96, 112; and Assiniboines, 87; and Big Bear, 89–90; and Bloods, 88; Brulés, 83; and Cowen Commission, 35; crossing the boundary before 1876, 32; and Crowfoot, 87–89; and Crows, 95; food crisis, 86; and Good Eagle, 87; hostilities with Blackfoot and Crees, 91–92; hostilities with Crows after Lakota peace attempts, 95–96; and Little Knife's rejection by Archibald, 38–39; and liquor/munitions trade with Red River Métis, 25–26; migration up Missouri River, 31; Minneconjous, 74, 75; Northern Lakotas, 4; Oglallas, 74, 75, 95, 98; opposition to Northern Pacific Railway surveyors, 50–51; opposition to boundary survey, 52–53; and peace negotiations with Gros Ventres, 93–94, 94; and Peigans, 88; raided by Crow scouts, 97–98, and response by, 98; relationships with Métis, 76, 79, 80, 84–85, and American perceptions of Métis arms trade, 79–80; and removal from borderlands, 102; Sans Arcs, 24, 50, 74; and ties with Yanktonais, 98–101; trading with Métis, 1860s and 1870s, 45; unsuccessful peace attempts with American Indians, 86; and Upper Assiniboines, 93–94
Lambert, Edward, 83
Lambert, Joseph, 67
Langer, Joseph, 70
Larivée, Andre, 89; saving lives of Martin Marty and John Howard, 77; facilitating Terry Commission, 77
Latta, Samuel, 108
Leaf, The: and Sioux-HBC negotiations, 19
Le Dow, Beth, 113
Légaré, Jean-Louis, 47, 53, 54, 68, 69, 70
Lestanc, Jean-Marie, 40, 42, 45
Leveillé, Louis, 77
L'Heureux, Jean, 81–82, 90
Lincoln, W. L., 80, 90, 93, 96, 99, 109, 111
Little Bighorn River, 63
Little Black Bear, 67
Little Bull, 33
Little Chief, 99, 109

Little Crow, 5, 9
Little Crow (d. 1863), 18–19, 31; and munitions from Red River Métis, 24; and Sioux-Métis peace negotiations, 21; and Sioux-Ojibwa peace negotiations, 28
Little Hawk, 74
Little Knife, 38, 43, 56, 67, 68, 70, 74, 75; as head of delegation to see Governor Archibald, 36–43; rumors concerning, 40, 42, 43
Little Knife River, 25
Little Pine, 100
Little Plume, 64
Little Rockies, 90–91
Little Six, 36
Little Souris River, 14
Little Wild Horse Lake, 73
Little Woody Mountain, 47
Little Wound, 34
Lodge Pole, 69
Long Dog, 34, 66, 67, 68, 69, 70, 72, 75, 79; charging Americans with sending Crow scouts to kill Lakotas, 97–98
Long Fox, 33
Long Lodge, 108; and Walsh, James Morrow, 109
Long Wolf, 68
Lorne, Marquess of, 23, 83
Louise, Princess, 83
Louisiana, 8; governor-general of, 9

Macdonald, Allan, 109, 110
MacDonald, Charles, 27
Macdonald, John A., 82
Macleod, James F., 75, 78, 82, 84, 88, 89, 90, 91, 102
Macleod, Norman T., 90
Mactavish, William, 18, 19
Mahpiyahdinape, 32
Mandans, 63
Manitoba, 4, 7, 9, 42, 43, 58
Manitoba Museum, 23
Man that Crawls, The, 70
Man that Owns the Horn, 98
Man that Wants the Breast, The, 69
Many Horns, 90, 99
Mapachong: and Sioux-Métis peace negotiations, 20
Maple Creek, 92
Marias River, 93
Marion, Alexandre, 47, 54
Martin, Joe, 27

CPSIA information can be obtained
at www.ICGtesting.com
Printed in the USA
BVHW031315130121
597756BV00010B/27/J